WIN ᴏʀ DIE

WIN OR DIE
LESSONS FOR
LIFE FROM
GAME OF
THRONES

FACE CONFLICT.

BUILD RELATIONSHIPS.

DEVELOP RESILIENCE.

BRUCE CRAVEN

BLINK
bringing you closer

Paperback – 9781788701990
eBook – 9781788702003

A CIP catalogue of this book is available from the British Library.

Printed and bound by Clays Ltd, Elcograf S.p.A.

1 3 5 7 9 10 8 6 4 2

Every reasonable effort has been made to trace copyright holders of material
reproduced in this book, but if any have been inadvertently overlooked the
publishers would be glad to hear from them.

Blink Publishing is an imprint of the Bonnier Publishing Group
www.bonnierpublishing.co.uk

Dedicated to Sherelle,
my khaleesi,
and mother of our two dragons

Contents

PREFACE

Leadership is difficult, but leadership is necessary. The achievement of good things requires our willingness to confront challenges and guide ourselves and our colleagues to achieve our objectives. In recent years, I have been using the fictional stories from George R. R. Martin's series, A Song of Ice and Fire, and the HBO adaptation, *Game of Thrones*, in my MBA and Executive MBA elective Leadership Through Fiction at Columbia Business School. The leadership decisions by the characters in *Game of Thrones* are often terrible and result in negative consequences, but the characters that survive are able to continue on their leaders' journeys because they learn how to improve their decisions and navigate the risks in front of them.

In *Game of Thrones*, what looks like a reasonable decision when you are attempting to lead a new team in a new role in a new city—such as trusting a supportive ally—can result in trusting the wrong person and end in your public execution.

Another decision that appears reasonable is to order your team to follow a strategy and plan that will save the organization and save many of your team from death. When you order your team to follow a strategy and plan they don't accept in the business world, this will generate resistance and ineffective results; in *Game of Thrones*, this gets you assassinated.

It appears reasonable to assume that when you help someone out of a bad situation and that person offers to help you in return, they will do so. This isn't true in *Game of Thrones*. It can be a terrible decision to trust the wrong person in Westeros or Essos, but if you don't find the right people to trust, you won't be able to lead and succeed. You won't win, you will die.

Terrible or not, we have to make leadership decisions in both the Known World of *Game of Thrones*, and here in our real world. Leadership calls to us.

When a huge dead mammoth blocks the gate at the Wall and the wildlings prepare to return with giants and attempt to slaughter the

Night's Watch, Maester Aemon tells Jon Snow, "You. You must lead."[1] Jon wants someone else to make the decisions. His team faces a crisis and he doesn't want to be in charge. Maester Aemon tells him, "It must be you or no one. The Wall is yours, Jon Snow."[2] Jon accepts this challenge, and many other challenges that follow. This is his Leader's Journey.

Each of the memorable characters face significant, often unbearable challenges. The environments of Westeros and Essos are brutal, unfair, overwhelming. Can the characters make it? Will their decisions help them . . . or hurt them? The fictional narrative sticks with us. Who will win . . . and who will die?

In the preface to his transformational *The Hero with a Thousand Faces*, published in 1949, Joseph Campbell, the author, mythologist, and professor of literature at Sarah Lawrence College, writes that the goal of his book is to *"uncover some of the truths disguised for us under the figures of religion and mythology. . . . The old teachers knew what they were saying."*[3] Campbell saw a pattern of common ideas in an array of myths and religious stories. He described an archetypal protagonist who could serve as inspiration, motivation, and guidance for us all. He identified a path each of us can choose to take to confront our fears and achieve fulfillment in our lives as we pursue our goals. This path became known as the Hero's Journey.

Win or Die: Leadership Secrets from Game of Thrones provides a similar path for each of us to follow as heroine or hero. This is a book for leaders at any level who want to accept their leadership version of the journey: the Leader's Journey. A phrase distilled from Campbell's teaching goes: The cave we fear to enter holds the treasure we seek. *Win or Die* is a book to prepare the reader to enter the cave and seek the treasure. The treasure that each of us seeks may translate into professional aspirations, including some combination of increased status, wealth, and skill; it may translate into the freedom to pursue dreams, spiritual growth, romantic fulfillment, or the ability to support the future of a worthy cause. It may translate into all of the above.

Whatever your treasure is, it requires you to pursue it . . . and that won't be easy. You can't do it on your sofa, watching a device. You have to go on the journey. You have to enter the cave. This is as true for each of us as it is true for the characters in *Game of Thrones*. We can't pursue our treasure if we don't take the first step and begin the journey on the path. We won't find the cave with the treasure without making decisions. If our decisions are terrible, we need to learn to make better decisions. This is an important element of leadership. Improve your decisions and stay on your Leader's Journey.

As Samwell Tarly scoured the books in Castle Black and then the Citadel for answers to the challenge of the White Walkers, we also search for answers to the challenges that will confront us in our efforts to achieve our objectives, pursue our purpose, and reach our version of accomplishment.

Each chapter of this book will provide challenges that are faced by the characters in *Game of Thrones*, offering frameworks to use in solving the challenges. Each chapter will offer real-world examples that use the frameworks, as well as examples of how the characters in *Game of Thrones* can apply the leadership insights to confront their own challenges. The chapters offer exercises to help the reader apply the leadership ideas in their own life. Each chapter references one or more stages of Joseph Campbell's seventeen-stage Hero's Journey model to help the reader think through their own path on their Leader's Journey.

Queen Cersei told Ned Stark, "When you play the game of thrones, you win or you die. There is no middle ground."[4] The Queen is wrong. There is a middle ground. The middle ground is the time when the decisions are made—both terrible decisions and productive decisions. The middle ground is the time for leadership. If you decide to play the game of thrones, learn to understand and leverage your abilities in the middle ground—play to win.

—B.H.C.
Desert Hot Springs, California
September 30, 2018

WIN OR DIE

Don't Be Ned Stark!

HOW TO LEAD WITH VALUES

In Westeros, Lord Eddard "Ned" Stark faces significant leadership challenges when King Robert travels north and requests Ned's services: "I want you down in King's Landing, not up here at the end of the world where you are no damned use to anybody."[5] Ned travels with his daughters to the capital. Lord Stark enters a city of potential allies and enemies. Exhausted and hungry from travel, he takes his seat at the table as Hand of the King. He studies the five men present at the urgent meeting of the small council called by Grand Maester Pycelle. Ned wonders which, in the words of King Robert, "were the flatterers and which the fools. He thought he knew already."[6]

DOWN IN KING'S LANDING

Ned reacts instinctively, guided by his personal values. He doesn't realize his values are subjective. He makes faulty assumptions. Ned fails to understand an important leadership insight: the people he has been tasked to report to, work with, and lead have different values from his own or share values but present themselves with less transparency.

As a result, Ned's biases about values trigger a disastrous argument with his boss, King Robert, and blind him to the advantages of a partnership with the Master of Whisperers, Lord Varys. Ned follows his values but doesn't factor into his decisions any of his subjective perspective on the values of other people on the King's Small Council or the values of people, such as Queen Cersei, who have influence with the King. Ned Stark underestimates Queen Cersei and he badly evaluates the Master of Coin, Petyr Baelish. Ned Stark isn't able to recover from his leadership misjudgment.

When King Robert Baratheon loses his temper with Ned in a Small Council meeting in King's Landing, it is because Ned, serving as Hand of the King, has questioned King Robert's *courage*. Ned is also courageous but his idea of courage is primarily about fulfilling his *duty* and obligation to his community, to act with *honor*, as well as to protect his *family*. This is where their problems begin. If King Robert thought he had hired Ned as a friend who would always defer to Robert's position as king of the Seven Kingdoms, he was mistaken. They share certain values but rank them differently.

Ned Stark assumes his values are a good method to evaluate all the members of King Robert's Small Council, as well as other stakeholders in the King's family, such as Queen Cersei and the Kingslayer, Jaime Lannister. Ned doesn't work to understand what values might motivate the other people who report to King Robert. Ned doesn't understand that the values that guide his decision making are irrelevant to colleagues he considers under his jurisdiction as Hand of the King. These people—potential colleagues or competitors—base their decisions on their own personal values. Ned also blinds himself to the opportunity of building partnerships with colleagues who have similar values because those colleagues aren't transparent and easy for Ned to understand and evaluate. If a colleague in a leadership role doesn't present himself exactly as Ned would present himself, then Ned decides that colleague cannot be trusted or can't have the same values that Ned considers important.

The Small Council is debating the news that a young woman, Daenerys Targaryen, is pregnant in Essos. Daenerys's long-dead father, King Aerys, held the Iron Throne before King Robert. If Daenerys gives birth to a baby boy, people could claim her Targaryen son has a right to King Robert's monarchy.

Ned and Robert, both allies and former brothers-in-arms during Robert's Rebellion, argue about a solution that involves sending an assassin to kill the pregnant Daenerys Targaryen:

Ned fought to keep the scorn out of his voice, and failed.

"Have the years so unmanned you that you tremble at the shadow of an unborn child?"

Robert purpled. "No more, Ned," he warned, pointing. "Not another word. Have you forgotten who is king here?"[7]

Ned had more luck swaying King Robert earlier by appealing to another one of his values: *pride*. The King wants to compete in a melee, a brutal fight with other knights that will turn into hand-to-hand brawling. The violence and danger don't trouble King Robert. What troubles him is Ned pointing out that the other knights won't fight hard against their King.

The king rose to his feet, his face flushed. "Are you telling me those prancing cravens will *let me win?*"

"For a certainty," Ned said, and Ser Barristan Selmy bowed his head in silent accord.[8]

King Robert realizes that fighting in the melee will not provide opportunity to prove his courage so he loses interest and returns to his vices. Ned appreciates having fulfilled his duty.

In leadership, we have a responsibility to understand our values. Our values motivate us. We also have a responsibility to not be owned and controlled by our values.

Queen Cersei knows that Robert's *courage* makes him vulnerable to wanting to prove it. When her initial plan to have him assassinated during the melee is foiled, she drugs his wine, aware he will attempt to prove his *courage* on a hunting trip. She is right and succeeds at using the King's values against him to achieve her personal ends: his mortal injury. King Robert never recognized that what he saw as his greatest strength was also his greatest weakness.

Ned suffers the same fate when he judges the Queen according to his own values. When faced with Ned's threat to reveal the parentage of her children, Cersei doesn't see a *duty* to gather her children and escape from King's Landing to protect her family from King Robert's wrath; rather, she sees an opportunity to prove her *courage* and *superiority*, defend her *family*, and increase her *power*. She won't run. The Queen will seize the Iron Throne.

Ned compounds his mistake by underestimating the cunning of

Petyr Baelish. He doesn't like Baelish but still finds the pact that Baelish offers easier to accept than trusting the Master of Whisperers, Lord Varys. Varys, also known disparagingly as the Spider, puts himself in a vulnerable position by approaching Ned in disguise and sharing confidential information with him. Lord Varys's attempt to communicate in private with Ned is in alignment with Ned's values. This is an act of *courage*, *duty*, and *honor* by Lord Varys, but Ned Stark doesn't see it that way. Ned only understands certain values if they are presented in a way similar to his own behavior. Varys can't be acting with *courage* and *honor*, thinks Ned, because if he was he wouldn't need to sneak into Ned's room in disguise. Ned believes in complete transparency and he rejects the possibility of an alliance with someone who uses deception.

On top of this, Ned Stark finds the political and tactical maneuvering of the various players in King's Landing to be a sign of their corruption. Ned is overwhelmed by the subterfuge Varys has revealed behind the murder of the former Hand of the King, Jon Arryn. "Wheels within wheels within wheels. Ned's head was pounding."[9] Ned understandably despises the subterfuge and betrayal that resulted in Jon Arryn's murder, yet he almost seems to blame Varys, the hopeful ally that brings him the information, for the murder. Ned has a colleague right in front of him with similar values, but Ned judges Varys and blinds himself to an opportunity.

Our values usually operate at a subconscious level, driving our behavior. Indeed, following our values often brings out the best in us, catalyzing our motivation and commitment. My colleague at Columbia Business School, Professor Paul Ingram, writes, "Your values are your internal control system. When moments of crisis occur, we rarely have time to explore options and consider alternatives in any depth. It is our core values that we rely on to guide us."[10] When possible, we should identify our values, recognize that they are motivating us, and use them as a way to build our leadership effectiveness. The more clarity we can elicit about how our values are impacting our leadership, the better.

VALUES

In 1965, William D. Guth and Renato Tagiuri published an article on organizational culture in the *Harvard Business Review* titled "Personal

Values and Corporate Strategy." The article points out "our values are so much an intrinsic part of our lives and behavior that we are often unaware of them—or, at least, we are unable to think about them clearly and articulately."[11] This lack of awareness is what happens when King Robert and Lord Stark fail at leading themselves and their colleagues. Their failures have a terrible cost and trigger the War of the Five Kings.

We owe it to ourselves, our colleagues, and our organizations to learn to operate with self-knowledge regarding our values and the opportunities and challenges that our values can present. If we derail because we mismanage our values, we can pay a high cost.

Leaders have an obligation to understand the challenges and opportunities presented by our values. Guth and Tagiuri explain: "Values are such an intrinsic part of a person's life and thought that he tends to take them for granted, unless they are questioned or challenged. He acquires them very early in life. They are transmitted to him through his parents, teachers, and other significant persons in his environment who, in turn, acquired their values in similar fashion. Child-rearing practices are expressions of a family's values, and of the values of the social group to which the family belongs."[12] This was written in the 1960s when use of the pronoun "he" was the habit. Of course the insight is true for everyone.

The Advanced Management Program (AMP) at the Columbia Business School uses coaching sessions where executives are led through the process of identifying their values. To be clear, in this process, the term "values" relates to "personal values" as opposed to "corporate values." Identifying values is used to help business leaders gain perspective on what is important to them on an individual level: what drives them, what contributes to their fulfillment, and what motivates and supports their leadership.

Paul Ingram, the faculty director of Columbia Business School's AMP, says, "We have been using a process for over a decade that, through one-to-one coaching, allows participants to highlight their eight key values, which they note on a Values Card. I continue to meet former participants years after they completed the program, who still carry their Values Card with them, though ironically they almost all have perfect recollection of their eight values."[13]

Working as director of AMP for over ten years with Professor Ingram, I have seen firsthand how coaching executives on their values provides insights about themselves and their leadership. These insights stick with them and continue to guide them as a resource in critical decision making. Professor Ingram, who also does research on values, writes, "Our research indicates that it is not the broad sweep of common values that hold people together (though not having that commonality certainly sets us apart), but our sense that we prioritize those values in a similar way. Work that we have done with Columbia Business School MBA students, over many years of intakes, shows that the single strongest predictor of who will become friends with whom in the program is if they have similar value priorities."[14] If you and your team prioritize your values in a similar way, it is easier to build strong relationships. This requires a reminder that leaders will prioritize values differently from others and must be aware of the challenges and opportunities that this difference in rankings will have on their leadership efforts.

Professor Shalom H. Schwartz, an expert in the field of values research, in "An Overview of the Schwartz Theory of Basic Values" writes, "Each of us holds numerous values (e.g., achievement, security, benevolence) with varying degrees of importance. A particular value may be very important to one person but unimportant to another."[15] Individuals and groups prioritize their values in varying orders. They may have similar values but assign them to greater or lesser degrees of importance. This prioritizing that each person does, usually subconsciously, is called a "values hierarchy." Professor Schwartz explains that there are six main features to values: 1) we believe in them and have emotional reactions to them; 2) they refer to goals that drive our actions; 3) we believe in them despite what outside norms are encouraged; 4) they are the way we decide what is good or bad, justified or unjustified; 5) they exist in hierarchies; and 6) we base our action on trade-offs determined by how we evaluate competing values. All values have these six qualities. "What distinguishes one from another is the type of goal or motivation that it expresses."[16]

Schwartz believes values serve to help us cope with three universal demands on our existence: 1) values help us get our needs fulfilled as biological organisms; 2) values help us coordinate our social interaction; and 3) values help with the survival and welfare of groups.[17] People's values cause them to pursue appropriate goals, communicate with others about those goals, and work in cooperation to achieve those goals. "Values are the socially desirable concepts used to represent these goals mentally and the vocabulary used to express them in social interaction."[18]

We are driven to satisfy our values. "Values can be guides to what needs, wants, desires people should have, what interests, preferences, and goals are seen as desirable or undesirable, what individual dispositions or traits one ought to have, and what beliefs and attitudes individuals should express."[19] Ralph H. Kilmann, CEO and Senior Consultant at Kilmann Diagnostics and former professor of organization and management at the Katz School of Business, published those words in 1981, pointing out that values are distinct from organizational norms, as well as from beliefs, attitudes, sentiments, and opinions. It is our values that drive the other behaviors and ways of thinking. "Values, as has been suggested, are seen as fairly independent from any one context."[20]

Values drive leaders forward in pursuit of achievement. Values may operate in some form of alignment with an organization's corporate values but they are individual, primary to how business leaders find motivation, focus, and the language to present themselves as leaders. Here are some examples of situations that can benefit from an awareness of values:

- Consideration of our values is helpful when we attempt to problem-solve and create positive opportunities in our organizations. If we understand our individual values, we are better prepared to see the opportunities and risks behind our value preferences.

- Understanding our values provides a lens to see what motivates us and reflect on how we can support others, understand their preferences, and offer to support them.

- Understanding our values allows us to be more specific in our communication with people. We can explain why certain decisions satisfy our values and are important to us, and we can ask questions to better understand the values and motivations of other people.

- Our anger is often triggered if our values are not satisfied. Understanding our values helps us see the catalyst to our emotional responses.

• In terms of selecting or leaving jobs, bosses, colleagues, subordinates, careers, and companies, it is important to understand whether or not our values are aligned. Even if our values are different in certain ways, it is important to consider that communication may be able to build win-win opportunities for our values to be satisfied. If not, we may have to reject or leave that working relationship, organization, etc.

VALUES IN THE WORKPLACE

Values are shaped by how we interpret the lessons of our lives. Objects are not personal values. For example, an executive, Sarah, may see her four-wheel-drive Jeep Wrangler as synonymous with spending time in nature. She may see the Rocky Mountains as the perfect environment to reach her top value of *peace*. The Jeep is not the value. The mountain range is not the value. Her value of *peace* may be fulfilled after a day of downhill skiing and a beautiful drive home to her family in Denver, Colorado, but her value of *peace* can also be fulfilled by her role as the chief development officer for a nonprofit organization.

Her effort and focus in generating support from corporate partnerships could catalyze an excitement similar to the feeling she gets navigating the Black Diamond runs at her favorite ski resort. Her value of *peace* isn't limited to one or two of her behaviors. She looks for the value in many different areas of her life. Sometimes she satisfies it, sometimes she doesn't.

In her role as chief development officer, Sarah focuses on supporting the organization's value of creating an inclusive culture. She believes in that value but is tested on a daily basis by a colleague, John, who supports the value of inclusion verbally in meetings, yet contradicts the organizational value in his daily behavior. He judges his colleagues, expressing biting condemnations about what he sees as their limitations. He is short-tempered, jumps to negative assumptions about their motivations, and is divisive during one-to-one interactions.

Sarah has a second value of *honesty*. Confronting John's behavior won't contribute in the short term to a feeling of *peace* for Sarah, but it is also important for her to act with *honesty*. She makes the decision to talk with John about the situation. Because Sarah and John have agreed verbally with the organizational importance of being inclusive, she can speak to that value. However, she should remember that her personal values are subjective: important to her but not necessarily to John.

If Sarah assumes John is also driven by the personal values of *peace* and *honesty*, she could put herself, unwittingly, into a vulnerable position. He might have different values, or similar values prioritized in a different order. John's top two values might be *recognition* and *achievement*. He might see the organizational commitment to being *inclusive* as being in fundamental conflict with his individual motivation to be *recognized* for *achievement*. This tension very likely won't be resolved without coaching aimed at gaining clarity on the mutual perspectives of John and Sarah, including defining a method to align the conflict in the values of the two colleagues and the organization. Sarah should follow her values but recognize that what motivates John in terms of his values might be different, and act with an awareness of the potential difference in what motivates her and John.

Satisfaction with our values stimulates the energy, confidence, and focus that drive our capability to be effective, but if our values aren't satisfied, frustration can occur. If you strongly value *accomplishment* and *independence*, yet you work in an environment where you are being micro-managed and aren't allowed to see projects through to completion, these constraints can keep you from reaching your primary value of *happiness*. You might recognize that you can't achieve satisfaction in that given role or organization or with a particular boss. You might recognize that you need to make a significant change in your professional situation. The motivation to fulfill one's value of *happiness* triggers impatience if the leader is blocked by an organization that keeps them from carrying their projects through to completion. I recently heard of exactly this situation in an executive coaching discussion with a graduate of Columbia's AMP.

The executive recognized that her efforts to improve her organization would not be supported. She was compensated well and her role was manageable, but she recognized that her top value of *making a difference* would not be supported by her organization. She would not be able to satisfy the one standard of criteria that mattered the most to her: *making a difference*. She realized it was time for her to talk to headhunters and develop an exit strategy.

EXERCISE: IDENTIFYING YOUR VALUES

Here is an exercise to help you identify your values.

STEP ONE: IDENTIFY CONCRETE ACTIONS

Write down five or six concrete actions that you enjoy. Some of these may be related to work, some related to hobbies, some to other commitments: family, spiritual development, sports, etc. You may prefer to use index cards or Post-its in order to move your responses and identified values into various hierarchies as you consider your priorities.

Be sure to write down the action itself, not the feeling you gain from the action; for example:

1) Play guitar

2) Shop with friends

3) Implement IT systems

4) Attend church

5) Scuba dive

6) Organize paperwork

STEP TWO: IDENTIFY ABSTRACT WORDS

Once you have completed Step One, write down an abstract word that captures the positive feeling you get when you do the above actions. Don't worry if the dictionary would use the word in that specific sense; write down a word that captures the action best for you. Push the abstraction as far as you can. For example, if you like to shop with friends, is it because you enjoy staying involved with current styles? Is it because you want to strengthen relationships with friends? It might be a combination of the two. What does the experience provide for you? Maybe finding the perfect dress that fits your style makes you feel *prepared*. Or *stylish*? Maybe shopping with your friends makes you feel *connected*. Or creates a sense of *trust*? Look for the best word to capture how the action makes you feel. Some actions might trigger a similar reaction. For example, *Attend church* and *Scuba dive* might both cause a person to feel *harmony*.

1) Play guitar = Engagement

2) Shop with friends = Connected

3) Implement IT systems = Focus

4) Attend church = Harmony

5) Scuba dive = Harmony

6) Organize paperwork = Responsible

Step Three: Organize the Abstract Words in a Hierarchy

Once you have completed Step Two, organize the abstract words in order from most important to least important. In our sample, the person might recognize that *harmony* is an abstract word that captures elements of how they feel when they are *responsible, engaged,* and *connected. Harmony* would be higher in their hierarchy. The other values lead up to the core value of *harmony.* The person might realize that the sense of *responsibility* they achieve from organizing paperwork is a nice feeling but not as important to them as the deep *focus* they achieve in working with IT systems and that playing guitar brings this *focus* up to another level where the focus, skill, and creativity trigger a feeling best described as *engagement.* This person's values hierarchy might be prioritized in this order:

1) Harmony

2) Engagement

3) Focus

4) Connected

5) Responsible

This isn't a negative judgment on the value of being *responsible.* It means that for this person, their values build toward achieving a sense of *harmony.*

If this person finds opportunities in their professional or personal life that fit these values, they will likely feel more involved, excited, and committed in their effort. Let's say this person works in the IT department. After thinking through their values, they can now see how most of the work they do brings a sense of *focus* and *engagement*. Plus, they feel *connected* to the whole organization's vision and *responsible* to their IT department. This suggests that their values are aligned with their professional effort. They find satisfaction in how they are motivated by what they do and what is expected of them. If they are asked to leave the IT department and take a new role in the Sales department, they will benefit from considering whether or not the role offered to them has the capacity to be aligned with their values.

If the new role requires them to interact with customers and potential customers on a constant basis, this may be a misalignment for them, depending on how much their other actions involve interaction with others versus working in isolation. For example, *attending church*, *playing guitar, shopping with friends*, and *scuba diving* could all be activities that involve interaction in an active way with a number of people, possibly even coaching and teaching. This might suggest that moving into the new role in Sales is a positive opportunity. On the other hand, if *shopping with friends* involves one friend and the other activities are solitary, they may need to consider carefully when deciding if the new role offered in Sales is appealing. They may decide to step out of their comfort zone and push their values in new directions. Or, if the role being offered is a bad fit, they may recognize that working in the Sales department will, for them, be a demotivating work environment.

VALUES IN KING'S LANDING

Our values drive us in the real world just as they drive the characters in the novels of A Song of Ice and Fire and the HBO show *Game of Thrones*. As leaders, it is our job to work to understand what motivates us. If we understand what drives us, we can make better leadership decisions for ourselves and clearly articulate what we stand for as leaders to those we serve to lead. It is also our job to communicate what we stand for so others can choose to follow us.

When Ned arrives in King's Landing, he is transparent, which can often be an advantage in leadership. However, transparency is not effective if it is misconstrued and pushes away productive dialogue. Ned is authentic, but transparency and authenticity can't be excuses for judging others and shutting down dialogue. Ned is vocal and reactive. His instinct is to be transparent, authentic, and accountable. This is exemplified by his commitment to swing the sword in an earlier situation at Winterfell where he is applying the King's Justice and executing a criminal. Ned shares this wisdom to his son Bran: "The blood of the First Men still flows in the veins of the Starks, and we hold to the belief that the man who passes the sentence should swing the sword. If you would take a man's life, you owe it to him to look into his eyes and hear his final words."[21]

This accountability is an admirable quality, but Ned also falls into judging everyone who crosses his path. He confuses his belief in his values with an expectation that everyone else should share his values.

Ned is not in control of himself as a leader. He reacts and judges his colleagues through the lens of his own values. He undermines the potential strength of following his values because he sees his values as absolute. He sees people with different values or ways of presenting similar values as flawed.

VALUES HIERARCHIES

We don't treat all of our values as equal. Our values are subconsciously organized in *values hierarchies*. In the words of Schwartz, "People's values form an ordered system of priorities that characterize them as individuals."[22] We prioritize certain values over other values. We might have similar values as our colleagues but prioritize those personal values in a different way, giving them greater or lesser emphasis. This prioritization can be a chance to build partnerships or they can initiate conflict.

If I am in a coaching session with a student, Alexandra, who defines her top three values as 1) *freedom*, 2) *duty*, and 3) *truth*, she will likely view the world from a different perspective than Rashmi, who defines her values as 1) *truth*, 2) *duty*, and 3) *freedom*. Although they both share the same three values, Rashmi might be more focused on the facts, contractual obligations, quantitative measurements, and clarified job responsibilities, whereas Alexandra might be more focused on pursuing

aspirational goals, fulfilling commitments to explore potential opportunities, and seeing her job responsibilities (*duty*) as the driver of
larger, big-picture (*freedom*) goals.

If we predict Ned's and Robert's personal values, I suggest the following *value hierarchies:*

NED	ROBERT
Duty	Courage
Honor	Reward
Courage	Honor
Family	Camaraderie

The *values hierarchies* show that Ned and Robert share some similar
values but care about those values to lesser or greater degrees. Robert
has a strong commitment to *courage*. He lives *courage* in each boar hunt,
in each melee, in each moment he can prove the value to himself and
to his entourage. Ned knows the importance of *courage* but holds that
value as less important than he holds *duty* and *honor*. This creates tension and puts the two colleagues in conflict.

KING ROBERT'S VALUES

Faced with the loss of Jon Arryn, King Robert follows his own values
hierarchy. He looks for an ally he trusts. He selects Ned, a colleague
and fellow brother-in-arms. The two men were raised together under
the mentorship of Jon Arryn. They share a long-standing friendship,
but that doesn't mean they understand their dynamic. King Robert
offers Ned a *reward:* the opportunity to bind their houses through
marriage of their children. Is Ned the best-qualified person to step
into the Small Council and operate effectively with the Spider, Littlefinger, Grand Maester Pycelle, not to mention Queen Cersei and the
rest of King Robert's circle of direct reports and family? Probably not.

Like Ned, King Robert sees the environment through his values and
doesn't recognize the subjectivity of his leadership decisions. Neither
leader recognizes Cersei as the greatest risk to their authority, their
own families' well-being, and the well-being of the Seven Kingdoms.
The two middle-aged alpha warriors choose to focus their leadership

energy in an argument about the best tactics to defuse the threat of pregnant Daenerys Targaryen on the distant shores of Essos. The two men worry about Daenerys because she is married to a Dothraki horse-lord. It is an unlikely possibility that Dothraki warriors—terrified of the ocean—will journey by boat across the Narrow Sea; yet, enraged nomadic warriors on horseback are a threat both Robert and Ned can recognize from past battles. The threat is unlikely, but it scares them. Neither of the men can see the danger in Cersei Lannister. Neither man is scared of the woman that will be involved in their deaths.

King Robert doesn't select a Hand of the King that has experience or expertise with office politics. The King wrongly believes that Ned's experience as Warden of the North has prepared him for the subter-fuge of King's Landing. King Robert selects a courageous, honorable warrior he trusts to keep an eye on boring management necessities. He selects a friend he believes will understand his daily debauchery and low prioritization of his monarch leadership responsibilities. King Robert hires a sanitized version of himself, a man that doesn't whore, booze, or fight in melees. King Robert misjudges Ned's strong com-mitment to the values of *duty* and *honor*. King Robert doesn't expect Ned to put his own values into action by engaging in leadership deci-sions. King Robert doesn't expect a direct report who will question his authority, who will cross the unspoken bond of their *camaraderie*, or brotherhood, and make leadership decisions, but this is exactly what happens when Ned issues the order for the arrest of Ser Gregor "The Mountain" Clegane.

The two friends make blinded decisions that put them in isolated, vulnerable positions with regards to their domestic enemies. This is compounded when Robert goes radio silent on a hunting trip, leaving Ned, sitting on the Iron Throne, making judgment calls above his pay grade as Hand of the King. Ned listens to the villagers' stories of ma-rauding attackers, rapine, plunder, and mayhem—then, without a mo-ment of reflection, information gathering, or the consideration of other opinions—issues the proclamation in the King's name against the apparent rogue terrorist Clegane. Ned's decisions to strip Ser Gregor of his rank and titles, all his properties, and sentence him to death; followed by Ned's command to Pycelle to send a raven to Cast-erly Rock, ordering Tywin Lannister to King's Landing to explain his possible involvement in the crimes of the Mountain are both leader-ship decisions true to Ned's values. It must be satisfying for Ned to do what his values tell him are the right things in a time of crisis, but Ned makes these calls unaware of the broader impact of his decisions. Ned also sees his values through the lens of the Smallfolk. He is derailed by a desire to answer their pleas for protection. This is a noble instinct but pulls him from clear analysis of the challenges in front of him. He sits on the Iron Throne as the direct report to King Robert. He lets his values trigger him into well-intentioned, questionable actions.

Lord Varys hints at the political ramifications of Ned's rash action. Ned fails to consider his decision from any objective perspective. He fulfills all four of his top values by indicting Clegane, but this satisfaction will be fleeting and will catalyze numerous challenges for himself and his team.

Both King Robert and Lord Stark share the value of *honor*, yet Ned puts the value above *courage* and *family* and Robert puts *courage* and *reward* as more important than *honor*.

Lord Stark takes immediate umbrage at the idea that the King's Small Council would send an assassin to murder pregnant Daenerys Targaryen. From Ned's point of view, there is a lack of *honor* in the Small Council's proposal. However, if Lord Stark could be persuaded that a Targaryen heir in Essos could lead a Dothraki uprising and an assault on Westeros, his concern for the values of *duty* and *family* might cause him to reconsider the responsibility to support the tactic of sending an assassin.

The potential exists for the King and the Hand of the King to find common ground and work to an agreement, but both men get angry when their values are called into question. King Robert takes offense when Ned challenges his *courage*. The two allies fall into a public, destabilizing argument.

CERSEI'S VALUES

Ned understands that King's Landing is "a nest of adders,"[23] yet he underestimates why he is vulnerable and which people are his biggest threats. In terms of values, Cersei can match Ned for *courage*. *Family* is a value that is important to Cersei but not on her husband's list of top values as shown by his marginalization of and disrespect for his brother Stannis, his limited regard for the children he believes are his own with Cersei, and his complete disregard for his illegitimate children. The children in these two categories don't appear to hold a priority for King Robert over his own desire to prove his *courage* and satisfy his desire for physical *rewards* and *camaraderie*.

Cersei doesn't consider her husband the King to be part of her *family*. This is an important distinction that Ned doesn't see until it is too late. For Cersei, Robert is just the drunk in the bed who has the *power* she needs and wants. Cersei doesn't give a damn for Ned's interpretation and priority of the personal value of *honor*. She doesn't care about his attempt to offer her the chance to save her children from the wrath of her enraged husband. Ned assumes Cersei will crumble in terror and be thankful for his effort to protect her family. He underestimates Cersei's commitment to her *family*, her *courage*, and her belief in her *power* and *superiority*. This error in evaluating Cersei puts Ned, his family, his boss, and his allies in a vulnerable position. Ned tells Cersei she should take her children to the Free Cities, the Summer Isles, or the Port of Ibben. "As far as the winds blow."[24] Ned tells Cersei she must escape Robert's wrath. "The queen stood. 'And what of my wrath, Lord Stark?'"[25]

Cersei explains to Ned Stark a fundamental rule of their leadership environment. "When you play the game of thrones, you win or you die. There is no middle ground."[26]

I suggest Cersei's personal values look like this:

CERSEI

Superiority

Power

Courage

Family

DON'T BE NED STARK!

King Robert and Ned Stark stand as powerful reminders that the pressures of day-to-day leadership can trigger conflict between colleagues, even colleagues that have strong mutual experiences, have extensive goodwill, trust each other, and share common goals. If we make assumptions about our personal values, we can commit the same mistakes. The two men lose critical time in assessing risks and developing action-steps to confront and defuse the external threats.

Values are an important instrument in our understanding of ourselves as leaders, but they are subjective. King Robert and Ned Stark were not explicit, or self-reflective, about the values that influenced their decisions and influenced their emotions. Values can be a source of mutual understanding among allies, but these values need to be made explicit through discussion in order to understand what motivates each member of the team.

We need to remind ourselves, under pressure, not to leap at the quick satisfaction of responding to our values without asking ourselves to see the bigger picture. Our values should be used as a map to help propel us forward. It is our job to read the map with care and understand the opportunities and challenges. The rash satisfaction of our values can have horrendous consequences, for us and for those we attempt to serve as leaders.

Our values motivate us and can help us become our "best self" in leadership. Understand your values and also operate with the insight that your values are not the same as other people's values. Even if you share values with colleagues or competitors, that doesn't mean you each prioritize your values similarly.

If you can align your values with your leadership role, you will maximize your motivation. If you assume other people need to prioritize their values in the order you prefer, you can blind yourself to other people's true motivations. As with Ned Stark and Robert Baratheon, this misjudgment can damage potential partnerships and opportunities.

Ned Stark didn't understand the reality of the relative importance of multiple values, of values hierarchies, and how these differently ordered systems guided the action of the various constituents vying for influence in the Seven Kingdoms during the rule of King Robert Baratheon. Ned Stark assumed that everyone would follow his values, or, if they didn't follow his values in a transparent manner, they were flawed and not worth trusting. In the end, Ned Stark, serving as direct report to King Robert, made these significant mistakes:

1) He harmed his relationship with King Robert by openly challenging the King's courage in a public meeting.

2) He turned away an important ally in Lord Varys, mistrusting the Spider because he didn't appear to represent the same values as Ned Stark.

3) He trusted the promise of a man that mocked him (and mocked his trust) when he conspired with Petyr Baelish.

4) He underestimated the courage, commitment, and cunning of Queen Cersei, assuming she would respond to his knowledge of her relationship with Jaime, take her children, and flee King's Landing.

5) Because he mismanaged potential allies and partnered with the wrong person, he was unable to protect his daughters in King's Landing and help them navigate a dangerous environment.

From the beginning, Ned Stark fails to understand the strength and risk inherent in his approach to his values. Because of his blind spots, his leadership fails and he can't bring any sort of productive gift, wisdom, or boon back to his community. His Leader's Journey needs to be picked up and carried forward by his family. . . . Any family members who survive.

THE LEADER'S JOURNEY: THE CALL TO ADVENTURE AND REFUSAL OF THE CALL

The decision to accept the Call to Adventure means making the choice to step out of the comfort zone of a stable environment on purpose and accept responsibility as a leader by entering a new environment. As the famed mythologist Joseph Campbell writes, "destiny has summoned the hero"[27] to leave the comfort of what is known and accept the challenge to work in an environment of potential risk in order to accomplish goals and achieve success. The hero may step into a complicated scenario, unaware of what he or she has triggered.

Joseph Campbell says our call to adventure, the first stage of the Hero's Journey, often begins with a "blunder,"[28] a mistake or stumble into something new that can bring danger and opportunity. The blunder is the trigger, but in that stumble is a chance to overcome and succeed. Ned stumbles forward in a blunder. He doesn't understand what is going on in King's Landing. Ned doesn't trust any of the Lannister family, including Cersei, whom Ned's sister by marriage, Lysa Arryn, has blamed for the death of her husband. This is smart, but Ned also doesn't respect Cersei's *courage* and her commitment to her personal values, including *family, power,* and *superiority*. It is not smart to underestimate your competitors.

When faced with accepting the call to adventure, Ned could have chosen instead to make his role as Warden of the North his priority. He had a job to protect the northern border against various threats to the Seven Kingdoms. But Ned didn't make that choice and his wife, Catelyn Stark, supported and in fact encouraged Ned's decision to travel south, adding their daughters, Sansa and Arya, to the entourage with hopes of future rewards.

The second stage of the journey is Refusal of the Call: "The myths and folk tales of the whole world make clear that the refusal is essentially a refusal to give up what one takes to be one's own interest."[29]

Ned hesitates at King Robert's offer, evaluating his own responsibilities to protect the north in Winterfell. He also considers the fate of his father and brother who traveled south to King's Landing many years before and were both murdered by Mad King Aerys, triggering the War of the Usurper, otherwise known as Robert's Rebellion. Ned hesitates. "My father went south once, to answer the summons of a king. He never came home again."[30] Yet Ned accepts the Call. "'A different time,' Maester Luwin said. 'A different king.'"[31] Despite misgivings, Ned passes through the second stage; he considers refusing but accepts the new job in King's Landing.

The choice Ned made was admirable yet mismanaged. Ned and Catelyn wanted to do what they could to protect their king and their kingdom, but they separated themselves from each other and bifurcated the family, putting everyone in vulnerable positions that didn't align with their strengths. Ned Stark needed to enter King's Landing with his eyes open; instead he allowed the immediate, unreflective satisfaction of his values to be his method of personal leadership. He blinded himself. He lashed out, judged and failed at leading himself, his potential allies, and his opportunities. Ned Stark could have pursued his leadership journey by staying in Winterfell and, eventually, confronting the true threat that faced Westeros, or he could have used his values more effectively in King's Landing. Ned could have acted judiciously instead of judging. He could have invited opportunities rather than limiting his network of resources.

For Ned Stark, the price of his mismanagement was tragic. His Leader's Journey ended on the King's Landing chopping block at the

Great Sept of Baelor, his head and chest thrust out, his neck naked. Ser
Ilyn Payne lifted Ned's own sword, *Ice*. The mob shrieked. Ned Stark
lost because he believed his values hierarchy would guide the decisions
and behavior of his boss, his colleagues, and his competitors. He
followed his values without reflection. He was wrong.

GOING FORWARD

It is important that we, as leaders, search for clarity on the values of
our allies and our competitors. What might Ned have learned from
Lord Varys if he had taken the time to ask and to listen? What if he
had chosen to push King Robert for clarity on what accepting the role
in King's Landing meant in terms of Ned's job responsibilities? What
if Ned had tried to understand Queen Cersei's motivations before assuming she would shiver in fear at his threat, weep thankfully at his
offer to save her children, and flee the capital?

It is important to remember that values are an effective way to understand what drives you, what opportunities might be natural for
you to accept, and what opportunities might require you to lead yourself in new ways if you are to succeed. You will find that reflecting on
your values will help you understand your past successes and challenges, as well as provide insights on future opportunities and what
excites you about them, and how they may offer challenges for you or
require additional resources.

Use your values as a map of what is internally important to you,
and assess what is important to other people in your professional environment as well. Don't fall into the trap of assuming that your values
also motivate your colleagues and competitors. Use the resource of
your values, but don't use the resource blindly.

Also, remember that sometimes people share your values and will
support your interests, but we have to see past our simplistic tendency
to judge people who are different from us in appearance. The bold,
courageous Lord of Winterfell would have benefitted in a significant
way from a partnership with the wily, strategic Master of Whisperers,
Lord Varys.

Keep your head where it can be a resource, not tarred on a stake
above the Red Keep.

SEE TRUE!

HOW TO COACH AND BE COACHED

Our leadership journeys are comprised of a series of critical decisions. No decision can be as important to our success—or detrimental to our success—than our choice of advisors and coaches. Indeed, the pitfalls of choosing poor advisors often drive the action of *Game of Thrones*, especially when it comes to Ned Stark and Daenerys Targaryen.

A NOBLE SPLASH

Ned Stark erupts in the Small Council, challenges the courage of his friend, and boss, King Robert, and triggers an enraged reaction. After the explosive meeting, Ned receives a visit from the Master of Coin, Petyr "Littlefinger" Baelish. Petyr tells Ned, "You rule like a man dancing on rotten ice. I daresay you will make a noble splash."[1] This moment of honesty from a dishonest, self-serving colleague is delivered before Ned's disastrous, brutal street brawl with Jaime Lannister and his soldiers. Petyr's guidance is also offered before Ned, sitting on the Iron Throne in the absence of King Robert, his shattered leg lit in pain, makes the rash decision to send a posse after Gregor Clegane. Ned sentences the rogue knight to the King's Justice and eases his wounded body back onto Aegon the Conqueror's jagged chair. Ned Stark would have benefitted from coaching before he made a series of emotional decisions.

Ned could have waited to pass judgment on Clegane until the King returned from his hunting trip. He also might have reflected more on the knight he chose to punish Gregor Clegane. As Varys points out, selecting Ser Loras Tyrell to lead the hunt for Clegane would have put the powerful Tyrell clan on Ned's side in the potential conflict with Clegane's allies, the Lannisters. When Ned leans back onto the Iron Throne, one can almost hear the loud *noble splash* as he falls through the rotten ice of his bad decisions. Ned didn't listen to Petyr Baelish when it would have been wise, and then later chose to listen to Baelish and partner with him to arrange for armed backup against Queen Cersei's unexpected insurrection.

Ned fails at having the ability to guide his colleagues and be guided by them. He decides to trust Petyr Baelish, instead of Lord Varys. Ned distrusts Varys because Lord Varys acts differently from Ned. Varys isn't rash; he listens, reflects, and proceeds with caution. Ned doesn't understand the strength in Varys's caution. "For all his protestations of loyalty, the eunuch knew too much and did too little."[2] Ned distrusts the Spider. Ned chooses to trust Baelish, even after Baelish warns him, "You are slow to learn, Lord Eddard. Distrusting me was the wisest thing you've done since you climbed down off your horse."[3] The selection of advisors and coaches is important. Ned Stark wasn't prepared to lead in King's Landing. Leadership requires listening to the right people.

DANY'S CHOICE

Ned's argument with King Robert was triggered by word of a pregnant Targaryen in Essos, across the Narrow Sea. After the War of the Usurper, Daenerys and her brother Viserys lived on the generosity of people interested in them because they were of the royal bloodline of the Mad King. Magister Illyrio Mopatis, in Pentos, is their most recent benefactor. He wants to become Master of Coin in the Seven Kingdoms and works to position Viserys to regain the Seven Kingdoms. He assures Viserys, "They are your people, and they love you well."[4] Magister Illyrio feeds Viserys's narcissism, assuring him that his fans in the Seven Kingdoms raise silent toasts in his honor and sew dragon banners, awaiting his return.

A young woman with no obvious credentials except for the questionable reputation of her family name finds her way forward into leadership. How should Daenerys choose the best advisors when she has been raised having others decide her fate for her?

We first see Daenerys when Illyrio Mopatis, her brother Viserys's advisor, promises him an army of Dothraki bloodriders. This promised army will theoretically transform the male heir to Mad King Aerys from a spoiled, insecure Beggar King into a charismatic warrior leader. Viserys's plan, based on Illyrio's coaching, is that the nomadic Essos bloodriders, used to following a Khal they chose, will decide to rally behind Viserys, with his silk trousers and borrowed sword.

At every level of leadership there might be people who will whisper what you want to hear; who might coach you into blindness and failure. Daenerys is young but smart enough to be skeptical of a man like Mopatis, a man who gives her and her brother fine clothes, sumptuous food and elegant accommodations, shares his home and wealth, and asks for nothing. Dany knows Illyrio will leverage his generosity. This moment arrives when Illyrio tells Viserys to offer his sister in marriage to Khal Drogo to secure his army.

Despite her fear of her nuptials, marital obligations, and married future, Daenerys finds her way forward in both her romantic partnership with Drogo and in her role as khaleesi. Her brother, Viserys, on the other hand pays a brutal price for his narcissism. He listens to the wrong guidance from Illyrio, which feeds Viserys's own vain clichés. He annoys then enrages Khal Drogo. Jorah Mormont and Daenerys attempt to guide Viserys in preparation for the leadership challenges ahead, but he won't listen. Jorah gives up trying. He asks Dany, "Truth now. Would you want to see Viserys sit a throne?"[5]

As Dany adapts to the challenges of the Dothraki culture, Viserys, untethered from common sense or good advice, derails. Drunk, enraged, and disrespectful of the culture of the Dothraki, Viserys disrupts the naming feast for his unborn nephew, the Stallion Who Mounts the World, Rhaego. Viserys understands the cultural norms in the sacred city, Vaes Dothrak, beneath the Mother of Mountains: no weapons. Yet Viserys draws his sword and demands his gold crown. Khal Drogo loses patience with this useless man without a horse, the Sorefoot King, the Cart King, and Viserys receives a crown of gold. As Drogo pours a pot of boiling gold over his head, Daenerys watches her brother's horrible death. The man Jorah Mormont had called "less than the shadow of a snake"[6] is not a dragon. Dany realizes, "He was no dragon. . . . Fire cannot kill a dragon."[7]

But even a dragon can choose poor advisors.

In her role as khaleesi, Dany has limited advisors capable of offering her guidance. Her handmaidens coach her on ways to please the Khal and on the norms of Dothraki culture. She defends the Lhazareen people as the plundering Dothraki rape and murder them. Her husband supports her kindness even though this sympathetic behavior is foreign to the Dothraki.

When Drogo is wounded in battle, a Lhazareen maegi who Dany attempted to protect, Mirri Maz Duur, offers her skills of healing. She claims she was trained by a maester from the Citadel in Oldtown. Drogo's men want to kill her, but Daenerys allows her to proceed. She rewards Dany's trust by possibly poisoning the Khal. More promised healing is followed by the stillbirth of Dany's baby, transformed in the black-magic tent into a nonhuman dead dragon infant. Khal Drogo, unable to ride a horse and abandoned by most of his people, stares incapacitated at the prairie sky, living but a vegetable. Magister Illyrio's support for Viserys and Daenerys appears to have been poorly planned and self-serving, but the maegi's support was deceitful, vengeful, and murderous.

Daenerys is taught three important lessons by Mirri Maz Duur. The first lesson is to "see what life is worth, when all the rest is gone."[8] The maegi's vengeful message to Daenerys is that the vulnerable can be destroyed and will be destroyed by those with the power to destroy. Life is worth nothing when all one cares about has been destroyed. Daenerys realizes that she cannot be a successful leader while only offering win-win solutions. She doesn't have the luxury of offering absolute trust to her followers. People will take advantage of leaders who trust too easily. Daenerys won't forget what the maegi has taught her: vulnerability leads to destruction. Dany loses her husband and her baby. She loses what she loves most but the Mother of Dragons, caught in the fever dream of her miscarriage in the bloodmage's tent, approaches an armored knight, her long-dead brother, Rhaegar. Daenerys lifts the black visor of his helm and sees . . . herself. "The face within was her own."[9] Her future is to fill the gap left when Rhaegar was murdered and become a leader.

The second lesson is to be very careful in the choice of coaches. The Mother of Dragons, Daenerys Stormborn, Daenerys of House Targaryen, of the blood of Aegon the Conqueror and Maegor the Cruel of Old Valyria, will no longer trust in the inherent goodwill of professed advisors. Daenerys understands there is an advantage in trusting colleagues. Her instinct is to select locals, such as the two slaves she will liberate into her service from Astapor (her advisor, the handmaiden, Missandei, and her eventual Commander of the Unsullied, Grey Worm), but even though Dany's instinct is to trust, she learns that she must discriminate and select the right people to trust. She must be objective in her selection process. She can't operate with wishful optimism. If she doesn't choose her coaches well, she will continue to pay the equivalent of the high price she paid by trusting the maegi.

Dany whispers to herself as she attempts to win back her leadership of the remaining Dothraki: *"If I look back I am lost."*[10] This is her third lesson. She has faced a terrible series of challenges, including the wrath of the vengeful Mirri Maz Duur, but Dany knows she must trust her strength, keep learning from every person and experience, and move forward. Dany confronts the possibility of burning herself alive. She watches the flames of the funeral pyre reach the body of her dead husband. The flames have already wrapped the bound figure of Mirri Maz Duur. The screaming maegi's "song became a shuddering wail, thin and high and full of agony."[11] Dany walks into the flames. "She saw a horse, a great grey stallion limned in smoke, its flowing mane a nimbus of blue flame. *Yes, my love, my sun-and-stars, yes, mount now, ride now.*"[12]

She steps from the immolated ruins of the pyre: "Dany had only to look at their eyes to know that they were hers now today, and tomorrow and forever."[13] Three pairs of dragon wings unfold from the colorful creatures that cling to her naked body. "The night came alive with the music of dragons."[14] Dany commits to protect what matters to her.

Unlike Ned Stark, the Mother of Dragons will carefully choose her advisors; she will trust herself and lead herself to be courageous. She will follow her vision and not look behind out of fear, doubt, or caution. She will look forward.

WHO WILL WE CHOOSE TO COACH US?

How are we to do the same? How can we recognize advisors and coaches that we can trust? We should start by finding people with skill in emotional intelligence, including the ability to listen and be 100 percent present during communication opportunities. Our selections of both advisors and coaches will depend on our circumstances and opportunities, but if our coaches and advisors can't listen, they can't guide us. We need commitment from them, and we need to be committed ourselves, even if the time to communicate is compressed with external obligations and pressures.

Howard Schultz, CEO of Starbucks, recognized Warren Bennis as the right person to serve as his coach when he wanted to grow Starbucks. Bennis was a world-renowned writer, consultant, professor, and leading-edge thinker on leadership. Schultz reached out to him and Schultz said of the encounter, *"Who do you talk to when you're afraid to demonstrate vulnerability and insecurity to others? You can talk to your wife or close friends, but you also need advice from someone who has been there before. I asked Warren for his help, calling him once or twice a month."*[15] Howard Schultz made a good decision. In his chapter "Moving Through Chaos" in his book *On Becoming a Leader*, Bennis writes, "Learning to lead is, on one level, learning to manage change. As we've seen, a leader imposes (in the most positive sense of the word) his or her philosophy on the organization, creating or re-creating its culture. . . . But unless the leader continues to evolve, to adapt and adjust to external change, the organization will sooner or later stall."[16] Bennis made a career of helping leaders do just that. And now eleven Starbucks open every three days.

I learned from Bennis myself. I had the honor to meet him briefly when he was a guest at the Arden House Conference Center during my early years with Columbia Business School. Years later, when I was promoted in terms of leadership responsibilities on the Columbia Business School AMP, I picked up his classic book *On Becoming a Leader*. It became a map for my new leadership role. Later, I wrote Bennis at the University of Southern California to thank him for the inspiration and guidance his book had provided me. He responded with generous and supportive comments, which is precisely what you would expect from a great advisor, even one you've only met once, tangentially, decades earlier.

The decision to accept the coaching of various bosses, mentors, allies, advocates, and colleagues is our responsibility. I have made good choices and bad choices. Either way, I can't blame my choices on anyone else. At certain points earlier in my career, I trusted the wrong people and paid a price professionally. Fortunately, the price wasn't too severe; I didn't lose my head like Ned Stark or my spouse and child like Daenerys. Still, I learned that I should not expect other people to be my strongest advocates. Fortunately, I have benefitted from great colleagues and bosses. I also benefitted from being coached using the practice of *Performance Coaching*.

PERFORMANCE COACHING

Over my almost thirty years of working in executive education, I have listened to and learned from many first-class speakers. In my early days at the Arden House Conference Center, we referred to the front of the auditorium as "the pit." No visiting lecturer held this space with more confidence, authority, and curiosity than author, consultant, and speaker Ram Charan. In the pit, Ram would teach in his dark blue slacks and pressed white shirt cuffs unbuttoned, shirtsleeves folded a few times. He wrote aggressively on flipcharts or the white board, his enthusiasm for leadership palpable, cerebral, and infectious.

Ram Charan has written twenty-five books on a variety of subjects related to leadership in business. He has advised a number of highly successful CEOs. In a 2009 *Harvard Business Review* (*HBR*) research report by Diane Coutu and Carol Kauffman, Charan wrote about the growing industry of executive coaching: "As coaching has become more common, any stigma attached to receiving it at the individual level has disappeared. Now, it is often considered a badge of honor."[17] Ten years after this *HBR* article, the belief by business leaders in the value of coaching has only grown and strengthened.

In Performance Coaching, the coach offers their objective coaching perspective, recognizing that the coachees might, depending on their careers and experiences, have more industry knowledge than the coach. The coach's role, as stated by Columbia Business School Professor Michael Morris, is to help the coachee "think through a problem and gain greater self-awareness in the process."[18]

The coach doesn't solve problems, provide answers, or guide the coachee with a specific career path in mind. The coach listens, asks questions, provides a helpful environment (i.e., a structure for the session) and helps the coachee think through their challenges and goals. The end goal of the coaching session is to prioritize what is important to the coachee, why it's important, and how they should proceed.

The act of coaching can focus on a variety of topics. The coach may be tasked with helping the coachee develop in specific areas, or the relationship may begin from an open-ended starting point. The coachee may be supported by his organization. The coaching contract may also be initiated and paid for by the coachee, who sees an opportunity for personal development.

DON'T HIRE A VAMPIRE

The craft of coaching has similarities to traditional consulting and to therapy. From consulting comes the idea of advising individual leaders on business matters, often involving management in goal setting, with the possibility of focusing on the values and ethics of the organization. As with professional therapists, coaches:

- are paid to ask the right questions

- tackle difficult issues at work and home

- focus on individual behavioral change

- explore subjective experience.[19]

"Coaching consists primarily of one-on-one conversations that help the person being coached figure out how to solve a current problem."[20] These conversations are often structured around a process to maximize the efficacy of the conversation, and secure action steps to make sure the insights don't evaporate with the conclusion of the discussion. Morris points out that the challenge with leading through the process of coaching is that it takes time. It is a slow process. The coachee can have a big insight, or be gently offered a suggestion that lands as a big insight, but coaching takes time. It is open to nuance and interpretation and benefits from reflection and follow-up actions. It depends on a dialogue—it's not about being told what to do. The coach doesn't point and command, rather, the coach asks and listens. The coachee reflects, decides, and acts. The goal of the process is to help the coachee develop insights, identify commitment to goals, and create a subsequent action plan.

The point of coaching is not to advance the fame, prosperity, or self-confidence of the coach. Self-aggrandizement in a coach is called *being a vampire*. This is what happens when the listener forgets he or she is listening, and sees the whole process as a promotion of his or her intelligence. I have had moments working as a coach where I have caught myself believing I had the answers for the coachee. A coach can make a suggestion, but the suggestion can't have the firm tone of a recommendation. A coach should focus on listening and helping the coachee see the best way forward. If your coach falls into the habit of providing answers, then it is likely that you will lose commitment to the thought process and disengage or defer to the coach without owning the decisions. You should benefit from a process that is controlled by the coach but "solved" by you. People get enough advice in their lives. The coaching process is about helping the coachee think, decide, and plan the necessary actions. Find a coach that listens, not a vampire that needs to feed his or her ego.

Miyamoto Musashi was an expert Japanese swordsman and ronin. Born in the final years of the sixteenth century, his life concluded in the seventeenth century. After years of combat he ended his days writing and living in a cave. He is famous for his sixty undefeated duels, his life of both warrior courage and wisdom, including his thoughts on strategy, tactics, and philosophy presented in *Go Rin No Sho* (*The Book of Five Rings*). His collection of warrior guidelines to living life, *Dokkodo*, is translated as either *The Path of Aloneness* or *The Way to Be Followed Alone*.

The fourth insight in the *Dokkodo* is: *"Think lightly of yourself and deeply of the world."* This encouragement is one I repeat to myself before engaging in a coaching session. It is an effective reminder to not take my opinion too seriously, while also recognizing the world is a complex environment, and to stay present in the goal of helping the coachee succeed in that environment.

Terrence E. Maltbia, Associate Professor of Practice at Teachers College at Columbia University, teaching to a class of our senior executives, said: "Great coaches ask questions that challenge think-ing."[21] They listen and help pull out ideas, a process that often bene-fits by the coach understanding and repeating back the thoughts of the coachee. This requires listening. Maltbia emphasizes, "The coach is not the performer." The goal is to help the coachee understand their cur-rent state and prepare for actions that will take them toward their de-sired future state.

Maltbia put it this way in our Advanced Management Program, "Coaching doesn't really mean anything until you put something in front of it." Your coach shouldn't be doing the heavy lifting; instead, they should be asking questions that help you build on the areas that are important for you to grow. The coach should help you work on the important goals you see in front of you. If coaching becomes important when you *put something in front of it*, the coach helps the coachee think through that *something*. The coach helps guide the think-ing, and the subsequent planning necessary to achieve the results the coachee identifies as important.

In my coaching with senior executives or when teaching a class on coaching to graduate students, I find it helpful to provide both models and encourage the coach to find a way to use the models that feels natural and encourages a productive coaching conversation.

The two models are: 1) Columbia Business School's Program on Social Intelligence (PSI) model: Entry-Insight-Action[22] and 2) the Columbia Coaching CCC model: Context-Content-Conduct.[23] Ultimately, the coach is best served by using the model that allows them to be natural, focused, relaxed, present, and committed to the coachee's challenges.

THE CCC MODEL

The CCC model comprises of three questions.

1) CONTEXT—"WHAT'S UP?"

    a. Understanding the events, challenges, opportunities presented

        i. Clarify expectations

        ii. Bring to the surface related hopes and concerns, get insights

2) CONTENT—"WHAT MATTERS?"

  a. Understand what really matters to the client

   i. Explore and outline options

   ii. Discuss possible steps to achieve options

3) CONDUCT—"WHAT'S NEXT?"

  a. Translate talking into action

   i. Observe their progress and possible learnings

   ii. Formulate action strategies and execution plan

   iii. Create a contract

Here is an example of how a coach might use the CCC model:

1) CONTEXT—"WHAT'S UP?"

Stage one in the CCC model—the stage of understanding the "Context" or "What's up?"—is comparable to two categories in the PSI model mentioned above: Entry Step #1 and Insight Step #1. In the recommended first stage of the model, the coach engages the person and earns the right to talk seriously by asking questions that build trust and help the coachee respond. For example, "What are you dealing with today?" The focus in this stage is to frame the process, by clarifying and establishing the goals of the coaching conversation. A related approach is to explore the story: help the coachee fill in the details and help the coachee see what they might be missing. This means helping the coachee pay attention to different aspects of the story. The coach can ask questions and move toward identifying a possible headline or thematic focus to the story. For example: What is at the heart of this challenge? What is it really about?

2) CONTENT—"WHAT MATTERS?"

Stage two in the CCC model involves asking about the "Content" or "What matters?" In the PSI model the second-stage categories are

Entry Step #2 and Insight Step #2. Essentially, here the coach focuses on helping the coachee gather facts. The goal is to ask questions that evoke detail but aren't limiting. This requires listening and avoiding the temptation to diagnose. Do not fall into the ineffective tendency to diagnose. This is not the job of the coach. Remember Terrence Maltbia's comment about how coaches should not do the heavy lifting: It is the coach's job to listen, be present, and ask questions or even offer suggestions. It is NOT the coach's job to offer solutions.

It is helpful for the coach to *play back*—to repeat—what the coach hears from the coachee. This supports the coach's effort to stay focused, plus it helps the coachee recognize the coach is engaged and processing the content the coachee is considering. Playing back what he or she hears is also a chance for the coach to help the coachee to ascertain what they intended to say was clear. The coach should ask questions that don't trigger a simple "yes" or "no," followed by silence. (If silence occurs because the coachee is thinking, that is part of the process. It is not the coach's job to fill that silence.)

In order to encourage more detailed answers, the coach might offer a question such as, "Do you have any sense as to why she might have reacted in that way?" or "If you didn't predict that reaction from the organization, did you have a different expectation and any thoughts on why you might have expected a different reaction?" Ask for examples, details, and thoughts to gain insight on what motivates actions and behaviors. Help the coachee remember that people's feelings can be ambivalent, nuanced; people can fall into the bad habit of seeing a negative self-evaluation as unquestionable and true.

Michael Morris points out that high achievers are often critical. Help the coachee see past what are referred to as Automatic Negative Thoughts (ANTs). It can be empowering to the coachee when they realize they have jumped to an automatic negative thought and have accepted their self-criticism as reality. As a coach, often just suggesting the possibility that the coachee's perspective is clouded by negative self-assessment is enough to open them to positive alternative interpretations. It may be clear that the coachee should collect more data about possible options. The end of this second stage is a good time for the coach to make sure they have pointed out positive qualities they see in the coachee and the opportunities they may have. It is now time to put an action plan together.

3) CONDUCT—"WHAT'S NEXT?"

Stage three in the CCC model is where the coach and coachee decide on the necessary action steps. In the PSI model, the categories are Entry Step #3 and Insight Step #3. This third stage of the model is critical because a contract, or set of agreed actions, puts steps into place that will prevent the coachee from a backsliding toward being reactive and passive in the face of personal leadership development opportunities. This is the part of the coaching process where the coach might see a benefit to move from inquiry more into advocacy, building on what the coachee has said up to this point. The coach is also helping the coachee do any final work in exploring useful strategies and moving from analyzing the challenges to planning. The coach and the coachee are moving toward the future. What are the options? What will the coach do next? How can the coach help the coachee commit to a specific plan?

What are tactical steps the coachee can take? Use the acronym S.M.A.R.T. to make sure the contract includes these categories: 1) specific; 2) measurable; 3) attainable; 4) realistic; and, 5) time-sensitive. My experience is that the contract will be followed if the coachee is motivated. The coach can't make this happen, but the coach can help the coachee be honest with themselves about their level of commitment to the challenge. If the coachee finds the motivation, new leadership opportunities will follow.

At the end of the coaching process it is suggested that the coach and the coachee sign a contract. The goal is for the coachee to commit to concrete behavioral steps and make a plan to communicate again after the coachee has attempted to fulfill the contract.

THE LADDER OF INFERENCE

The coach brings a perceptive guidance into the process that helps the coachee "step down the ladder of inference and back to the common ground of objectively observable behaviors."[24] The challenge of coaching, as Michael Morris writes, is "people sometimes have exaggeratedly self-critical thoughts and feelings that are irrational. Irrational self-criticism often takes the form of simplistic self-theories that support self-sabotaging strategies."[25] Morris gives examples of coachees who decide they will never be good at numbers or never be charismatic. He points out how these ways of thinking can defeat us before we make the effort to try. These strategies put us in the perspective of not having power. We believe that we will never be good enough.

We may have developed Automatic Negative Thoughts. These ANTs could have developed in our past to protect ourselves from trying to process negative feedback we received. If ANTs become familiar to us, we will continue to buy into believing the ANTs are true. We blind ourselves to options that may be available for us. The coach has the advantage of offering objective perspectives to the coachee, helping them understand they might be viewing their situation with a bias that isn't useful to their potential success.

The coachee needs to be helped back down from the ladder to solid ground, where they can see their challenges with clarity and avoid unproductive self-judgment. This *stepping down the ladder* process requires the ability for two people to enter a conversation about the context of the situation, gathering insight through exploring the content, and then deciding upon appropriate actions.

A COACHING EXERCISE: WORKING WITH AMBITION

One way to practice coaching is to identify an area where the coachee wants to develop. When I teach coaching, I ask people to identify an area in which they have an ambition to see change. This could be around professional or personal development. For example, in professional development, the coachee might want to improve their ability at selling a product; in personal development, the coachee might want to incorporate more healthy habits and practices into their daily life.

The first step is to identify that area where the coachee has an ambition to develop.

1) Arrange for a partner to work with you on this coaching exercise. It is preferable that the person is not a family member or close friend, as people close to us can jump to assumptions about what is in our best interest. Try to select someone who believes they can offer you objective coaching and who is comfortable

being honest with you. If you select someone you know well, be aware of your mutual need to be objective and not prescriptive.

2) Prior to beginning the exercise, identify one way you would like to improve yourself in the area of *ambition*. It might be helpful to reflect first on a time in your life when you were ambitious and you benefitted from the effort. Write down how you felt during the pursuit of that ambitious goal. What was your energy level? What was motivating you? What concerned you? What did it feel like if you achieved your goal? What did it feel like to pursue an ambitious goal, even if you did not hit your target completely? Our most aspirational efforts, even if unachieved, can remind us of the energy that motivated us.

   a. Write down the goal you have regarding ambition. Is there a particular goal you want to achieve? Is there a particular habit or quality you want to develop?

3) Identify which of you—yourself and your partner in the exercise—will go first as the coach and which as the coachee.

4) Take 20 to 30 minutes each and use the CCC model as a structure. Move through the coaching steps and conclude by creating a contract. Reverse roles as coach and coachee.

5) It is helpful when you are being coached to be open and available to help your coach work with you on the following questions:

   a. What story are you telling?

   b. What behaviors are you showing?

   c. What needs are driving your behaviors?

   d. What questions would help you sharpen your thinking?

   e. How can you move your insights into action?

Follow the coaching process, but also trust your natural instincts. When you are being coached, the goal is to see your situation as clearly as possible and then decide what can be done to bring about the most positive results.

When you are coaching, remember Musashi: "Think lightly of yourself and deeply of the world."

Coaching Senior Executives

In my experiences coaching senior executives, the coaching process is accelerated when the coachee recognizes a future leadership opportunity and understands the need for development to make that opportunity a success, as the following examples illustrate.

Peter's Developmental Goal:

Build the Organization's Confidence in His Ability to Drive Innovation

Two years ago, Peter, an AMP participant, accepted the optional post-program coaching session with me. Peter worked for a successful non-US bank positioned in an area with significant emerging markets. In our first coaching conversation, Peter told me that his finance skills within the bank had him pigeon-holed in terms of his perceived leadership capacities. He realized that part of this perception was based on his own unwillingness to take risks. If he wanted to be recognized as the leader he knew he could be, he needed to step outside of his comfort zone. His aspirations were to stop putting up unnecessary barriers for himself, and to make sure he came across as less aloof and less focused on just the technical aspects of his role. He wanted to be seen as a leader who could drive transformational change for the bank in the area of innovation.

Peter understood that as a CFO it was easy for him to fall back into cost reduction and risk management, but he chose to push himself into asking for a role leading innovation. Peter did exactly what Ned Stark was unable to do in King's Landing: Peter reflected upon his emotional tendencies to build his self-awareness and respond to the opportunities through self-management. He developed his leadership skills with action steps that included consciously guiding himself internally and presenting himself in a new way to stakeholders both inside and outside of the organization. By actively working more to present his abilities as a conceptual, innovative thinker and an empathetic, enthusiastic leader, Peter changed how the key decision-makers at his bank saw him. Peter was aware of his own tendency to be cautious and the perceptions of the colleagues to identify him as cautious, not innovative. He also recognized he needed to earn the trust of the Board of Directors. Peter was able to motivate and lead himself based on a contract he created through the coaching process. Despite previous perceptions of his skills as well as his limitations, he adapted and was able to present himself as capable of driving change in organizational areas that required creativity. He began to be perceived differently and was chosen to run innovation projects.

One year later, he was traveling from Africa to meetings in Silicon Valley, leading a team within his bank that was excited by the technological opportunities; while also running IT and Finance within the bank, he was guiding other stakeholders still moving up the curve to see the possibilities of his vision for the role of innovation at the bank.

Six months ago, Peter told me the bank was looking at seven possible new business ventures. He told me that his focus on learning from coaching was a critical part of the process. He is involved with technology and fulfilling an organizational mandate to build new business and revenue models. He is incubating a second new business and soon will be taking the first new business to market. In his own enthusiastic words: "So all is happening!"

Peter recognized the need to stay driven by his purpose of helping the organization see new opportunities. He understood that coaching would be the way for him to figure out how to reinvent himself as a leader. He pursued coaching in various ways. Phone sessions with me were just one of his approaches to self-development. Peter was aggressive in evaluating his potential areas for growth, and he worked hard to see himself objectively and identify ways to expand his skills and effectiveness in leadership within his organization.

In addition to leading himself, he told me that the process of being coached helped him focus on the people he worked with. He found an ability to pursue what excited him and also stay true to the interests of his direct reports and colleagues. It was energizing and deeply rewarding.

LAURIE'S DEVELOPMENTAL GOAL:

Clarify Her Boss's Understanding of Her Role and the Required Resources

One of the consistent challenges for senior executives is facing the disconnect between how they envision their ability to contribute to the organization and how their potential is evaluated by their boss.

Laurie, an executive in the medical insurance industry and a recent graduate of our AMP, was frustrated. She knew she had a decision in front of her, as a job offer from another organization was heading her way. The new job would entail an increase in responsibility, as well as other appealing benefits. Her current job had been exciting and she had achieved success. She was proud of her efforts but also faced issues that seemed unlikely to be reconciled in her current role. She needed her boss to make certain decisions about her responsibilities and resources, but it didn't look like that would happen. Laurie faced reality: she would need to decide if she should leave her current organization in order to take a job better aligned with her aspirations, even though taking the new job meant giving up her role with an organization that was important to her.

During a coaching session, I asked Laurie to tell me more about the context and answer the question: *What's up?* The answer was that she wanted a more strategic role in her organization. She felt constrained on the intellectual side and was leaning toward taking the new job because it offered a clear opportunity to pursue a strategy, to possibly step into part-time teaching at the university level, and to be around people involved in trying to solve ambitious challenges, including bringing new solutions to her industry. The salary in Laurie's current role wasn't an issue. The issue was around her engagement and energy for the role as her boss defined it versus the possibilities Laurie saw for herself to offer transformational solutions to industry challenges.

She had, until recently, loved her job. She had just returned from the Columbia AMP and wanted a chance to apply the leadership knowledge she had been developing to make a positive impact on the organization. The trajectory of the organization had become focused on doing more with less. In her words, "It's not fun. . . . I felt a bit empty. I couldn't free myself. I felt a bit stuck." It would be rational to suggest that most of us on any given day aren't always having fun, and might feel a bit empty and stuck. That can be the normal situation for an adult with responsibilities. Still, if one's daily emotional reaction to a job involves feeling stuck and the job not being fun then there is a tension that demands answers.

What matters to Laurie is to be able to do more . . . to make big things happen. When we discussed the question *what matters?*, she said, "I have never met an unknown I can't tackle." Laurie needs to make an impact. In health care, this involves being able to approach persistent challenges in innovative ways. She knows it could happen at the new organization, but she's not sure she wants to leave her current company. She believes that if she was given the right support, she could contribute in a significant way to solving big challenges for her current organization and the industry. But this requires being empowered to attack the big challenges. As she put it, "I can't get outside of the organization and learn what options might work, if I'm always in the weeds." The job feels boring and she feels stuck.

Her *what's up?* (context) is that she's not satisfied in the current dynamic. Her *what matters?* (content) is that she wants to contribute to her organization by taking on significant challenges. This isn't an opportunity presented to her. Ideally, the new role offered would be at a strategic level, but if not, it will still offer her the chance to pursue ambitious goals and not limit her to conserving resources. Laurie needs to decide if she should take the new job offer.

The question on the table: What should she do? *What's next?* (conduct).

In our coaching session we looked at options. One option was for Laurie to make the effort to gain absolute clarity about the situation from her current boss. Laurie decides to initiate a discussion that will resolve where her boss stands on giving Laurie more independence and the resources to get out of the weeds. This will provide Laurie a chance to fulfill her own commitment to being authentic by being clear about what she looks for in her role. It will provide a chance to discuss with her boss how Laurie's values drive her effort and why she has aspirations to put her efforts behind big goals and not just do more with less. This conversation would also open the door to discuss their mutual challenges and potential successes and what Laurie can do to support the goals of her boss. Focusing on core values will help Laurie clarify what is important to her and also raise ways that she can discuss how to help her boss achieve success as a leader. Laurie is excited about the idea of making her own values clear to her boss with the purpose of helping her boss also succeed. This would be a win-win arrangement.

Laurie realizes that in addition to this win-win perspective, she will also need to get into specific tactics with her boss. If not, the talk could all be warm and positive, but then Laurie would be in a position to have to sell any new arrangement to the executive team without clear support from her boss. This conduct—her decision on *what's next?*—will also help Laurie make a decision regarding her outside job offer. If her boss doesn't agree with Laurie's aspirations and potential to support the company, then Laurie will move on and take the job with the new organization. The conversation can provide the clarity necessary for Laurie to make the right career move.

Ten days after our coaching call, Laurie wrote me. The job offer from the new organization had arrived. Laurie spoke with her boss and explained her aspirations, focusing on her core values. They discussed how she faced unworkable constraints if she stayed in her job the way it was designed. If her role was redesigned, she could stay. Her boss agreed and provided Laurie with additional staff so that she could delegate her operational duties and focus on the bigger challenges.

Our two coachees, Peter and Laurie, both took the initiative to choose a coach to help them gain clarity on their challenges, define their potential constraints and opportunities, and then pursue their goals. Peter responded to his opportunities by working on self-management and developing action steps that could prepare him to be seen by his colleagues in a new way. Peter transformed the limiting perception of him as always acting cautiously, to being known as someone acting innovatively. Laurie recognized that in her professional life, she was successful at taking on big challenges. She had confidence in her capabilities and needed to test them. Her work responsibilities weren't offering her the chance to take on the big challenges. She decided not to accept constraints that limited what she could accomplish.

ARYA'S DANCEMASTER

Like Peter and Laurie, Arya Stark searches for coaches to advise her on her unpredictable, dangerous, and important path. The youngest daughter of the warden of the northernmost of the Seven Kingdoms doesn't want to be limited by the ways other choose to see her. She doesn't want to feel stuck.

Let's apply the CCC coaching model to Arya's situation when her father is imprisoned in King's Landing:

1) WHAT'S UP FOR ARYA? WHAT'S THE CONTEXT?

Arya has been brought to a foreign city by her father. She has no interests other than learning to fight with weapons. Arya learns fast that power matters . . . and skill with weapons offers power.

2) WHAT MATTERS FOR ARYA? WHAT'S THE CONTENT?

Most of Arya's allies don't understand her or they minimize her interests as unbecoming of a young lady. Her father is arrested and she is sought out by the Queen's soldiers. She is trapped in an environment where no one can protect her. It appears that her swordsmanship teacher, her dancemaster, Syrio Forel is killed by Meryn Trant and the White Cloaks of the Kingsguard. Syrio urges her to flee. Arya wants to survive, to secure her freedom, and continue to train in the combat arts.

3) WHAT'S NEXT FOR ARYA? WHAT'S HER CONDUCT?

Arya escapes King's Landing and fights for her survival and revenge.

Arya, like Peter and Laurie, decides to evaluate her situation, identify her options, and act on her insights, which include a strong encouragement from her coach at a life-threatening moment.

Peter and Laurie make the choice to attempt to push their careers in a new, aspirational direction. Peter and Laurie choose coaches to help them think through their leadership options, find the necessary action, and then take it.

Arya also makes the choice to pursue her aspirations. Her early training prepares her to deliver on Forel's encouragement that she not let herself get arrested by Cersei's soldiers. Syrio has left five men on the ground, dead or dying, armed only with a wooden staff. Ser Meryn Trant approaches him, armored, a steel sword in his hand. Syrio has resumed his stance, after decimating the men that attacked him. His future is dire. "'Arya child,' he called out, never looking at her, 'be gone now.'"[26]

It takes grit to confront authorities and flee into the unknown. Arya runs. "All that Syrio Forel had taught her went racing through her head. *Swift as a deer. Quiet as a shadow. Fear cuts deeper than swords. Quick as a snake. Calm as still water. Fear cuts deeper than swords.*"[27]

We will look at Arya's journey and the influence of the mentors—both positive and negative—that offer coaching. Arya has the tenacity to pursue what matters to her: fighting and the use of weapons. She has full commitment. Arya is focused. She finds a meditative attention in the details of her new craft. She knows what she wants and pursues her goal. In *Grit: The Power of Passion and Perseverance*, Angela Duckworth writes, "Grit is about working on something you care about so much that you're willing to stay loyal to it."[28] Though Arya Stark is not the only person that will depend on grit to survive and succeed in Westeros and Essos, this young woman exemplifies the benefits of grit. Arya escapes, whispering the guidance of her teacher. She enters her warrior's path. Let's consider her journey and how she learns from coaching.

TRUE SEEING: THAT IS THE HEART OF IT

The ronin, Musashi, would appreciate the teaching methods of the former First Sword of Braavos, Syrio Forel. Musashi insisted that a person needs to conquer himself or herself before he or she can take on the world. This is the journey Syrio coaches Arya to begin: 1) conquer internal conflict, and 2) conquer external conflict. Syrio Forel advises his young student on the importance of practice, the value of listening, and the ability to see what is real.

Syrio Forel has unique training methods. Ned finds his daughter chasing a tomcat, who is "older than sin and twice as mean."[29] The Hand of the King smiles when Arya Underfoot explains that she chases cats to develop her agility. She has caught many cats Syrio has set for her, but this tomcat is the big challenge. Arya likes a challenge. She studies with Forel, but she could also be learning from Musashi, who wrote: "It will seem difficult at first, but everything is difficult at first."[30] The former First Sword of Braavos serves as Arya's coach in significant ways. He gives her a language to keep her spirit calm, even as her mind and body must perform for survival under great pressure. This is a challenge that applies to chasing cats through the tunnels beneath the Red Keep, and also applies to the challenges Arya faces when she travels out into Westeros, hunted by the Queen's men, after watching her father's execution. The ronin Musashi advises, "Even when your spirit is calm do not let your body relax, and when your body is relaxed do not let your spirit slacken."[31]

Syrio has prepared Arya for conflict, asking her questions, guiding her insights, developing his young Stark pupil. He had shared with Arya a story that he said explained why he was the best swordsman in Braavos. There were younger men, faster men, stronger men, but Syrio, her coach, had once been the best. Curiously, it was his monarch, the Sealord, who tested him in a simple way. Syrio was shown an exotic animal from a distant land, and asked to identify the strange creature. He could see past the mythmaking and understood that the exotic animal was just a tomcat. "The seeing, the true seeing, that is the heart of it." He tells Arya the story and she says, "You saw what was there." The Braavosi tells her, "Just so. Opening your eyes is all that is needing."[32] True seeing is critical in battle, as Syrio and Musashi would agree, and it is critical in leadership. Coaching is a method we can use to build our own abilities to succeed against conflict. Seeking coaching, and offering coaching, is one path toward true seeing. Coaching is a powerful tool in our effort to learn from Syrio and *see true*.

FEAR VERSUS SWORDS

Arya develops a fierce will, to gain revenge but also to survive and to build her skill and knowledge. She learns to control her immediate urges for the long-term fulfillment of her development and her vision. She repeats the guidance of her guru, her coach: *"Fear cuts deeper than swords."*[33]

In the *Harvard Business Review* reading "Fear of Feedback," Jay M. Jackman and Myra H. Strober emphasize the importance in our organizational environments of learning to handle feedback and not let fear contribute to "maladaptive behaviors such as procrastination, denial, brooding, jealousy and self-sabotage."[34] This ability to learn from feedback is what the ronin Musashi and the former First Sword of Braavos encourage. Arya is told by Syrio to recognize fear as a danger that is sharper than a blade. Syrio prepares Arya to understand the brutal feedback of fear when it arrives.

In our world, as in Westeros and Essos, we can benefit from the insights in "Fear of Feedback." People in organizational life can "learn to acknowledge negative emotions, constructively reframe fear and criticism, develop realistic goals, create support systems, and reward themselves for achievements along the way."[35] Arya learns this skill. She can acknowledge her fear, which is necessary to her escape from King's

Landing. She reframes her fear into a nightly reminder of her goal to exact what we in our modern world call "closure" to those that betrayed her. She wants revenge. These nightly revenge prayers are one step she takes to make her goals realistic. The second step she takes is to learn how to fight. In a third step, she creates support systems from colleagues as diverse and dangerous as Tywin, Jaqen, the Hound, even the Waif. Arya never quits. She chooses to learn and develop skills, even learning skills from coaches willing to kill her. Arya rewards herself for her patience and effort when she exacts her revenge on Trant, Frey, and Baelish.

She understands that she will benefit from taking the long view. Excellence won't happen overnight. In the words of Musashi: "Step by step walk the thousand-mile road. . . . Today is victory over yourself of yesterday."[36] Arya goes through many tests, not fleeing them but inviting them. Her pursuit of these tests takes her across the Narrow Sea to the city of her dancemaster: Braavos. She requests training and mentorship at the House of Black and White. Jaqen allows Arya to train as a Faceless Man. Arya doesn't lack courage or commitment, but she decides not to abandon her humanity after killing the Waif. She has completed her transformation into *no one*: an assassin for the Many-Faced God. Jaqen sees the removed face of the Waif placed in the Hall of Faces in the House of Black and White. He says to Arya, "Finally, a girl is no one." But Arya *is* someone. "A girl is Arya Stark of Winterfell."[37]

Arya will be cut and wounded, threatened and chased, from Winterfell to King's Landing, from Harrenhal to Braavos, and back to her northern home. But fear won't stop this young woman from returning to protect those she loves. She pursues her Leader's Journey and finds her way back home, against great odds, with the boons of fighting skill, courage, and a deeper commitment to those she has privately sworn to protect. She succeeds due to her ability to learn from coaches, both good and bad.

THE LEADER'S JOURNEY: SUPERNATURAL AID AND CROSSING THE FIRST THRESHOLD

Campbell believes myths provide us with metaphorical examples that can help us lead ourselves to a fulfilling life. "What is it we are questing for? It is the fulfillment of that which is potential in each of us."[38] Fulfilling our potential matters. "There's nothing you can do that's more important than being fulfilled. You become a sign, you become a signal, transparent to transcendence; in this way, you will find, live, and become a realization of your own personal myth."[39]

Campbell believed we have a wisdom inside of us and that *bliss* is an effective adjective to describe the welling up of this energy. Myths can help us find our bliss. We need to turn to these mythologies, these stories, to guide us to achieve our potential. We hold the choice to live our lives in the pursuit of becoming fulfilled—a sign, a signal, transparent to the possibility of transcendence. We have the choice to improve ourselves in an effort to achieve success.

Myths and stories guide us. Myths have similar structures and recurring themes. The idea of help from the outside, from some force beyond ourselves is appealing, recurring; it can motivate us, drive us forward, encourage us to locate and allow aid from unpredictable sources, but we can't accept any coach. We must listen, consider, and choose which voices are important.

Coaching and being coached are methods to pursue fulfillment and success. Daenerys Targaryen follows her democratic, protective, and trusting instincts in the tall grass on the Dothraki Sea. This leads to the horrible destruction of her husband and stillborn baby, but this betrayal of trust is her crucible.

As Nick Craig writes in *Leading from Purpose*: "Challenges on any scale—ranging from personal problems to disasters—can bring us to rock bottom. When we find ourselves in one of these crucible experiences, we rely on our innermost resources for a way out. We reach for and find the purpose that will lead us out of trouble."[40] Her loss sharpens Daenerys's commitment to her greater leadership capabilities and the risks that go with her choice to lead.

In Joseph Campbell's monomyth, Supernatural Aid is his name for the stage where the hero meets up with a figure that represents the benign, protecting power of destiny. This figure offers a talisman. Obi-Wan Kenobi, in *Star Wars: A New Hope,* gives Luke Skywalker his lightsaber: a talisman for self-defense to achieve Luke's goals. This protecting, benign figure of Obi-Wan, in the words of Campbell, is a fantasy, "a reassurance—a promise that the peace of Paradise, which was known first within the mother womb, is not to be lost."[41] The maegi in Essos appears to be this figure, offering magic to help Daenerys. According to Campbell, "The higher mythologies develop the role in the great figure of the guide, the teacher, the ferryman, the conductor of souls to the afterworld."[42] But the idea that this guide or teacher exists doesn't mean that all who present themselves this way are trustworthy.

The maegi isn't the old man or woman that Campbell argues will offer amulets and magical support to assist the hero in his or her journey, "For those who have not refused the call, the first encounter of the hero-journey is with a protective figure."[43] Mirri Maz Duur is not an ally. She is revenge of the Lhazareen on the Dothraki, which includes the khaleesi. Supernatural Aid does arrive for Daenerys, but it is not in the form of the maegi. "What such a figure represents is the benign, protecting power of destiny."[44] No, this protecting power of destiny doesn't arrive in the grateful presence of a Lambwoman healer pulled from violent rape. The power of destiny arrives for Dany in the wedding gift offered by Magister Illyrio Mopatis: three fossilized dragon eggs from the Shadow Lands beyond Asshai.

The adventure won't happen without the courage, vision, and motivation to Cross the First Threshold. "The adventure is always and everywhere a passage beyond the veil of the known and the unknown."[45] Arya has crossed beyond the veil of the known and the unknown. She has been thrust past the threshold of community and has no choice except to run but still has been preparing for this moment. Her sister, Sansa, isn't prepared. The pretty one that bought into the story of an easy, perfect married life to her handsome prince, will stay locked under house arrest, prisoner of House Lannister, a teenage gamepiece for Cersei, King Joffrey, Petyr Baelish, and Ramsay Bolton. The days ahead for Sansa will be horrible, filled with psychological and physical suffering, a fate only slightly better than what her childhood friend from Winterfell, Jeyne Poole, must face in the novels.

Arya, the brawler, disparaging of surface appearances, crosses the first threshold and finds her way forward, angry, scared, and hungry to fight. She benefits from coaching, which can make all the difference: "The powers that watch at the boundary are dangerous; to deal with them is risky; yet for anyone with competence and courage the danger fades."[46] The danger escalates, but Arya trains herself to keep confronting the danger. Her courage combined with her skill with weapons becomes her strength and her shield. The danger doesn't fade for Arya, but the constant noise of threat lessens for her because she develops skills to face it.

Through learning from all her coaches—both the favorable ones serving Arya's best interest, and the riskier ones who serve their own ends—Arya keeps developing competence and courage. In volume one of *The Hagakure: A Code to the Way of the Samurai,* Yamamoto Tsunetomo argues for the importance of surpassing others by listening to them. "Consulting others is the foundation for making a leap ahead of others."[47] Arya takes this quiet counsel in her approach to her mentors, whether Syrio Forel, Tywin Lannister, Sandor Clegane, or Jaqen H'ghar.

In volume two, Tsunetomo recommends the importance of knowing the nature of others in order to resolve or settle issues with them. "To settle matters, one should understand the other man's nature quickly and deal with him accordingly."[48]

It takes Arya Stark time to develop the skills necessary to respond to the natures of the people that hurt those she loves, but she has the courage to enter her journey and cross the first threshold. She learns the natures of both enemies and allies. Her grasp on Walder Frey's nature helps her poison his followers who executed her family at the Red Wedding.

Arya enters her trials. Her fighting spirit in A Song of Ice and Fire's Known World emboldens her and reminds us to choose to accept our adventure. Arya develops her warrior skill through her commitment to courage. Her heroism can remind us to use courage. She delivers us the boon of courage.

George R. R. Martin said, "We read fantasy to find the colors again, I think. To taste strong spices and hear the songs the siren sang. There is something old and true in fantasy that speaks to something deep within us."[49] When Ned Stark stumbles in his decision making, we stand in the crowd at the Great Sept of Baelor. A street urchin mistaken for a boy, Arya Stark, watches the terrible result of her father's misdirected noble leadership turned into tragic sacrifice. We are at the foot of the statue of Baelor the Blessed as two soldiers pull Lord Stark in front of King Joffrey. We are in the language of dreams, and we are also in the metaphor of fiction, ready to be coached as our terror lifts us. The screaming crowd rants for the head of the supposed betrayer of the Iron Throne. We are with Arya and Sansa as the sisters watch the unwatchable event of their father's public execution. What could Lord Stark have done to prevent this fate? What can we do to make the most of our leadership opportunities . . . and the challenges that face us in our world? Can we respond with the immediate resourcefulness of Arya? Can we learn as Sansa learns through her resilience?

We can build our leadership skills, both internally and externally, and learn from George R. R. Martin's myth to prepare ourselves to write the Leader's Journey our ancestors will read: the story about our courage and the skills, including wisdom, we developed with the guidance of our coaches.

GOING FORWARD

Coaching is one method to bring out the best in ourselves and our people. Daenerys Targaryen accepted the wrong advisor, the wrong coach, and trusted the wrong supernatural aid. The result was the deaths of those she loved, but she learned to be careful about her future selection of coaches. She learned through her mistake and was able to leverage the support of liberated slaves, outliers from a foreign government, and the supernatural aid of her dragons. Daenerys learned that at the end of each intense workday, whether she is on the Dothraki plains or on Slaver's Bay in the Ghiscari city of Meereen, or on Blackwater Bay at the castle Dragonstone, she must be aware of the stakes of the game she plays; she must evaluate her advisors and then walk forward, able to find confidence, confront the risk, and not look back in fear.

Arya Stark was given the sword she named Needle by her brother (later revealed to be her cousin), Jon Snow. Neither Arya nor Jon recognized how soon Arya's future would depend on that weapon. She had a coach, Syrio Forel, who saved her life by preparing her for the conflict that would arrive on the path to achieve her goals. His spirit has lived in her and built her wisdom, skills, and success.

We all face blind spots in our leadership. We all can benefit from identifying and learning from the right coaches. Coaching matters when, in the words of Terrence Maltbia talking to the senior executives at the Advanced Management Program, you put "something in front of it." That something will consist of goals that contribute to our success. Find coaches that will help you challenge your automatic negative thoughts, that will help you climb down the ladder of inference, and that will help you pursue what matters on your Leader's Journey.

If you have the chance to coach: listen. Think lightly of yourself and deeply of the world.

BE A PLAYER, NOT A PIECE!

HOW TO BUILD RESILIENCE TO CONFRONT ADVERSITY

Sansa Stark had a serene childhood, enlivened by Septa Mordane's dark stories of long winters and otherworldly creatures descending from north of the Wall. When faced with adversity, we can decide to be a *player* or a *victim*. The victim, as described by Littlefinger to Sansa, is being a *piece*. The victim doesn't choose to be responsible for his or her situation. The external problems from the perspective of the victim are just too big. The player takes responsibility and responds to the situation. If remorse is looking back and realizing we did something poorly and regret is looking back and feeling pain over not trying something, Sansa is unfairly thrust into situations where remorse and regret appear to be her future. She fights and creates a different future.

After her escape from King's Landing, Sansa realizes she has been a victim, a piece. She needs to find a way out of her victimhood and become a player.

THE PRETTY ONE

Sansa grew up with a stable family dynamic. Her little sister was annoying and embarrassing, but her brothers were what brothers should be: handsome, courageous, and kind. Her parents were responsible, committed romantic partners, protective of their clan. Her uncle and grandfather had died brutally in a civil war, but that was ancient history. Sansa wasn't forced to connect the dots between irrational authority figures and make sense of a toxic environment filled with trauma. The path stretched ahead from their castle gates and the journey appeared idyllic. It wouldn't be.

Leaving Winterfell for King's Landing, Sansa Stark is winsome, lovestruck, and trained by Septa Mordane to be a success in courtship and court life. As her sister, Arya, notes, "She blushed prettily. She did everything prettily."[1] Sansa joins her father and sister on the journey to King's Landing. Catelyn Stark believes her oldest daughter will find happiness through marriage to Prince Joffrey, as well as a likely future as queen of the Seven Kingdoms.

When Sansa first sets off from Winterfell, joining her father, sister, and the Baratheon entourage south to the sun-splashed capital, she reveals hints of moody independence, teenage impetuousness, and understandable vanity. Sansa is the good daughter; the one with auburn hair that catches the winter light; she has the cheekbones. Whether true friend, promised friend, or obvious foe, people call her sweetling. Even the Queen recognizes and acknowledges Sansa's beauty. Sansa knits with precision, plays instruments, and recites poetry. Confronted on proper behavior by Septa Mordane, Sansa still insists on feeding Lady, her direwolf, by hand at the table. She has just enough rebellion to be an adorable teenager, full of promise.

The rest of her actions are committed to fulfilling the perfect fate promised to her by the idealized stories she has been told and retold, stories that sanitized the conflicted motivations and behaviors of past figures in Westerosi history. Even after the petty, vicious, unjustified execution of her direwolf on orders of the Queen, Sansa buys into the appealing narrative: love will protect you, your future will be perfect, your children will be blond.

Sansa's trip to the southron capital goes wrong when she is caught up in the murderous drama of Prince Joffrey, Arya, Mycah (the butcher's son), and Queen Cersei's power play against the Starks. Even when Lady is executed by her father at the order of the King, Sansa is confident all will be right in the realm and her future. While Arya follows the training advice of her Braavos dancemaster and chases tomcats in the bowels of the Red Keep, and while Ned Stark works to solve the mysterious death of Jon Arryn, Sansa is happy. "She loved King's Landing; the pageantry of the court, the high lords and ladies in their velvets and silks and gemstones, the great city with all its people."[2]

At her first public joust, Sansa sees nothing but the fulfillment of the ancient songs of heroism and romance. After the news of rape, thievery, and murder, when her father selects Beric Dondarrion to lead the sortie and track down the *false knight* Ser Gregor Clegane, Sansa is deeply frustrated that the Knight of Flowers isn't selected. While "nibbling delicately at a chicken leg,"[3] she reflects on how the glamorous Loras Tyrell would have been the logical choice. Ser Loras was even younger and more handsome than Beric. If *The Mountain* was the monster, then the *Knight of Flowers* should be the hero to slay him. Sansa believes her journey will deliver to her the romance of the songs. She is mistaken. Sansa looks for leadership by those in authority. Sansa wants to follow. She will do things prettily in exchange for being rewarded. This strategy doesn't work.

Sansa will realize that everything depends on her ability to learn and her courage to act to secure her freedom. Her courage to act will depend on her resilience—in particular two social constructs related to it: grit and sisu. How can we learn, like Sansa, to move from being a piece to a player? We can be conscious of the way grit and sisu can support our choice to build our resilience.

RESILIENCE

Angela Duckworth suggests grit is "a passion and perseverance for very long-term goals."[4] Grit depends on recognizing that achievements come to us due to our extensive effort and not from a sudden burst of interest. Research shows that having talent doesn't necessarily lead to operating with grit, but it helps to have what Carol Dweck defined as a *growth mindset*.[5] The growth mindset is about recognizing that you are not born with a limited amount of ability but can develop and learn. You always have the choice of taking action to pursue your development. This perspective supports a positive impact on one's development of grit: people persevere because they don't believe failure is a permanent condition.

My colleague at Columbia Business School and partner in running

the AMP, Paul Ingram, uses the example of Josh Waitzkin to introduce the growth mindset to our classes of senior executives. Josh Waitzkin made the choice to work as a student and transform from a
world-class prodigy in chess—a cerebral, stationary sport—to a world-
class fighter in combative martial arts.

In *The Art of Learning: An Inner Journey to Optimal Performance*,
Waitzkin talks about the importance of having a beginner's mind and
being aware of the value in investment in loss. "In all disciplines, there
are times when a performer is ready for action, and times when he or
she is soft, in flux, broken-down or in a period of growth."[6] During
these latter times, the learner is vulnerable, but it is important to recognize what is going on and give yourself *protected periods of cultivation*.

How does this relate to our work lives? Waitzkin points out that in
the business world, "there are seldom weeks in which performance
does not matter."[7] It is one thing to have a beginner's mind and focus
on investment in loss when we are novices in a chosen hobby or sport,
but can we have that incremental approach that allows us to learn from
investment in loss even as we are being expected to perform in our
profession? Waitzkin's message is to keep the growth mindset while
under pressure. In Waitzkin's words, "The key to pursuing excellence
is to embrace an organic, long-term learning process, and not to live in
a shell of static, safe mediocrity. Usually, growth comes at the expense
of previous comfort or safety."[8]

SISU

Sisu, a Finnish concept more than five hundred years old, is related to
grit. As Emilia Lahti, a mentee at Penn of Angela Duckworth, says, "Sisu
begins where perseverance and grit end."[9] At the 3rd World Congress
on Positive Psychology in Los Angeles, sisu was further described as a
psychological key competence which enables extraordinary action to
overcome a mentally or physically challenging situation, "the ability to
endure significant stress while taking action against seemingly impossible odds and extreme adversity. Sisu is what we depend on when we
have nothing left. It provides us with the final empowering push when
we would otherwise hesitate to act."[10] Sisu is a catalyst. It is "more about
the short-term intensity in that moment."[11] Sisu is about taking action,

displaying resoluteness; it is "similar to equanimity, with the addition of a grim kind of stress management."[12]

In 1940, *Time* magazine wrote about it when describing how the Finns held off the Russian army, despite being badly outnumbered. "It is a compound of bravado, bravery, of ferocity and tenacity, of the ability to keep fighting after most people would have quit, and fight with a will to win."[13] Grit is long-term. Sisu is courage driven by a back-against-the-wall desperation. In addition to being a catalyst, sisu can be a bridge to keep us persevering and help us guide ourselves and our colleagues toward resilience. It is a pathway that arrives when we need it. In the words of Emilia Lahti, it "helps us fight the fight first."[14]

Two figures from history demonstrate how grit and sisu enable resilience.

VIKTOR AND FREDERICK

Viktor Frankl's *Man's Search for Meaning* and Frederick Douglass's *Narrative of the Life of Frederick Douglass, an American Slave* are nonfiction narratives where the authors are placed unfairly in the category of a piece. These two men worked with what they had available, including a belief in themselves, a desire for freedom, and resilience to transform themselves and those around them into players. They fulfilled the definition of resilience provided by Rick Hanson in his book *Resilient*: "Mental resources like determination, self-worth, and kindness are what make us *resilient*: able to cope with adversity and push through challenges in the pursuit of opportunities."[15]

Viktor Frankl, neurologist, psychiatrist, and survivor of the Holocaust, describes the vicious *capos*, prisoners selected by the Nazi SS for their ability to be brutal to the other prisoners. He also writes about the prisoners who found survival to be their ultimate purpose, even at the expense of any other moral focus. "On the average, only those prisoners could keep alive who, after years of trekking from camp to camp, had lost all scruples in their fight for existence; they were prepared to use every means, honest and otherwise, even brutal force, theft, and betrayal of their friends, in order to save themselves."[16] Frankl goes on to write that it was a miracle to survive if you didn't follow this strategy. He writes: "the best of us did not return." Yet, some prisoners he observed chose to honor their commitments to their morals and to humanity, even in the face of imminent death. They chose, under the most horrendous of circumstances, to be players and maintain their moral compasses. They faced their mortality with resilience. Frankl saw prisoners—including himself—who made the choice to confront the horror of their imprisonment with a moral commitment to hold true to their beliefs under incredible pressure. Regarding resilience, Duckworth writes, it's "not just falling in love— *staying* in love."[17] The same is true for prisoners that sustain their moral code when others are betraying and abandoning it. They didn't fall in brief affection for their moral code; they stayed committed to it while under terrible threat of harm. Grit is ultimately about stamina.

Frederick Douglass, orator, abolitionist, writer, and statesman, escaped slavery as a young man. While enslaved in the Southern United States prior to the Civil War, he was subject to the violent discipline of Mr. Covey, a white man recognized as a slave breaker, who beat Douglass. Exhausted, wounded, desperate, Douglass faced the reality that he had no choice left but to fight even though choosing to fight back could lead to his execution. He accessed the equivalent of the Finnish social construct of sisu and decided to confront the slave breaker, raising his fists and punching back, even at the likelihood of his own death. "Mr. Covey seemed now to think he had me, and could do what he pleased; but at this moment—from whence came the spirit I don't know—I resolved to fight."[18] Douglass ended up fighting two men. The fight extended for two hours. Later, after he escaped slavery to freedom, Douglass became an orator, speaking on the horror of living in slavery. He described this moment of confronting the slave breaker as the catalyst to his freedom, writing that it was "the turning-point in my career as a slave. It rekindled the few expiring embers of freedom, and revived within me a sense of my own manhood."[19]

With his back against the wall and the stakes as high as possible, he chose to fight. After his choice, he recalled, "I did not hesitate to let it be known of me, that the white man who expected to succeed in whipping, must also succeed in killing me."[20] Douglass applied grit to his effort to escape. He recognized it would take significant time and effort. A first attempt was a failure and almost cost him his life. He described the great difficulty in staying focused on reaching his goal and not losing hope. He found work in a shipyard but was forced to give a significant part of his pay to the white man who owned him.

He operated with sisu when he confronted Mr. Covey. He continued to operate with grit in his commitment to secure his escape from slavery and become a free man. "My discontent grew upon me. I was ever on the look-out for means of escape; and, finding no direct means, I determined to try to hire my time, with a view of getting money with which to make my escape."[21] He found his way forward with the help of his wife. He impersonated a sailor on a ship, but first he had to persevere and be resilient against the various adversities that confronted him daily and throughout his young life. "The wretchedness of slavery, and the blessedness of freedom, were perpetually before me. It was life and death with me. But I remained firm, and, according to my resolution, on the third day of September, 1838, I left my chains, and succeeded in reaching New York."[22]

In the direst of circumstances, both Frankl and Douglass found a path forward to approach the hardships of their journeys as players, not pieces. As Douglass operated with sisu and grit to support his resilience in slavery, Viktor Frankl also relied on sisu and grit to develop his resilience during the Holocaust. He tried to help those who were vulnerable, and keep a grasp on what he believed was morally correct behavior. He also reminded himself that he always had the power of choice. He bravely fought (sisu) his internal mental battle and reminded himself that someday in the future he would use what he learned in the concentration camps to contribute to the knowledge of humankind (grit).

RESILIENCE DEVELOPMENT EXERCISES

Our leadership challenges will hopefully never put us in situations as dire as the fictional situations faced by Sansa Stark, or the real-life situations that were faced by Frederick Douglass and Viktor Frankl, but we still want to leverage our resilience. The following two exercises will help with staying in a player mode when facing challenges.

Exercise #1—The Living Case—offers a chance to gain advice from peers. This is an external exercise that relies on the consulting of advocates.

Exercise #2—Your Resilience Story—is an internal exercise that offers a chance to prepare oneself to face challenges in the future.

Both exercises are opportunities to leverage Josh Waitzkin's idea of "investment in loss." You are not ready to act and resolve the challenge, but you are preparing for action. The choice is not to live in what Waitzkin called "static, safe mediocrity" but to take responsibility for your challenges and pursue excellence.

RESILIENCE DEVELOPMENT: EXERCISE #1

The Living Case

In the senior executive Advanced Management Program, we have a project called the *Living Case*. Executives write three to five pages describing a leadership challenge they face at their organization. The objective of the exercise is to provide leaders with diverse perspectives on the challenge they face. Each executive describes their challenge, answers questions to a small group of colleagues to provide necessary context, and then the executive leaves the room. Their colleagues work together as a consulting team to provide solutions to the challenges. This builds resilience for the executive by providing fresh insights. The executive will frequently say after the exercise that they realized he or she had been analyzing their challenge in a myopic way, seeing it through one limiting lens of possible solutions. The diverse perspectives of their colleagues—from different industries and cultures—energized them to move forward and win.

The process of the workshop is simple: 1) each executive provides a clear description of his or her challenge, 2) a selected team of classmates serves as consultants; the team comprises people with different industry experience and a range of functional, cultural, and leadership backgrounds, 3) the executive answers questions about his or her Living Case and then leaves the room, 4) the teams work on each participant's case and then present their suggestions.

Each Living Case takes ninety minutes; this doesn't sound like much time and it's not unusual to have participants go into the workshop skeptical about the process in advance, but the process works. Consistently, the recipients of the consulting advice gain insight from seeing their problems through the fresh perspectives of their colleagues. Their post-workshop enthusiasm is strong and the majority have immediate *aha* moments and return to their organizations with solutions to put into action.

The Living Case produces results because the executives on the teams are business leaders that have persevered through challenges throughout their careers. They are proactive and expect to find solutions. They have learned to bounce back from adversity and they bring this energy and curiosity to learn; they are hungry to solve the problems presented by their classmates' cases.

Some recent Living Cases in the AMP have included:

1) *Culture (Germany)*: Sustain and develop creativity on a service industry team that is having resources taken away by headquarters.

2) *Persuasion (Australia)*: Support the growth of a company involved in large infrastructure projects, where the use of tax dollars and value added to the community must be demonstrated to gain buy-in with politicians representing the voting public.

3) *Motivation (Denmark)*: Manage an impending change in CEO leadership, which could include new reporting relationship to a colleague with opposing leadership behaviors and values, and could impact team's ability, opportunity, and commitment.

4) *Strategy (Thailand)*: Lead a mission to regulate and moderate health-care products, help consumers gain knowledge, and confront the dangers of purchasing illegal health-care products.

5) *Multigenerational Workforce (USA)*: Bridge the gap between millennials and boomers.

6) *CEO's Work-Life Balance (UK)*: Confront a personal leadership habit to get "in the weeds" and be too operational; instead learn to trust people, effectively communicate the organization's vision, and hold people accountable.

The Living Case works because of the trust created in the group. It operates under the idea that people from diverse industries who have a strong bond can help one another see their leadership challenges from a new perspective. Look for a group of people that have different professional experiences and, ideally, can bring emotional intelligence and commitment to advising on your challenge.

One approach is to get together a group of colleagues in your organization, especially people from different parts of the organization that face different challenges, or different elements of similar challenges. Another option would be to reach out to people you know in different industries and arrange a plan to write and distribute the Living Cases, read them, and then work together in groups to develop guidance.

How to Write a Living Case

Draft the following description of your business challenge:

1. Succinct problem statement.

2. Brief analytic discussion of the situation.

3. Brief company description.

4. Description of key players, including you.

5. Related information as necessary.

6. Relevant exhibits, such as organizational charts or financial statement.

Your Living Case should describe your challenge in three to five pages. Tell the story of your challenge.

Some Additional Guidelines

When describing key players, you might want to use names. These don't have to be actual names of the real people, but names can help present the material or the story of your challenge.

In describing the challenge: What is not working right? Why is solving this challenge important? Describe the situation in detail to help your colleagues understand the challenge. Tell them the story.

Don't write your Living Case strictly in bullet points. My experience is that your case will benefit from detailed description.

What will the future state look like? If the problem is fixed or the new goal is successful, what will it look like to the outsider?

What are some possible solutions and related concerns? What has been tried and/or what are your concerns about possible action steps you have considered?

Obstacles: Clearly state obstacles that you believe will prevent you from solving the challenge.

Resources: Clearly state resources that you believe will help you solve the challenge.

Title: You might find it helpful to give your Living Case a title. This could involve a description of the challenge you want to resolve.

How to Time a Living Case Discussion

- Ninety minutes per case as follows:

    –Briefing by you, questions from the group (fifteen minutes).

    –Group discussion without you in the room. Aims to reach a consensus recommendation and implementation (forty-five minutes).

    –Group presentation to you, your response (thirty minutes).

THE LIVING CASE:
A FOLLOW-UP COACHING CALL

I recently held a follow-up coaching call with a chief executive who was considering the next step in his career. During his time at the AMP, he worked on his Living Case with his colleagues and took the feedback home. David expects to transition to a professional director role after almost ten years as CEO for a national automotive road-side assistance and service business. He discussed his recent work in guiding a turn-around effort for one of the company's businesses that had performed poorly. This was a leadership task that consumed his time. He had thought the business was in better health and had expected to be able to grow it, but that wouldn't happen until the challenges and opportunities were better understood. The business had been part of their organization for seventeen years but hadn't been given much focus. "IT was poor. Finance was poor. . . . I had to take a deep dive to build the foundations again."[23] This required David to learn all about the business, not just the strategic piece. They were eventually forced to write off a significant amount of money, and it had taken a great amount of effort just to "get to the place to see if we can worry about growth."[24] This was a demanding effort for David and his team. In his words, "It's been a rocky road," but David explained, "They have things in place and the management team is coming back up for air after the effort."

Leading this turnaround wouldn't have been David's first choice of roles but it was necessary. He was asked to take on the responsibility and he did it. This is an example of the kind of humble, focused perseverance that one sees in successful senior executives. David wasn't looking for a pat on the back or extra credit; he was looking forward to stepping into his leadership responsibilities. He was also excited around the whole new space of connected homes, wearables, and the Internet of things. Closing in on turning sixty, David is looking at the next stage of his career and he wants it to involve the chance to teach and build talent. When I encounter an executive who doesn't have this hunger, regardless of their age or role, it stands out. Perseverance is a leadership behavior that goes with success and drives resilience.

This last year I worked with the CEO of a successful bank. His Living Case was focused on identifying what he didn't see or understand in his professional environment *because his bank was too successful*. He understood that not seeing the challenge meant he needed to be proactive, persevere, and find the challenge. I've worked with many executives that use their Living Case to focus on the problem they can't see, the vulnerability that could hurt their organization, identifying their blind spot, and then preparing to stand firm against adversity.

Senior executives have a hunger to be effective; otherwise they wouldn't last long in their roles or continue to be promoted based on their accomplishment. They recognize the importance of learning and teaching. They have a commitment to fight adversity in order to lead their teams to success.

RESILIENCE DEVELOPMENT: EXERCISE #2

Your Resilience Story

In *The Power of Story: Rewrite Your Destiny in Business and in Life*, author Jim Loehr explains, "*Every story we tell has some effect.* Stories move the needle every time we tell them."[25] He writes that "we constantly need to infuse our story with new thinking, new energy. To do so can bring about shifts in happiness, excitement, enthusiasm, joy, inspiration that are not temporary but sustained."[26]

We can help prepare ourselves to be able to bounce back from adversity. "Crafting a new story is liberating. Also challenging, scary, and painful."[27] Loehr encourages us to evaluate our assumptions, identify where they are faulty or misleading, and create a new story that can guide us forward with more honesty and less delusion. I developed a workshop around a similar idea. I have taught this exercise for a decade to business leaders of all ages from organizations located all over the globe. The workshop involves writing *Your Resilience Story*. The writing exercise helps participants envision how they will confront their future challenges.

The writer predicts the adversity he or she might face and envisions how to handle the challenge. This involves confronting internal and external threats, considering solutions, and looking for a path forward toward achieving the desired objectives.

Your Resilience Story can be written in roughly one hour, which includes five ten-minute sections as described below. You will notice that these five stages have a similarity to Joseph Campbell's seventeen stages, using an abbreviated Departure-Initiation-Return structure and a focus on facing internal and external challenges, stepping up to take action, and persevering through difficulty in order to achieve success. I created this model with the goal of using Campbell's roadmap to function in a three-hour leadership development workshop.

Confront Your Future

Identify a future business challenge you can imagine yourself confronting. This could be related to your current professional role or to an aspiration you have for a different role or career. This could be based on a challenge you have faced in the past or could be a challenge you predict could be in front of you. Take a few notes on what kinds of reactions you might have that would be counterproductive. What could you do that would lead to you stumbling, failing, making a mistake? Take a few notes on what success will look like and what kinds of behavior and results you think you will need to achieve your goal. Remember: your challenge is in the future. It may be based on past experiences or things you have seen with colleagues, including challenges you may have read about faced by other people in the industry you have selected, but the challenge is in the future. It has not happened yet and you are preparing for it by writing about your choices to engage with the challenge. Duckworth puts it this way: "Grit is more about stamina than intensity."[28] Prepare yourself to approach your challenge with stamina.

Five Ten-Minute Stages

1. **First Stage: Stability**—Write for ten minutes. Imagine yourself in the near future, maybe a few weeks from now, or a few months from now, or a year from now. Everything is going very well with you! Describe what you are doing, maybe having dinner in your favorite restaurant or enjoying a favorite sport? Maybe you are in your current role and have faced real success and are expecting a promotion? Maybe you have moved into a new industry that you aspired to enter? Write for ten minutes and capture what it feels like to be in this perfect, pleasant space.

2. **Second Stage: Looming Crisis**—Write for ten minutes. Imagine yourself in that stable time you just described, except now something happens that suggests the stability won't last. This will be the first hint that adversity is headed your way. Your goal is to build your resilience, which may benefit from a conscious effort to lead yourself with grit and sisu. Remember, grit is committing to a long-term goal. It's a marathon, not a sprint. Sisu is recognizing that your back is against the wall and you need to fight. Your challenge could arrive in a phone call from your boss, a colleague, a customer . . . this could be an email or an article in the press that changes the calm future you were imagining where everything was going your way professionally. One way to think of this looming crisis is that suddenly you see a fire in the distance and you know this fire will have a professional impact on you, if not immediately, then very soon.

3. **Third Stage: Falling of the Hero**—Write for ten minutes. Imagine that the looming crisis has arrived as a full-blown crisis. The fire is not in the distance. It is happening right now. This is impacting your professional goals and can't be ignored; however, for the sake of this exercise, imagine yourself trying to ignore the problem. We often hesitate to act during a crisis and assume that someone else will solve our challenges for us. If you were to hesitate, why would you be hesitating? Could this be due to an internal doubt or fear? Maybe you don't believe you are the right person for the job? Think of *Star Wars: A New Hope*. What happened when Obi-Wan Kenobi asked young Luke Skywalker to fulfill his legacy, train as a Jedi, and fight for the Rebel Alliance? Luke said he couldn't help. He was needed at home for the crops. He changed his mind when the crisis escalated and he found his stepparents murdered by stormtroopers. What will hold you back when the crisis arrives?

Do you have allies that could arrive at this point of your story? Maybe they are people you currently know in your industry. Maybe they are people you envision could be available in the future to help you. Luke Skywalker had C-3PO, R2-D2, and Obi-Wan Kenobi. We can't create allies out of thin air and guarantee their arrival, but we can remind ourselves that allies might arrive in a time of crisis. We can remind ourselves to be available to the support of our allies.

4. **Fourth Stage: Hero Faces Internal Fears**—Write for ten minutes. How are you able to face your internal doubts, fears, and resistance to confronting the challenge? You are writing the story and the story is about you. You are the protagonist. The situation is very serious right now. You need to find all the resources that are available and push to succeed. If sisu hasn't been called on yet in your challenge, this could be the moment. Your back is against the wall.

5. **Fifth Stage: Hero Faces External Enemy and Succeeds**—Write for ten minutes. Envision what success will look like for you and how you will win. If the external enemy is an actual competitor, how will you succeed in confronting this competitor? If you need to overcome a transformation in the industry or some change in

the external environment, how will you do it? Describe your role in leading yourself and others to confront adversity, be resilient, and succeed.

6. **Rewriting**—Take five bonus minutes and review your story. One of the pleasures of writing is rewriting. As you reread your story, do you see opportunities to add more descriptive detail? Are emotions involved that would benefit from further description? How about ideas that could impact your industry or your own ability to succeed?

Writing Your Resilience Story will prepare you for challenges ahead. This exercise can work without the aid of a group. However, you can also have a team of colleagues write their stories and then share them. My experience from teaching this workshop for many years is that teams learn about each member in a significant way that builds cohesiveness and the ability to support one another in working on future challenges.

ADVERSITY WILL ARRIVE

The Dalai Lama reminds us that, "Good fortune is not permanent; consequently, it is dangerous to become too attached to things going well. An outlook of permanence is ruinous. . . . An outlook of impermanence helps."[29] These words can be seen as an encouragement to remember that adversity will arrive because permanence isn't real. He also reminds us that, "A strong ego is needed, but without becoming egotistical. You need a strong will to achieve the good."[30] We need a strong will in our effort to be resilient against adversity. The reality of impermanence and the fact that everything will be fine, until it isn't, is a constant driver in business leadership. Don't have an outlook of permanence, but do believe in your capacity to develop your resilience through grit and sisu.

RESILIENCE IN WESTEROS

In Blackwater Bay, the burning dinghy and immolated knight drift away as Petyr Baelish tells Sansa that she is the daughter he was never able to have with Catelyn Tully. "You are safe now, that's all that matters. You are safe with me, and sailing home."[31] This is a lie. Baelish had warned Sansa earlier that life was not a song, but he also promised her that even though the game of thrones operates on lies, competition, and self-interest, their relationship was similar to the unique song of father and daughter. Sansa will learn that her Stark name delivers political legitimacy to whomever can control her through marrying her, or bartering her marriage to another House: Lannister, Arryn, Bolton, even Baelish. How will she develop into a great leader?

The *Belly of the Whale*, in Campbell's language, is when the hero is unsuccessful at "conquering or conciliating the power of the threshold." Basically, forces antithetical to her survival capture her because she didn't successfully navigate the threat. She "is swallowed into the unknown, and would appear to have died."[32] This is the trail Sansa follows: from the perfect daughter that blushes prettily, to the terrified young woman threatened by a drunk Cersei and trapped in Maegor's Holdfast during the Battle of Blackwater Bay, to the young woman who watches an almost disinterested Petyr Baelish push Lysa Arryn through the Moon Door, to the maiden bride of Ramsay Bolton, raped on her wedding night. Sansa is trapped at a threshold, a crossway into either the idealized future she was taught would be her destiny, or a wasteland fraught with risks where she finds herself imprisoned by various tormentors. She does have one genuine ally: Brienne. The Maid of Tarth will not abandon her own quest and her promise to both Catelyn Stark and Jaime Lannister: "There are others looking, all wanting to capture her and sell her to the queen. I have to find her first."[33] Sansa will survive the belly of the whale.

Sansa made a mistake that any person can make: she believed the pretty story and got trapped and used by the powerful people that offer the pretty stories. Sansa got tangled in the hope of her exceptionalism. Like Sansa Stark, most of us would prefer to not have to leave the comfort of focusing on ourselves: our opinions, our accomplishments, our plans. But like Sansa Stark, we are forced to recognize constraints, challenges. Like Sansa Stark, we will face long odds. It will be a time for agency. We will all face a time to show resilience.

Sansa can't escape the embrace of terror, but she stays capable of learning. Later, when it is finally time for her respond to Petyr's deception and play the game of thrones, Sansa emphasizes to Baelish her capacity to learn. Enveloped in the horror of her marriage to Ramsay Bolton, she sees an opportunity and escapes. Ramsay follows her. Sansa operates with a consistent level of grit in her passion to find her way back to her surviving family. She relies on sisu, when her situation is past desperate, leaping with Theon from the castle wall of Winterfell, her home turned prison. She steps into leadership when Jon Snow leaves her in the top leadership role as Warden of the North, but she still appears to be a piece, used by Baelish.

Littlefinger attempts to destroy the trust between Arya and Sansa, as he once broke the trust between two other sisters: Catelyn Stark and Lysa Arryn.

Sansa has Arya brought to her for an apparent trial. She looks at her sister. "You stand accused of murder. You stand accused of treason." All eyes are upon Arya, until Sansa says, "How do you answer these charges, Lord Baelish?"[34]

Littlefinger, smug and observant, leaning against the wall of Winterfell's Great Hall, is surprised at the accusation. He tries to lie his way out of the trial, but Sansa has survived and has transformed herself from a piece to a player. She tells Baelish, "I'm a slow learner. It's true. But I learn."[35]

THE LEADER'S JOURNEY: BELLY OF THE WHALE

It is important to remember that we have choice in how we face immersion into the stage Joseph Campbell calls the Belly of the Whale. We will face moments on the threshold, surrounded by threats and constraints on our aspirations, and challenges to our current and future success. Our path forward will appear blocked. We may seem lost to ourselves and from the perspective of the outside world. Like Sansa Stark, we may seem imprisoned. But we must remember it is our choice. We can commit to rely on grit, and sisu, to lead ourselves with resilience and bounce back from adversity.

In the famous PBS interviews, *The Power of Myth*, Bill Moyers asks Joseph Campbell about his phrase "the soul's high adventure."[36] The phrase is a version of an encouragement Campbell would offer his students. He would tell them to follow their bliss. Campbell wasn't asking his students to simply find what pleased them at a given moment and pursue pleasure. He was insisting that they needed to decide what goals mattered—their purpose—to the extent that they would fight to make those goals happen. What aspirations would be worth the difficult tests that waited down the road? "I don't know what being is. And I don't know what *'consciousness'* is. But I do know what *'bliss'* is: that deep sense of being present, of doing what you absolutely must do to be yourself."[37]

Campbell said, "Life is a manifestation of bliss."[38] He explained that "bliss" could be a guide. "Your bliss can guide you to that transcendent mystery, because bliss is the welling up of the energy of the transcendent wisdom within you."[39]

The world can be competitive and brutal. Campbell describes the world we live in with an adjective Sansa Stark would understand in Westeros as her family is systematically murdered. "The world is a wasteland."[40] Campbell insists that a person must find what makes them the most alive and pursue that thing with full engagement. This is *the soul's high adventure*: to bring life to the brutal world. This is what gives us the strength to be resilient, finding grit and sisu when necessary. If we choose to follow our bliss, we can be sure we will face serpents in the wasteland. We can confront our serpents or we can quit. Campbell argues for engaging with the adventure. If we bring a fighting spirit, the adventure can offer salvation for both the adventurer and those impacted: "The influence of a vital person vitalizes."[41] This is resilience. This is what we will all need at some point on our Leader's Journey when we are trapped in the belly of the whale. We will all need the resilience of Sansa Stark.

GOING FORWARD

The piece, knowingly or not, is a victim. The victim doesn't choose to be responsible for their situation. The external problems from the perspective of the victim are just too big. The victim chooses resignation and resentment. The player takes responsibility and responds to the situation. The player accepts exposure to anxiety in the effort of pursuing important goals. The player chooses to control their thoughts and actions as they work on influencing those they need to influence. On the road to King's Landing, Sansa is a victim, but by the time of her leadership in Winterfell she has become a player.

Successful leaders can write their Living Cases and present that exercise to trusted advisors to gain insight. They can also write their Resilience Story and prepare themselves to confront future challenges. We can choose right now to put full effort into building resilience against the inevitable arrival of adversity.

We can remember Viktor Frankl, who faced brutalizing, inhuman conditions during the Holocaust. He found his way forward. We can remember Frederick Douglass, born a slave, who felt himself completely broken before he fought back with his fists. He taught himself to read as a young boy and never quit on his commitment to escape to freedom. Both men chose to fight against adversity to be players. Both men showed grit and sisu.

We can look to Sansa's Hero's Journey. She finds her way across the threshold. She fights against adversity. She continues to learn. She transforms herself into a leader. Her sister, Arya, tells her she has become the Lady of Winterfell. The two young women acknowledge their respect for each other's abilities to persevere and be resilient. Now, they are together and face another brutal challenge, yet they are sisters and are together. Sansa quotes their father: "The lone wolf dies, but the pack survives."[42]

4

Be More Than
a Sword-Hand!

HOW TO LEAD WITH EMOTIONAL
AND CONTEXTUAL INTELLIGENCE

Our excellent training, sharp minds, and technical abilities can build our reputation in specific functions, but if we want to become organizational leaders, we will need to develop our emotional intelligence.

THE KINGSLAYER

Jaime is a warrior in a warrior culture. Jaime has one skill acknowledged by Westeros: he excels in armed combat. Released by Catelyn Stark without consent of her son Robb, Jaime is sent off in shackles from the King in the North's iron cell. Brienne of Tarth is tasked with taking him back to King's Landing in exchange for Catelyn's daughters. Jaime committed to the Kingsguard to be close to Cersei. He sees himself as unique, true to himself. He has his warrior's code. His romantic choice his whole life has been his twin sister, Cersei. He holds a cynical view of everyone else in Westeros. He doesn't live for anyone beyond himself and Cersei.

While captive and drunk, he tells Catelyn, "I told you, there are no men like me."[1] Jaime tells Catelyn, "I've never lain with any woman but Cersei."[2] On the road toward King's Landing, Jaime tries to provoke Brienne into a fight. He looks for chances to steal her dirk and stab her in the abdomen. He mocks her. Yet, despite himself, Jaime begins to recognize the strength in her commitment to knighthood and her sworn vow to defend Catelyn's daughters.

The Kingslayer protected the people of King's Landing at the cost of his own reputation when he murdered the Mad King. Now, with Brienne vulnerable, he faces a similar decision to either do what is expected of him (in this case, return to his father and sister in King's Landing) or support the vulnerable (in this case, Brienne). The Roman Stoic philosopher Seneca wrote: "You must live for your neighbour, if you would live for yourself."[3] Jaime allows himself to respect Brienne. This gives him the courage to care about her, listen to her advice, save himself, and save her. Jaime learns to live for his neighbor. This is part of the development of his emotional intelligence.

At his lowest ebb, a prisoner of the Bloody Mummers, severely wounded, and close to death, Jaime realizes that his pride in his warrior skills can't be all that he represents. Jaime wants to die. Brienne whispers to him, encourages him back to life. "'Live,' she said, 'live, and fight, and take revenge.'"[4] She challenges Jaime to find courage, drawing on her social awareness. She doesn't try to motivate him with a soft message; she calls on him to fight back. Jaime responds to her challenge with self-awareness and self-management, which results in the motivation to fight for his survival. *"Was that all I was, a sword-hand? Gods be good, is it true?"*

"The wench had the right of it. He could not die."[5]

Jaime sees Brienne's captors have mockingly dressed her in an unflattering, pink dress. "Pink was not a kind color for her either. A dozen cruel japes leaped into his head, but for once he kept them there."[6]

Jaime saved Brienne when she faced gang rape, likely mutilation, and inevitable murder. He lost his hand in the process. Jaime is provided with an armed escort back to his sister and father in King's Landing. Jaime knows Brienne is in peril if she is left with the Brave Companions. Leaving the Maid of Tarth to her horrible fate in Harrenhal would serve Jaime's interest, as she had been his captor and the sworn ally of the enemy at war with his family. But on his way to King's Landing, Jaime has a dream. He is in the bowels of a cave beneath his family home, Casterly Rock, and is joined by Brienne. There, they are confronted by his sworn brothers—the Kingsguard—and Prince Rhaegar. These men died after Jaime killed King Aerys. Only Brienne stands by Jaime and is willing to defend him in his dream. Jaime recognizes her emotional commitment to knighthood is the same as the brothers who died on both sides of the civil war. He also realizes she stood by him when others would have forsaken him. The Kingslayer decides he must return and save the Maid of Tarth. He finds her in a bear-baiting pit, armed with a useless wood sword, attempting to not be mauled to death. His heroic return saves her.

Jaime subconsciously acts with emotional intelligence. Like Jaime, we often act with emotional intelligence, although we may not be familiar with the concept. If we understand emotional intelligence, we will be better able to lead ourselves when faced with challenges.

EMOTIONAL INTELLIGENCE

Emotional intelligence, or EQ, is the foundation to effective emotional leadership. Daniel Goleman, psychologist and author of *Emotional Intelligence* and many related books, argues that without emotional intelligence, "a person can have the best training in the world, an incisive, analytical mind, and an endless supply of smart ideas, but he still won't make a great leader."[7] In the *HBR* article "Primal Leadership: The Hidden Driver of Great Performance," republished in *HBR's 10 Must Reads: On Emotional Intelligence*, Goleman writes: "If a leader's mood and accompanying behaviors are indeed such potent drivers of business success, then a leader's premier task—we would even say his primal task—is emotional leadership." EQ is about leading the challenges of the inner emotions in order to get effective results "so that the right emotional and behavioral chain reaction occurs."[8] Leaders need to manage themselves and create that chain reaction.

The concept of emotional intelligence, presented by Goleman in the 1990s with the acronym *EI*, soon morphed into *EQ*. Emotional intelligence is a set of skills different from our Intelligence Quotient, or *IQ*. Here are the four skills Goleman presents in his recent *Adaptability Primer* on the building blocks of EQ.

Self-Awareness:

  The ability to recognize and understand your moods and emotional tendencies, and how they impact people.

Signs of Self-Awareness include: self-confidence, realistic self-assessment, self-deprecating sense of humor.

Self-Management:

The ability to lead oneself through controlling disruptive impulses; the ability to not be reactive in judging other people.

The ability to pursue goals with energy and persistence. As described in *Emotional Intelligence 2.0*: "Self-management is what happens when you act—or do not act."[9]

Signs of Self-Management include: trustworthiness and integrity, comfort with ambiguity, openness to change; a strong drive to achieve and optimism, even when challenges arise.

Social Awareness:

The ability to understand the emotions of other people. It is important to be able to listen and take the time to observe people. The challenge is to understand their emotions when you are in the middle of the interaction.

Signs include expertise in building and retaining talent; cross-cultural sensitivity; service to clients and customers.

Relationship Management:

The ability to find common ground and build networks. This skill depends on your mastery of the three previous elements of EQ. It depends on your effectiveness in the use of your own emotions and your understanding of the emotions of other people to build a strong relationship through positive communication.

Signs of Relationship Management include effectiveness in leading change; persuasiveness; expertise in building and leading teams, also the willingness to interact in constructive conversations to resolve conflict.

Self-Awareness and Self-Management can be thought of as Personal Competencies. Social Awareness and Relationship Management can be thought of as Social Competencies.[10]

Although Jaime does not think of his actions in terms of EQ, the four EQ skills manifest themselves in him as follows:

Self-Awareness: He recognizes that his code of valor urges him to help Brienne in her time of need.

Self-Management: He wants to return to his sister, Cersei, but he controls himself and acts with integrity by returning to Brienne.

Social Awareness: There is no advantage to put himself in harm's way and defend Brienne, but he is motivated to pursue her safety. He understands what Brienne will face at the hands of the Bloody Mummers. He chooses to be sensitive to her situation and protect her.

Relationship Management: He builds a relationship with her by returning to rescue her; he follows this heroic act by gifting her a Valyrian steel sword and supporting her mission to find and protect the Stark daughters. He has gained an unlikely ally.

These four competencies are difference makers when it comes to being an effective leader, and in Jaime's case, his decision to return to Harrenhal and defend Brienne is what turns him from the Kingslayer into something more kingly.

EMOTIONAL INTELLIGENCE: SENIOR EXECUTIVES

When I first started highlighting my copy of Goleman's book *Emotional Intelligence* in the nineties, the term EQ was not recognized by corporate audiences. This quickly changed. It would be surprising now if an executive from almost any large organization located in any country couldn't make at least a rough guess at the meaning of EQ. That's not to say a majority of current business leaders could provide the four categories off the top of their head, but they would likely say EQ is different from IQ and that EQ involves managing the emotional side of leadership in order to bring out the best in one's self and one's team. They might use the term *soft skill*, to describe emotional intelligence. The adjective "soft" doesn't do justice to the rigor required to operate with effective emotional intelligence. If we look at Jaime's decision to return and save Brienne, it wasn't a soft decision—it was difficult and put Jaime at risk, required self-control, and put his other goals at risk.

Some might mistakenly think that EQ is about being nice. The advantages of being nice in leadership are dependent on many factors. Being nice can be an authentic and/or effective approach. As a leader, one may choose to be nice. From my experience working with successful business leaders, most enjoy the opportunity, advantages, and pleasure of treating people nicely. But emotional intelligence isn't about being nice—it is about maximizing our abilities by understanding and managing ourselves and those around us. As Goleman puts it, "Emotional intelligence skills are synergistic with cognitive ones; top performers have both. The more complex the job, the more emotional intelligence matters—if only because a deficiency in these abilities can hinder the use of whatever technical expertise or intellect a person may have."[11]

In my work with executive education leadership programs, the presence, or absence, of emotional intelligence is noticeable. Emotional intelligence is the first competency I find myself evaluating when meeting a new group of senior executives or graduate students. The on-site educational environment is geared to be supportive and collegial but also challenging. On rare occasions, I have watched people turn that positive atmosphere dysfunctional by not understanding how to operate with the categories of self-awareness, self-management, social awareness, and relationship management. I have seen a business leader's behavior, even when well-intentioned, trigger discord if they were caught up in their emotions and disregarded the emotions of their classmates.

Anyone can have a low-EQ moment. I have watched myself as if from a distance saying something that was not productive, often because I was derailed and failed at applying EQ insight to my situation. On our executive education on-site program team, we often remind ourselves to "H.A.L.T." This acronym captures four triggers to a low-EQ moment. We are human and have to lead ourselves. It is also helpful to realize that other people can fall into the H.A.L.T. categories, which might explain when a high-EQ leader succumbs to low-EQ behavior.

The acronym represents:

H—hungry

A—angry

L—lonely

T—tired

Regardless of what triggers our reaction, our response in a low-EQ moment is important. Whether we are reacting in a low-EQ way or the target of low-EQ behavior, we can choose a high-EQ reaction.

Five years ago, during the first week of the four-week Advanced Management Program, Ian, an Australian executive, asked me what I thought he should do in order to gain the most from the senior executive education program. What would make the difference between his having an effective experience at the program or him having an exceptional experience and gaining the most possible from the time and commitment? I suggested he practice the skills of EQ, which we discussed. In hindsight, I realized he was already practicing EQ, either consciously or subconsciously, by asking me the question.

His question was framed with humility and curiosity: *What can you see based on your experience that can help me?* This simple question holds all the components of the EQ in practice:

1) Ian asked the question with *self-awareness*, confident about his abilities, thirsty for feedback, even if critical; he spoke with a hint of self-deprecation, showing he was eager to learn;

2) He was *self-managing* in that he took time out from his lunch to engage with me in a respectful way;

3) He had the *social awareness* to make it clear he wanted to learn from myself and our team; he had prioritized the program, his development and wanted to help us help him;

4) He understood *relationship management* was an important opportunity and he was committed to the twenty-eight days of education, to bringing energy to the work, and being both optimistic and accountable; he showed that team-building started with earning my trust and offering his openness to help the class.

On the other hand, when a participant acts with low-EQ, it surprises me. Low-EQ behavior won't deliver productive results. It doesn't happen often, which I attribute to the emotional intelligence of people in leadership roles who are supported by their organizations to attend executive development programs, but it does happen.

In one particular instance, a participant named Laurette raised an opinion in class about an element of the course that didn't satisfy her educational expectation. She made a point that our team believed we had addressed yet we were open to discussing it. However, she made her argument in a strident, accusatory way. Her humor wasn't self-deprecating but sarcastic. Her statements and rhetorical questions seemed intended to preclude debate. She didn't initiate a discussion. It felt more like a trial with one possible verdict: guilty.

In terms of self-awareness, she didn't recognize that her negative emotion caused the actual discussion to shut down. She might have consciously decided to introduce a confrontational approach to the discussion, but if she was in control of herself and her goal was to build group learning around her concern, she failed. Her decision didn't lead to building common ground with the rest of the class or myself in the role of facilitating the discussion. If her goal was only to be disruptive and not impact positive change, she succeeded. It is hard to *agree to disagree* with someone that is accusatory. It is difficult to find common ground and new solutions.

Yet, it was an opportunity to develop my EQ. Just because a conversation is difficult, it doesn't mean there aren't effective ways to approach the confrontation.

It is important to realize that you always have the ability to decide how to respond to a low-EQ situation. After Laurette's haranguing, I reminded myself to evaluate the categories of EQ and decide where I responded with EQ and where I didn't respond with EQ. What could I learn from the experience? I decided I had a chance to reach out to Laurette later and practice a more calm social awareness: I would start with a personal focus on my self-awareness and self-management, and work at building my relationship with her, finding common ground and following up on the subject of our conversation. It was my responsibility to act with EQ. That didn't mean I would be 100 percent satisfied with that first conversation, but EQ offers each of us a chance to be a player, instead of falling into the victim—or piece—mentality.

If we operate with the components of emotional intelligence, we are *"recognizing our own feelings and those of others, for motivating ourselves, and for managing emotions well in ourselves and in our relationships."* Goleman's core message is that EQ is critical because "Many people who are book smart but lack emotional intelligence end up working for people who have lower IQs than they but who excel in emotional intelligence skills."[12]

In *Emotional Intelligence 2.0*, Travis Bradberry and Jean Greaves write, "Of all the people we've studied at work, we have found that 90 percent of high performers are also high in EQ. . . . You can be a high performer without EQ, but the chances are slim. People who develop their EQ tend to be successful on the job because the two go hand in hand."[13]

When a senior executive acts with high emotional intelligence, as when Ian asked me his question, I want to do whatever is in my power to improve that person's educational experience. EQ builds partnerships because it strengthens motivation by managing the emotions of the people involved.

When a senior executive acts with lower emotional intelligence, as Laurette did with her effort to make her point, regardless of the impact on the class, I can recognize the negative impact on my own motivation, including my emotional reaction. I try not to allow myself to stumble on my self-management, but I do realize the impact. I see low-EQ behavior, my own or someone else's, as misguided, ineffective revenge. It is a conscious or inadvertent attempt to lash out in response to something negative from the past. It doesn't help.

Low-EQ in other people is a reminder that we can choose to act with high-EQ. We must ask ourselves to respond to interpersonal tensions with emotional intelligence.

EMOTIONAL INTELLIGENCE IN WESTEROS AND ESSOS

Underestimating EQ will have a cost, but Goleman writes that EQ can be learned. "The process is not easy. It takes time and, most of all, commitment."[14]

Emotional Intelligence 2.0 explains that we all have a mix of IQ, our personality, and EQ. Combined, these three categories impact how we think and act. "It is impossible to predict one based upon another. People may be intelligent but not emotionally intelligent, and people of all types of personalities can be high in EQ and/or IQ."[15] We can't change our IQ, but we can impact our EQ. "EQ is the foundation for a host of critical skills. A little effort spent on increasing your EQ tends to have a wide-ranging, positive impact on your life."[16]

DAENERYS, ARYA, AND JAIME

On the Dothraki Sea, Daenerys Targaryen realizes she can't look back with yearning for some idealized past that never existed. The world is difficult and dangerous and she must take responsibility to move forward. Self-awareness taught Dany she must depend on herself. She must operate with self-management. "*I am afraid*, she realized, *but I must be brave.*"[17] In Meereen, this lesson holds true, as it will when she sails her ships to Dragonstone and on to Westeros.

Daenerys is a perpetual outsider and first envisions her role of khaleesi as synonymous with protecting the vulnerable. Mirri Maz Duur teaches her that even the vulnerable can turn on you and repay your trust with harm. The maegi had told Daenerys she wanted to help protect Khal Drogo because she had been taught that "all men are one flock."[18] Dany buys the lie . . . the sweet promise about humanity in Essos. After the loss of her baby and her husband, Daenerys learns she must be more careful and thoughtful about who she selects to trust. She would identify with Seneca's recommendation: "Ponder for a long time whether you shall admit a given person to your friendship."[19] When the maegi offers to help, Dany thinks for a few seconds before embracing the support of the healer. This learned moment of self-awareness helps her understand that kindness and trust can't be freely given. She steps into the burning pyre because she has had another moment of self-awareness: she has realized that fire will not hurt her. "She was the blood of the dragon, and the fire was in her."[20] With the insight based on her self-awareness, Dany operates with effective self-management, which is dependent on the ability to manage one's emotional reactions, tolerating uncertainty until it is clear how to act. So Daenerys finds her way forward, guided by self-awareness and self-management.

Her Dothraki followers lie prostrate on the ground. Her self-awareness about the flames not hurting her helps her to find the confidence to use self-management to get past her fear and step into the fire with her dragon eggs. Her self-awareness about being susceptible to trusting the wrong people will ignite her wrath when she discovers Jorah Mormont has lied to her about his allegiances. She will rely on the skill of self-management to control her anger with Jorah over time, as she will control, eventually, her desire for the sellsword, Daario, who she decides she cannot marry. The young woman that she is hungers for him but the queen that she also is knows that this is not the partnership necessary for her future. Faced with the deceit and support of terrorism by the Grand Masters, Daario suggests tricking them into a public appearance, then betraying and killing them.

"Dany was appalled. *He is a monster. A gallant monster, but a monster still.* 'Do you take me for the Butcher King?'

'Better the butcher than the meat. All kings are butchers. Are queens so different?'"

Daenerys's answer is significant:

"This one is."[21]

Daenerys develops the personal competency—the self-awareness and self-management—to not make a leadership choice she believes is contrary to her larger vision, purpose, reputation, and values.

Arya Stark operates with emotional intelligence when she watches her mentor, Syrio Forel, surrounded by armed, aggressive City Watch. Arya is filled with terror. She is reacting, but she is also self-aware and she self-manages, fleeing at the shouted counsel of her embattled Braavos mentor. Paralyzed in the stable, after killing the stable boy, she realizes she must get out of the castle before the gates close and the hunt for her intensifies.

"She had to leave *now*, she told herself, but when the moment came, she was too frightened to move.

"*Calm as still water*, a small voice whispered in her ear. Arya was so startled she almost dropped her bundle. She looked around wildly, but there was no one in the stable but her, and the horses, and the dead men.

"*Quiet as a shadow*, she heard. Was it her own voice, or Syrio's? She could not tell, yet somehow it calmed her fears.

"She stepped out of the stable."[22]

Daenerys Targaryen and Arya Stark recognize their emotions and think about their reactions, with consideration given to their past experiences. In Dany's case, she put aside urges ranging from a physical desire, to a desire to locate and trust a leader, to a desire to exact revenge, and she managed herself to pursue larger, more important goals. Arya recognized the immobilizing capacity of her fear, saw it for what it was, listened to her guiding internal voice, and stepped from the stable in time to escape Cersei Lannister's soldiers.

If self-awareness is to understand your own emotions accurately and if self-management is to choose to act or to not act, a high-EQ moment for the Kingslayer is when he realizes that he admires Brienne of Tarth and he chooses to defend her from the Brave Companions, persuading their mercenary leader that he should protect Brienne from physical abuse and try exchanging her safely for payment from her father, Lord Tarth. Jaime is faced with new emotions: empathy for an enemy who is also female, and who is both vulnerable and courageous. He confronts his self-awareness about his feelings for Brienne. He understands that self-management is about action and he chooses to act.

JON AND TYRION

Jon Snow's childhood as the bastard son of Ned Stark, unwanted at Winterfell by Catelyn Stark, resulted in the development of Jon's social awareness. When King Robert traveled north to make his offer to Ned Stark, Jon saw Lord Stark was troubled during the great feast in Winterfell. "A bastard had to learn to notice things, to read the truth that people hid behind their eyes. His father was observing all the courtesies, but there was tightness in him that Jon had seldom seen before."[23] For a child raised as an outsider, acceptance, even survival, could depend on understanding and being able to respond to insights gleaned from social awareness. Jon loses track of this skill when he attempts to impose his leadership decisions on the Night's Watch. This misstep at social awareness impacts Jon's ability at relationship management during his effort to bring the wildlings across the Wall.

Tyrion is similar to Jon Snow. When Tyrion was an infant in his crib, his older sister, Cersei, tells the young visitor from Dorne, Oberyn Martell, that her brother was a literal *monster*. (Oberyn later tells Tyrion he wasn't impressed or scared by him as a baby.) Throughout his life, Tyrion, due to his physical difference in size, has been treated as an outsider. He has needed to use social awareness and relationship management as much as Jon Snow. Both men developed EQ from an early age as a reaction to environmental pressures.

Tyrion is strong at his ability to bring people to his side, even people intent on killing him. His vices are minor in the bloody atmosphere of Westeros and Essos. His decadent habits are a form of escape, but also of network building. When confronted on the amount of time he spent with people on the fringes of society, people he met due to his vices,

Tyrion said, "I try to know as many people as I can. You never know which one you'll need."[24]

In "Building Success Habits: Networking and the Science of Self-Change," Professor Ko Kuwabara, writes "networking has to be like exercising: habitual (i.e. long-term, strategic, and semi-automatic)."[25] Tyrion's most effective networking connections are primarily the result of bonding with people outside proper King's Landing society— including people who have some involvement with his survival, such as Bronn the sellsword and Shagga and the Hill Tribes. The exception is Lord Varys, who sits on the Small Council, and is a significant power broker. Varys approaches Tyrion and plays an important role in Tyrion's network.

Tyrion could have done more to build his network with leaders on the senior levels in Westeros. Tyrion's lack of effort at scaling up a traditional power base in Westeros contributes to his vulnerability when he is railroaded by his sister and father and made to look guilty in the death of his nephew, King Joffrey.

In relationship management, Tyrion has the strength of speaking honestly, often with the intent of helping those less advantaged. He tells Jon Snow to embrace and acknowledge the term *bastard*, giving the young man advice based on what he himself has learned as a mocked outsider in House Lannister. "All dwarfs are bastards in their father's eyes."[26] He orders a special saddle made for young Bran, saying, "I have a tender spot in my heart for cripples and bastards and broken things."[27] He defends a terrified Sansa from being beaten and molested on King Joffrey's order. Tyrion confronts King Joffrey in defense of Sansa despite the risk to himself. He leads the military defense of King's Landing in the Battle of Blackwater after King Joffrey is hustled off at the request of his mom to cower in safety, and after the Hound falls apart in fear of the flames.

Tyrion steps into the breach, gives a rousing speech, and heads out the Mud Gate. "'This is your city Stannis means to sack, and that's your gate he's bringing down. So come with me and kill the son of a bitch!' Tyrion unsheathed his axe, wheeled the stallion around, and trotted toward the sally port. He *thought* they were following, but never dared to look."[28]

Tyrion finds courage when people need him to bring courage. His defense of the vulnerable is not appreciated in Westeros, but in Essos he finds the support of Daenerys Stormborn, the Mother of Dragons.

CONTEXTUAL INTELLIGENCE

Tarun Khanna, economic strategist and professor at Harvard Business School, writes in "A Case for Contextual Intelligence" about the importance of understanding context, distinguishing between *knowing the facts* and *making a judgment*: "Understanding the limits of our knowledge, which is at the heart of contextual intelligence, is a very basic component of human comprehension."[29]

Leadership demands navigating the context of the turbulent external environment, making productive decisions, avoiding toxic associations, and building support from true allies. Warren Bennis and Joan Goldsmith in their workbook *Learning to Lead* describe external context as "the larger environment in which we live and work—specifically, the culture of our organizations as well as the political, social, and economic realities that shape our lives."[30] They point out that each of us has an internal context "comprised of our values, political, social and religious beliefs, and our intellectual commitments that guide us to solutions for the problems we face."[31] Our leadership is optimized if we can master the context. "When we perceive the elements of the *big-picture context* and understand the forces and opportunities inherent in it, we can be responsible leaders who can shape our time and place in history."[32]

Khanna emphasizes the importance in adapting that "knowledge to an environment different from the one in which it was developed."[33] It would have been helpful to both Ned and Catelyn Stark if they had been able to abstract specific learnings from their life experiences in both Winterfell and Riverrun and realize they had to adapt to a new location. This might have given them the motivation to work proactively to understand their new environments instead of reacting. As Khanna puts it: "Trying to apply management practices uniformly across geographies is a fool's errand."[34] The conditions in various regions can be significantly different in ways that are hard to discern. The generic approach won't work.

Contextual intelligence, according to Bennis and Goldsmith, can be learned by anyone who works to "understand the cultural and personal contexts"[35] of the new environment. It would have been helpful for Ned if he had learned earlier that Lord Varys was an ally. It would have helped Catelyn if she had understood that her betrayal of Robb's leadership by releasing Jaime Lannister would offer leaders willing to break moral codes, such as Roose Bolton, Walder Frey, and Tywin Lannister, the alliance and opportunity to betray the young King in the North in pursuit of their enrichment and victory.

Catelyn's contextual intelligence failed her, but contextual intelligence can be learned. It is knowledge—as opposed to data or information—and requires awareness, analysis, and understanding of raw facts. Building this knowledge reveals patterns of influence that might otherwise be misunderstood. Bennis and Goldsmith argue, "Leaders with *contextual intelligence* seek to understand the impact of external events on their life choices."[36] In order to understand cultural and personal contexts, the aspiring leader should focus on four categories of knowledge: self-knowledge, social-network knowledge, organizational knowledge, and stakeholder knowledge.

Self-Knowledge includes an awareness of one's history, role models, and current choices and lets you see the impact of these influences on your leadership values and choices. For example, Jaime—forced by his captors to drink horse urine, his severed hand hanging in a leather pouch around his neck, starving, feverish, and sick—shivers in the cold mud and chooses to define himself as more than just a "sword-hand."

Social-Network Knowledge draws on your recognition and assess-ment of the information flowing around you from friends, colleagues, and acquaintances. This is an area of contextual intelligence that would have helped Lord Stark in King's Landing by improving his ability to see his personal values as subjective.

Organizational Knowledge comprises a picture of the different cul-tures of your workplace, school, community, volunteer site, and family. The Lannisters usually benefit from the belief across Westeros that they will always pay their debts. Lannisters have access to credit. Public opinion assumes they are good for their promises, as well as aware of what is owed to them. But in one flawed moment, Jaime com-municates ineffectively to the leader of the Bloody Mummers, which results in this Organizational Knowledge being used against him when his sword-hand is cut off. Queen Cersei does benefit from the global belief in the Lannisters' reputation, and the fact they do pay their debts. The Iron Bank extends her credit after her successful military assault on Highgarden. This allows Cersei to purchase the services of the mercenary Golden Company in Essos.

Stakeholder Knowledge includes the history, thoughts, expectations, needs, and desires of those who depend on your leadership. This is composed of an understanding of the central interests of all who have a stake in the organization's success. Jon Snow and his struggles with relationship management at Castle Black are a clear example of one of the benefits—and costs—of managing or mismanaging *stakeholder knowledge*. He didn't achieve the buy-in of his stakeholders. It cost him his life.

CONTEXTUAL INTELLIGENCE
EXERCISE #1—YOUR RESOURCES

Here is a Contextual Intelligence Exercise you can do to consider resources that will help you to develop your capabilities when moving into a new situation or context. When completing the exercise, think about your strengths and gaps when you are in the new environment. An example follows from the perspective of Jon Snow when he moves into his role as Commander of the Night's Watch.

Write in possible resources to develop your capabilities

Capabilities	Resources
Self-Knowledge	
Social-Network Knowledge	
Organizational Knowledge	
Stakeholder Knowledge	

CONTEXTUAL INTELLIGENCE EXERCISE #1: JON SNOW

Capabilities	Resources
Self-Knowledge I am younger than many of my direct reports. I assume people will be courageous, honorable.	Speak to Maester for guidance Can I build allies, question assumptions?
Social-Network Knowledge What resources does Castle Black have in Westeros? Essos? Do the wildlings have skills that will matter to the Night's Watch?	Communicate with Houses Shared skill training
Organizational Knowledge The Night's Watch are sworn to guard the Wall. The top priority is to guard Westeros.	How can we redefine success? Surface implicit values/opinions
Stakeholder Knowledge My stakeholders are isolated, emotional, and vulnerable. Re: Wildlings on our side of Wall? Don't expect the Night's Watch to agree....	What can appeal to the Night's Watch?

CONTEXTUAL INTELLIGENCE EXERCISE #2—YOUR CHALLENGES

In the following exercise, the goal is not to collect data but to extract knowledge that will provide perceptions and solutions. The exercise provides eight categories that can help the leader evaluate the challenges in their external context.

Build your contextual intelligence by noting challenges you currently face. You may choose to fill this out from the perspective of the industry where you work, or where you would like to work in the future.

- **Demographic:**

- **Social Contracts:**

- **Modern Technology:**

- **Social, Economic, Political Unrest:**

- **Public Mistrust:**

- **Disparity between Rich and Poor:**

- **Inversion of Trust:**

- **Failure to Learn and Act:**

Review the Contextual Challenges faced by Daenerys Targaryen below and add your own additional insights that relate to her challenges. If Daenerys were to evaluate the answers below, she could continue to use the categories to reflect on upcoming risks that confront her leadership. For example, under Public Mistrust, you might add that Dany faces distrust when Khal Drogo is unable to lead the Dothraki. Her power as khaleesi is called into question. She navigates this challenge but then in Meereen, after freeing the slaves, must confront the terrorism of the Sons of the Harpy.

CONTEXTUAL INTELLIGENCE
EXERCISE #2: DAENERYS TARGARYEN

Use the free space to add additional challenges in Daenerys's journey.

Demographic: She is ex-pat Westerosi royalty, living in Essos.

Social Contracts: She is khaleesi and a "Beggar Queen."

Modern Technology: She has dragon eggs, and then dragons. This ancient power appeared lost but is returned and she has limited control of the resource.

Social, Economic, Political Unrest: The Dothraki are prairie warriors, nomads who live for honor through battle; they also take slaves in Essos where slavery is common. Daenerys doesn't agree with this system and leverages power by freeing the slaves.

Public Mistrust: Her reputation is a combination of her famous name and her warrior husband. She loses the husband and faces the skepticism and hostility of various stakeholders and competitors.

Disparity between Rich and Poor: Daenerys must accrue resources. Born of noble blood but no wealth, she has relied on others her whole life for financial support until she becomes a khaleesi. She is sensitive to the disparity between those with wealth and those without access to it.

Inversion of Trust: Daenerys doesn't know how far her power extends with the Dothraki or fully grasp her risks when the Khal is poisoned. She must come to terms with the maegi's betrayal and she also discovers that Jorah Mormont had been sending news of her to King's Landing in hopes that his loyalty to the realm would gain him a pardon for his past crimes. Dany becomes aware of the risks of trust.

Failure to Learn and Act: Daenerys acted to help Khal Drogo and a terrible cost was paid. She recognizes the importance of acting upon the wisdom she learns.

THE LEADER'S JOURNEY: ROAD OF TRIALS, MEETING WITH THE GODDESS, AND WOMAN AS TEMPTRESS

On our Leader's Journey, we might remind ourselves how Jaime Lannister realized he was more than a sword-hand. He developed his EQ during a terrible stage in his journey, abused by the Bloody Mummers, wounded and tortured and close to death. Jaime's choice to defend Brienne exemplifies Seneca's reminder that "you must live for your neighbour, if you would live for yourself." Yet we shouldn't forget Seneca's own former student Emperor Nero turned on him, and Seneca paid the King's Justice. He was forced to drink poison: an execution similar to Lady Olenna's final moments in Highgarden, speaking her last words to Jaime. Our Leader's Journey is a choice. Danger is part of our choice to confront our challenges and pursue our goals. The ability to maximize our understanding of the internal and external contexts will help us live for both our neighbors and ourselves.

The Kingslayer and the Maid of Tarth find support in each other in the sixth stage of Joseph Campbell's monomyth: The Road of Trials.

"Once having traversed the threshold, the hero moves in a dream landscape of curiously fluid, ambiguous forms, where he must survive a succession of trials."[37]

Campbell tells us "in the multitude of myths and legends that have been preserved to us, or collected from the ends of the earth"[38] we may see something that can guide us . . . something that can help us. Yet part of the problem is that to "hear and profit, however, one may have to submit somehow to purgation and surrender."[39] In other words, we can't sit back on our sofa, tweak the controls on our devices, and expect to benefit from learning from our history of narratives. We have to live. We have to mix it up. We have to face trials, divinities, and temptations. The Road of Trials will involve suffering. This chapter of *The Hero with a Thousand Faces* reminds us: "One by one the resistances are broken."[40] It is through this suffering that "the hero, whether god or goddess, man or woman, the figure in a myth or the dreamer of a dream,[41] discovers that he or she has what Campbell calls an *unsuspected self*. This revealing of the unsuspected self is what happens to the survivors in A Song of Ice and Fire.

Jaime does choose to live. Campbell describes the Road of Trials as a part of the journey where we are faced with "ageless perils, gargoyles, trials, secret helpers, and instructive figures and in seeing them, we see both the whole challenge we face but also the clue to what we must do to be saved."[42]

Jaime's perils, gargoyles, and trials are right in front of him. The Bloody Mummers torture him to the verge of insanity and death. Jaime's secret helper and instructive figure at this moment is Brienne. She questions his courage, challenging Jaime to realize he adds up to more than his lost skill with a sword. Her intention lands. He follows her leadership.

Campbell describes the seventh stage of the monomyth as "the crisis at the nadir, the zenith, or at the uttermost edge of the earth."[43] In other words, the Hero's Journey at a peak location somewhere in the firmament, what Campbell refers to as the "central point of the cosmos, in the tabernacle of the temple, or within the darkness of the deepest chamber of the heart." This could be Dragonstone, former roost to dragons and Targaryens, a vantage point symbolized by the Chamber of the Painted Table. True scholars of the history of Westeros know that the ancient dates are not precise; what is known is that the isle of Dragonstone is where the Targaryens collected their power before overtaking Westeros. Many years before Stannis Baratheon chose to also hide on this outpost on the Narrow Sea, Aenar Targaryen arrived. "The Targaryens were of pure Valyrian blood, dragonlords of ancient lineage. Twelve years before the Doom of Valyria (114 BC), Aenar Targaryen sold his holdings in the Freehold and the Lands of the Long Summer and moved with his wives, wealth, slaves, dragons, siblings, kin, and children to Dragonstone, a bleak island citadel beneath a smoking mountain in the narrow sea."[44] The key word in this description is: *dragons*. The Targaryens had a technological advantage over the iron weapons of the Westerosi.

Many years later, Stannis doesn't have dragons. He has a claim on the Iron Throne as the older brother of the assassinated King Robert. Stannis isn't wealthy enough to buy mercenaries. He is not effective at the EQ categories of social awareness or relationship management. He lacks allies ready to raise their banner in support of his claim on the

Iron Throne. Stannis has the Onion Knight and Stannis has the Red Woman.

Melisandre has put her faith in Stannis as the Prince That Was Promised. Born centuries ago, she is not the divinity. She is not the Lord of Light but a priestess committed to carry out the vision of her god. The Meeting with the Goddess stage from Campbell's perspective "is the final test of the talent of the hero to win the boon of love."[45] It is about learning from the narrative to find some element of eternity here in the messy, temporary struggles of our lives. Stannis pursues the Iron Throne but appears to be looking to fill some personal emptiness.

In the myths, the struggle is a powderkeg of violence, of desire, of power, of salvation; and it happens between male protagonists and female divinities. In the twenty-first century, I suggest we consider the genders as metaphors representing differences that seek a merging and fulfilling. You don't have to be male to have your Meeting with the Goddess. The female protagonist will also confront this stage of mystical marriage to a force that represents creation and annihilation. Male or female heroes meet, confront, achieve, partner with, in Campbell's language, "the incarnation of the promise of perfection,"[46] which involves both the healing and destroying element of the feminine. This is an image the hero remembers from their past and there won't just be benign memories, regardless of the hero's gender.

While Melisandre proves to be human, she presents herself with elements of a goddess. Campbell writes of the Cosmic Mother at Dakshineswar, who "was Cosmic Power, the totality of the universe, the harmonization of all the pairs of opposites, combining wonderfully the terror of absolute destruction with an impersonal yet motherly reassurance."[47] Another goddess is also Melisandre-esque. "The goddess is red with the fire of life; the earth, the solar system, the galaxies of far-extending space, all swell within her womb."[48]

In Westeros, our Red Woman, Melisandre, with her swollen womb rides in a rowboat with the Onion Knight and delivers a black demon with the face of Stannis to murder his brother, Renly.

Melisandre is able to trick mortality with her ruby necklace, but she is also a servant, decrepit and ancient, crawling into her bed—the illusion of strong, fertile beauty dissolving into the husk of an old woman. She is not divinity. Melisandre is a human, a sorceress with tricks that hide her mortality. She is a disciple, a true believer in the god R'hllor, searching for a solution to a terrible threat. She gets it wrong. Stannis and Melisandre were not Campbell's *harmonization of all pairs of opposites;* they were the failed partnership of a low-EQ, aging prince and a decrepit priestess, dressed in beautiful magic. She wanted to believe she had found the hero necessary to stop the annihilation of humanity. She must carry her despair at the failure of her leadership, including the loss of innocent lives. She burned Shireen alive. Stannis agreed to this murder in the name of victory. This is not Campbell's *harmonization*. Brienne answers her pledge to revenge Renly and kills Stannis with her sword, Oathkeeper. Melisandre survives, shaken in her ability to read the flames.

Campbell describes the eighth stage of the monomyth, The Woman as Temptress, as the situation where "the mystical marriage with the queen goddess of the world represents the hero's total mastery of life."[49] Campbell writes: "The whole sense of the ubiquitous myth of the hero's passage is that it shall serve as a general pattern for men and women, wherever they may stand along the scale. . . . Who and where are his ogres? Those are the reflections of the unsolved enigmas of his own humanity. What are his ideals? Those are the symptoms of his grasp of life."[50] Arya Stark enters the House of Black and White. She prostrates herself to make a mystical marriage, a lifetime commitment, to Jaqen H'ghar and the rules of the temple of the Many-Faced God. She is drawn to the House of Black and White because it suggests an education in control over fear and vulnerability. To be *no one* is to have power. After great personal suffering, Arya develops mastery in the fighting arts. The marriage is temporary, due to her choice. She abandons the promises of Jaqen and the Many-Faced God. She achieves answers to solving her nightly list of vengeance. She also needs to be a wolf.

Campbell writes, "Every failure to cope with a life situation must be laid, in the end, to a restriction of consciousness."[51] The hero—male or female—faces the Woman as Temptress stage of the journey—a symbol for the gift of life and the eventual loss of life and journey past death. The hero develops the ability to learn and find the knowledge to cope with life. Arya goes through difficult series of tests, yet the greatest test is her battle in Braavos to fulfill the rules of the Faceless God, followed by her rebellion against assassinating the actress in the traveling troupe, and her fight to the death with the Waif. Her open consciousness and courage allows her to navigate death and win. She walks away from the House of Black and White. The Arya that leaves Braavos is a true warrior, ready to confront the ogres in Westeros.

The heroes in Westeros and Essos journey through the stages of Road of Trials, Meeting with the Goddess, and Woman as Temptress in pursuit of fulfillment. We can watch, listen, pray, and use their strength to lead ourselves.

GOING FORWARD

We are wired for competition and survival. As Campbell puts it, "The crux of the curious difficulty lies in the fact that our conscious views of what life ought to be seldom correspond to what life really is. Generally we refuse to admit within ourselves, or within our friends, the fullness of that pushing, self-protective, malodorous, carnivorous, lecherous fever which is the very nature of the organic cell."[52]

There are places on the road of our leaders' journeys where we will face extreme trials as we pursue our dreams. On this road, we will also meet temptations and spiritual advisors. We will interact with people who represent so much to us—our aspirations, fears, beliefs, insecurities, desires. These people will be caught up in their own journeys. They will not be here for us but for themselves. All of this will happen on a constantly changing landscape.

Two core, impactful skills to lead ourselves and lead our colleagues and stakeholders are emotional intelligence and contextual intelligence. If we build these capacities, our leadership, both externally and internally, has less chance of being reactive, more chance of supporting the achievement of our desired goals.

We can recognize how to manage ourselves and bring out the best in our colleagues. We can read the narrative unfolding around us by asking the right questions to understand the situation, control our emotions, respond to the emotions of other people, learn to master the context, and guide ourselves and our team on our Leader's Journey.

RIDE TO MEEREEN!

HOW TO BE YOUR BEST
AUTHENTIC ADVOCATE

Leadership roles don't arrive wrapped in a red ribbon with a bow. We have to fight for the chance to lead. The hero must see him- or herself from a new perspective, often confronting the resistance of disbelievers. This can require the hero internally to establish their identity and promote themselves, despite the opinions of disbelievers. Leaders learn to be clear on what motivates them; they learn to not confuse extrinsic rewards with internal rewards. The former can be materialistic and ephemeral, the latter can provide strength against adversity.

THE IMP

After killing his ex-lover and his father, Tyrion must find atonement for his past. This includes atonement for his perceived failures, the failures blamed on him, and the emotions he carries inside himself. When Tyrion's journey across the Narrow Sea is complete, and his box with airholes arrives in Pentos, he has lost the confidence to move forward. He is consumed with a mix of rage and guilt. He consumes Illyrio's wine and brandy and ruminates on what has been done to him and what he did in return. His challenge is that he needs to earn another chance. He needs to be a leader.

Tyrion fell into a trap in King's Landing, one set by his father,

Tywin, and his sister, Cersei. Both were comfortable with the idea of his public execution as the assassin of King Joffrey. Both were willing to bend the facts to confirm Tyrion's guilt. But the real trap that caught Tyrion was that he took employment as Hand of the King from people who operated with principles he didn't respect: his own family. He looked to those people for affirmation. He abandoned what mattered to him and filled that emptiness with pleasures he could purchase. When the professional environment where he worked turned against him, he responded with hurt feelings, confusion, and rage.

Bill George writes in *True North* about the importance for leaders to understand their motivation in order to operate with sustained energy, and stay balanced in how they apply their energy to various tasks and goals. Leaders need to be clear on their extrinsic and intrinsic motivations. One can't take the place of the other.

When serving in support of the Lannisters in Westeros, Tyrion is driven by extrinsic motivation. He wants to do well and prove himself. As George puts it, many leaders are "measured by the outside world. They enjoy the feelings of success, recognition, and status that come with promotions and financial rewards."[1] We see this motivation in Tyrion in his role as Hand of the King, including his heroics at the Battle of the Blackwater. We see this even earlier in the pride Tyrion takes in explaining to Varys how well the sewers ran at Casterly Rock when Tywin put Tyrion in charge of castle plumbing. But extrinsic motivation can be dangerous. Tyrion succeeds in the roles offered to him, yet he is hungry for praise and acceptance into his powerful family. He wants the extrinsic reward of their approval, while he offers them a steady amount of sarcasm and criticism. He tries to drink and whore his way past the imbalance between the extrinsic rewards of having access to Lannister wealth, and the intrinsic emptiness of not being able to fulfill his values and prove his leadership abilities.

Intrinsic motivations are within us and they are subtler than our extrinsic motivations. It can be dangerous if we fall in the trap of pursuing extrinsic motivations—and the rewards that come with achieving success in our extrinsic efforts—but don't find the satisfaction of fulfilling our intrinsic motivations. George reminds us that chasing the extrinsic has a price: "Many people never tap into their most powerful motivations."[2] This is what happens to Tyrion in Westeros. He pursues the extrinsic but can't find a path to achieve his intrinsic motivations while reporting to Tywin, Cersei, and King Joffrey.

These motivations are linked to our life stories and the meaning we extract from the experiences in our lives. "Examples include personal growth, helping other people develop, taking on social causes, and making a difference in the world."[3] Tyrion's life story is infected with hurtful behavior from his father, sister, and community. He attempts to help people. He continues to develop his mind. He wants to make a difference for the people of Westeros. Unfortunately for him, his efforts are often irrelevant to the Lannisters that run the kingdom.

Tyrion performs heroically in the Battle of the Blackwater, risking his life to hold back Stannis's army at the walls of King's Landing. During the battle, King's Landing is surrounded. Joffrey's men are dying. The odds are high that Stannis's army will breach the city walls. Even the leader of King Joffrey's Kingsguard—the Hound, Sandor Clegane—puts his sword into the earth and quits fighting. Tyrion, who had lured Stannis's armada of ships into a horrific inferno of wildfire, recognizes further leadership is needed to avert horrific results: "In the distance, Tyrion heard another great crash. Above the walls, the darkening sky was awash with sheets of green and orange light. How long could the gate hold? *This is madness*, he thought, *but sooner madness than defeat. Defeat is death and shame.* 'Very well, *I'll* lead the sortie.'"[4]

Tyrion seizes direct leadership of the remaining Kingsguard at a moment of ultimate risk to King's Landing . . . and to himself if the defense of the city fails. He fights with courage. He achieves success and holds back the enemy assault until Tywin arrives with the Lannister and Tyrell armies.

King's Landing would not have held without Tyrion's heroic decision to lead the sortie. In addition to his success at repairing the sewers at Casterly Rock, the Halfman succeeded at restructuring and managing the finances at King's Landing during his tenure as Hand of the King, and he succeeded, despite anyone's expectation, at defending the capital from armed assault. His military successes included both his strategy to trap the attacking navy in the bay, immolating them in wildfire, and his crisis decision to lead the desperate fight at the city walls. Without his contribution on both fronts, the city would have fallen before Tywin arrived.

How is Tyrion rewarded? In the heat of the battle, Ser Mandon Moore, at the behest of Cersei, Petyr Baelish, or King Joffrey, tries to kill him. Moore is only stopped by the quick thinking and courage of Tyrion's squire, Podrick Payne.

That blade attack leaves Tyrion with a mangled face. His father will further mangle his emotions.

Tyrion wakes up after the battle to find himself drugged and locked in a solitary room in the Red Keep. When he recovers from the drugs, he enters his former office to find his father has retaken the position as Hand of the King. Tyrion is stunned by what feels like a betrayal by his father. He uses humor to communicate with Tywin. This is often a good EQ approach to a difficult conversation. The problem is that Tywin doesn't respond to humor. Tyrion says, "The badge looks good on you. Almost as good as it looked on me." He points out all he did to protect the city. He complains that he didn't receive gratitude. Tywin says, "Jugglers and singers require applause. You are a Lannister."[5] Regardless of what one thinks of Tywin's and Cersei's leadership, they were focused on their family, both in terms of present achievement, status, and the family legacy. It is easy to see how a drunken jokester in the arms of paid women might be irritating. They didn't see the man that quietly contributed to their efforts. They saw the inebriated critic.

Tyrion is locked into wanting to be praised and awarded for his effort. Cersei and Joffrey won't reward or empower him. Tywin might be persuaded, but Tyrion doesn't approach this challenge with skill. He needs approval from a boss that won't give approval. He also brought Shae to King's Landing, despite his father's insistence he not bring a whore to the capital. Tywin tells his son why Tyrion has failed in his leadership role and refuses to acknowledge his accomplishments.

When we discuss season one of *Game of Thrones* in my Columbia Business School MBA and Executive MBA course Leadership Through Fiction, I have heard persuasive arguments in defense of Tywin Lannister as an effective leader. If his son Tyrion Lannister were sitting in one of those classes, swigging Arbor Red, he might argue that Tywin is limited in his leaderships skills, both self-serving and ungenerous. As a father, Tywin's leadership decisions have caused Tyrion to suffer. During the sham trial to railroad Tyrion as the assassin behind Joffrey's wedding-day death, Tywin accepts Jaime's suggestion that Tyrion admit his guilt and be allowed to *take the black* and spend the rest of his days at Castle Black. But Tywin doesn't seem concerned with protecting this son from public execution. Tywin tells Tyrion that he was fortunate that he was not drowned as an infant. Drowning would have been the socially acceptable solution for a powerful house in Westeros to dispose of a physically unacceptable child.

But if we want to consider Tywin a villain, let's remember that the villain is always the hero of his or her own story. What did Tywin see in Tyrion? Why was this father so tough on his son? Tywin saw a drunk. Tywin saw a lecher. Tywin saw someone who, despite his moments of success, brought dishonor to House Lannister. He may have also seen in Tyrion the true son of Mad King Aerys, and a symbol of his own wife's betrayal of their marriage or even a symbol that his wife was a victim of rape from the Mad King. (We know Tywin saw Tyrion as the cause of his beloved wife, Joanna Lannister's, death during child-birth.) At best, Tywin saw Tyrion as a self-centered clown, unwilling to focus on fulfilling his role as a Lannister.

GET FEEDBACK

Leaders can benefit from gaining objective feedback from colleagues, including direct reports and bosses, within their organizations. Tyrion could also have benefitted from feedback. Tyrion was a bit too comforted by his ability to escape into his pleasures, too easily pleased by his chosen role as degenerate truth-teller. This role worked for him in Westeros, until it didn't work. When it didn't work, the role failed in dramatic fashion.

We don't want to get to the point in our careers where our reinvention is as desperate as Tyrion's reinvention. Terrified and betrayed in King's Landing, and suicidal in Pentos, he claws his way back into functioning in Meereen, but it's touch and go for the Halfman. We want to be able to pitch ourselves for new opportunities in leadership without having to overcome the perspective that we don't deserve the chance, can't handle it, or won't succeed. If we do make it to our own Meereen, we can learn from Tyrion's journey and lead ourselves to improve our odds.

In Westeros, Tyrion does a poor job at marketing his potential to key decision-makers. This is easy to understand. The key decision makers are his unlikable, unapproachable family. Queen Regent Cersei was a step up from psychopathic King Joffrey. Tywin is an arguable step up from Cersei. Family Lannister is not easy senior leadership to approach with the request for career-building opportunities. Still, the responsibility is Tyrion's. He is not proactive at self-advocacy. The Halfman doesn't elicit feedback; he only receives it when the decision makers, such as Tywin, are enraged.

Tyrion's strengths also contribute to his weaknesses. He seeks information from a wide swathe of people. He identifies with the fringe, including those that make their living on the edges of appropriate society. Despite his physical constraints, he speaks truth to power.

Tyrion's anger is triggered when the vulnerable are abused. He proves adept at leading himself and his allies out of dangerous situations; this allows him, in addition to his time in brothels and pubs, to build his network. He forms alliances with the Hill Tribes, with Bronn, with Lord Varys, and, most important, with Daenerys Targaryen. He pursues knowledge and is proud of his intellectual interests and attendant capacities with language. "A mind needs books as a sword needs a whetstone."[6] Yet, for all of his intellectual and emotional intelligence, he never dispassionately explains his strengths with clarity to Tywin.

Tyrion is very confident and proactive when he is making independent decisions, such as developing a strategy to defend King's Landing, or fulfilling his duties as Hand of the King, but he is derailed when he confronts a powerful leader he can't outwit, charm, or pay: Tywin.

Tywin's judgment of Tyrion might not seem fair, but we have, and will, face being judged by leaders that have influence over our careers. They most likely won't be parents, but they may give that parental impression, regardless of their age and our age. They may not approve of our leadership decisions and they may not approve of our behavior. This is reality. We need to learn to advocate for ourselves to those who are positioned in relation to us as Tywin is to Tyrion.

SELF-ADVOCACY

INTEGRITY

True North's chapter 8, "Staying Grounded: Integrating Your Life," offers the reader guidance on self-advocacy in the leadership area of *integrity*. The metaphorical message is simple. I often share George's idea with students to encourage them on how to apply integrity and authentic leadership on a daily basis. "What does it mean to live your life with integrity? Real integrity results from integrating all aspects of your life so that you are true to yourself in all settings. Think of your life like a house, with a bedroom for your personal life, a study for your professional life, a family room for your family, and a living room to share with your friends. Can you knock down the walls between these rooms and be the same person in each of them? When you can act the same in each setting, you are well on your way to living your life with genuine integrity. Living that way, you will be an authentic leader who leads a fulfilling life."[7]

Tyrion Lannister is challenged to live this way in Westeros. The Imp faces practical considerations. Prior to his wrongful arrest for the assassination of King Joffrey, Tyrion already had problems with the different areas of his metaphorical house: first, his father and sister had both threatened to harm his romantic partner, Shae, and second, his closest ally in the family, Jaime, is (overly) committed to his primary antagonist, Cersei. Tyrion should follow the encouragement to see his life as a house and walk into each room with integrity, but he must be careful. Integrity can be difficult. In Westeros, integrity can get you killed. Just ask Ned Stark.

AUTHENTICITY DEPENDS ON THE *WHY*

Tyrion falls into chaos in Westeros. He loses his moral center because he reports to leaders who operate with leadership behaviors he despises, driven by values that he wouldn't accept. His primary desire is to gain the approval of Tywin Lannister. This is a plan guaranteed to pull him away from authenticity. This is a plan focused on securing another person's opinion. Effective leadership depends on following intrinsic motivations, which depends on understanding *why* you are doing something. That *why* has to be about more than a pat on the head.

As Bill George writes, "Without a real sense of purpose, leaders are at the mercy of their egos and narcissistic vulnerabilities."[8] This is part of what contributes to Tyrion's difficulties in Westeros. He tries to align his purpose with the purpose of his father, his sister, even King Joffrey. But their purpose is not his purpose, and so he continues to speak truth to power and enrage them. He continues to pursue his passions, including his romance with Shae, and his value-driven desire to defend the vulnerable, such as the imperiled Sansa Stark. Tyrion's integrity is tested as he continues to exert effort to win extrinsic approval while following his personal, intrinsic motivations that are not in alignment with his bosses'. He continues to fail.

In Westeros, some extrinsic rewards are available to Tyrion, but intrinsic rewards aren't available. Tyrion fills up on extrinsic rewards, but it won't help fulfill his authentic leadership. Bill George describes the five key principles of authentic leadership:

1) Pursuing purpose with passion

2) Practicing solid values

3) Leading with the heart

4) Establishing connected relationships

5) Demonstrating self-discipline

Tyrion is not able to fulfill these principles when he works for the monarchy of King Joffrey. Tyrion is provided with very specific *what* tasks: as Hand of the King, he has been tasked with managing the finances involved in King Joffrey and Queen Margaery's indulgent wedding. He has even developed a military strategy to defend the capital. But Tyrion doesn't have a clear *why* to motivate him. His only *why* is to prove himself to Tywin and the people Tywin controls or has influence on.

Simon Sinek, author of *Start with Why: How Great Leaders Inspire Everyone to Take Action*, makes the point that leaders must understand why they are supporting an organization; otherwise, they can't be authentic leaders. "Authenticity cannot be achieved without clarity of WHY. And authenticity matters."[9] You have to believe everything you say and everything you do. Tyrion manages to be authentic in crisis, but when the crisis stops, his frustration with the *why* that drives the Lannister government is too much for him.

After he strangles Shae and murders his father on the privy with a crossbow, Tyrion escapes to Pentos with the one person who believes in his leadership abilities—his one true advocate and ally: Varys.

Tyrion has been mocked as the Halfman, the Imp, and other derogatory terms, but now he must accept: *Kinslayer.* He is in a dark place of anger at the family that betrayed him, as well as filled with self-loathing aimed at his reactions to those betrayals. With the guidance of Varys, he looks for a new kind of boss in Daenerys. He must find a *why* he can accept. His intrinsic motivations can't commit completely to Cersei's primary values of superiority and power and Tywin's primary values of superiority and legacy. He will travel to a besieged city along Slaver's Bay where the Mother of Dragons offers a new vision of *why*. It won't be an easy trip or a welcoming environment. The mercenary Sons of the Harpy lead a terrorist guerrilla war against the liberated slaves and Daenerys's army of the Unsullied. On the plus side, Tyrion will meet his first dragon.

SELF-ADVOCACY AND PERSONAL DEVELOPMENT

Positive Qualities and an Integrated View

The Columbia CaseWorks "A Primer on Personal Development" (the Primer), written by Daniel Ames, Malia Mason, and Dana Carney, encourages the importance of understanding our strengths and weaknesses. "The plan we've set forth here is not about outsourcing your convictions: *it's not for other people to decide what you want in life.* However, in order to get what you want, you need to understand how people see you."[10] The steps they suggest to guide us forward require doing an initial analysis of our strengths and weaknesses. Our strengths and weaknesses can be the double-edged sword we saw with Tyrion. Our strengths often have a way of also supporting the continuation of our weaknesses. Tyrion is a creative, intelligent, charismatic loner, great at building network connections with people on the fringe, but he was not effective in Westeros at building strong relationships with people in positions of authority, including his family. He trusted people more if they were vulnerable or depended on him for payment. Tyrion didn't understand his true weaknesses. He defended his small stature on a regular basis but was blind to weaknesses he could control, such as his capacity to attempt to persuade people with power.

Ames, Mason, and Carney write that it is critical to understand our strengths, so that we don't undermine our strengths in an effort to target and respond to our weaknesses. When Tywin Lannister first orders Tyrion to travel to King's Landing and take Tywin's role as Hand of the King, he is dumbstruck, asking his father, why me? Tywin responds, "You're my son." Tyrion sits in stunned silence as he processes this acknowledgment. Then Tywin adds, "Oh one more thing, you will not take that whore to court. Do you understand?"[11] Tywin believes Tyrion spends too much time with prostitutes. Despite the flaws Tywin sees in Tyrion, the father recognizes his son as a Lannister. That counts for something. Tyrion chooses to rebel and takes Shae into King's Landing. Tyrion is hooked on Shae—she is sexy, full of life, courageous, uncompromising. She professes strong feelings for him, calling him *my lion*. Shae is Tyrion's chance to remake what he lost as a young man when Tywin manipulated the end of Tyrion's impetuous marriage to the crofter's daughter, Tysha.

Tyrion wants Shae in King's Landing. He also wants to defy his father's command because it strikes him as unreasonable and it might be, but Tyrion could also evaluate his own weaknesses and realize his immediate effort to deceive the man who has offered him a promotion is worth reconsidering. He doesn't follow his father's command and believes he has no choice. He has a choice.

Tyrion ends up working in conjunction with Varys to keep Shae hidden from the Lannisters' view. It's easy to blame Shae's betrayal and death on Tywin's behavior, but in addition to Shae's strengths, she was also naïve, vulnerable, and not prepared to take the situation seriously. She became jealous of Tyrion's unconsummated marriage to Sansa. The stress of putting Shae in danger was more than Tyrion could handle. It wasn't worth the thrills or fulfillment of a romance. He pushed her away out of fear for her safety. He wasn't clear to her that he was attempting to protect her. This left her confused and feeling betrayed. Stepping into court as a defendant in the assassination of King Joffrey, Tyrion is shocked to find Shae as a witness for the prosecution. She tells lies about Tyrion, presenting him in a harsh light, and follows this betrayal by having sex with Tywin. Tyrion strangles her to death.

The Primer suggests we identify our *signature positive qualities*. The goal is to decide what kinds of adjustments can be made in our behavior to turn the way we are perceived into a positive direction. However, that won't work if we ignore feedback or decide all feedback directed toward us is flawed. *"The challenge is to pick out a small number of observations and data points that link together to tell a story about how you're seen and why that matters."*[12] Tyrion could have linked the data points together. He might have taken in the sharp criticism he received from Tywin as motivation to monitor his vices. His signature positive qualities are his leadership, not his drinking and whoring. Success at the former could have happened if he controlled the latter. Tyrion has operated for many years in a style of his choice—the cynical, decadent, self-deprecating outsider—and it's not surprising that Tywin doesn't leap to acknowledge Tyrion's positive qualities, because the Imp is known throughout the kingdom for his vices.

When it came to positioning himself for opportunities, Tyrion was a failure as an advocate for himself, until he met Daenerys. Tyrion had to face the reality that the key decision makers—Tywin and Cersei—saw him as a self-centered person who was a risk. (Cersei saw him as an aggressive antagonist.) If we can objectively answer the question about how colleagues see us, this can provide us with greater understanding of what we can do in our actions to send the best message to those deciding on our future possibilities.

Tyrion's goal, and our goal, should be to evaluate our strengths and weaknesses in an unemotional process with the intention, as the Primer recommends, of trying "to develop an integrated view of your behavior and others' perceptions of you, including both positives and negatives."[13] You want to get an understanding that you can prioritize, in order to help you concentrate your effort on development. It is likely that your strengths and your weaknesses don't seem to have a connecting thread, but you may find that you can identify one.

Tyrion's strengths involved his empathy, creativity, and his curiosity. Those three qualities are an advantage to anyone who has him as a direct report. His empathy is clear in his ability to identify with people in vulnerable positions, and to see their perspective as one that should not be ignored by the senior leaders, as well as his ability to build relationships with outliers such as Shagga and the Hill Tribes.

At the Battle of the Blackwater, his creativity and curiosity contributes to his idea to bring the pyromancers' arsenal of wildfire into the conflict and trap the ships behind a huge chain submerged in the bay. His weaknesses include his expectation that other people will understand his motivations and respond in support of his interests. If they don't, he is wounded. The two men he doesn't pay to support him—Varys and Jaime—are the two men who help him escape from the Black Cells. Tyrion has told himself a story where he is the unloved child and has no option except to rebel and accept being unloved. His story has some truth, but he also feeds that truth through his behavior. He takes pride in overcoming the limitations and judgment put on him due to his short stature, but he also keeps fueling the narrative of his decadence. He thinks his weakness is that people treat him unfairly and he can't catch a break. His weakness is that his brand limits how others trust him.

The Primer reminds the reader that "it's essential to consider the effects of context, be careful about mistakenly attributing your weaknesses solely to misunderstandings or the effects of situations."[14] Tyrion makes this mistake. He has options in Westeros. In addition to not bringing Shae to King's Landing, he could have disciplined himself to not need his father's approval. He could have tried to get an objective understanding of his strengths, and weaknesses. He took pride in defending the vulnerable and took pride in his performance at demanding jobs, but he had trouble understanding why he was never appreciated for his accomplishments and why his defense of the vulnerable triggered rage in those with power.

The Primer suggests *"seemingly contradictory responses can signal a boundary or trigger of some sort that, when understood, can reveal an important insight."*[15] Tyrion succeeded but was never truly acknowledged for his success. This was a *seemingly contradictory response*. He might have realized he needed to stop working for his family and get out of King's Landing. He might have realized he needed to stop playing the lovable degenerate. But he was also fascinated by the roles he chose, including being adept at political intrigue and being a charming rascal. He was hooked on Shae, and being a bad-boy, but he was much more hooked on his desire to prove himself in the hallways of power to his family.

The context of a situation may impact our behaviors, but "our abilities and personality eventually express themselves over time. . . . In short, people's impressions of us are driven both by the contexts in which we act *and* by our underlying abilities and personality."[16] We can ask ourselves to follow the chain of causality and try to figure out why unwanted behaviors keep happening. Tyrion should have asked himself what he might be doing that contributed to the cold judgment he received from his family. Tyrion might have turned to his brother, Jaime, sooner for guidance and support. Tyrion needed to learn from people that wanted him to succeed. Instead, he surrounded himself with people he could pay and he ignored any seeds of truth from people who criticized him.

If Tyrion were to follow the Primer's advice, he would look at his past interactions with members of his family and ask why he behaved in the manner he did. The goal is not to get entangled in the emotions of past failures but to gain understanding. The purpose is to "extract some ideas about future change and development."[17] Once we have effectively gone through analysis, and collected a variety of feedback and targeted our strengths and weaknesses, we can work to understand our potential for more effective future behavior. We need to focus on what we can change for the better.

The Primer recommends that, even if you decide on "broader, long-term action, which might feature multiple interwoven issues," also "include a short-run entry point that allows you to make changes within days or weeks."[18] If Tyrion were to look back to the moments of his greatest frustration at attempting to achieve leadership opportunities, his *short-run entry point* could have involved making a specific request where his leadership skills would have offered value to his father and House Lannister. This was part of his success when he meets Daenerys in Meereen.

Instead of offering specific skills to Tywin, Tyrion asks his father to give him the Lannister castle of Casterly Rock. He demands his inheritance. His short-run entry point should have allowed him a small step in establishing a functional, productive relationship with his father.

Tyrion would get mad at Cersei and enraged by King Joffrey, but he was the most hurt, and derailed, by his father. Tyrion was effective in group meetings with various constituents but lost control of himself in one-on-one meetings with Tywin. The Primer recommends looking for areas to focus. "Indeed, some of the best analyses takes seemingly separate initial issues—like conflict avoidance and difficulty delegating—and finds a single core underlying issue to be addressed."[19] If Tyrion applied the insights from "A Primer on Personal Development" to his challenges in Westeros, he would recognize the importance of creating a plan to help himself develop his working relationship with Tywin Lannister. When we recognize we need a plan of action, we can use the S.M.A.R.T. model: 1) specific 2) measurable, 3) attainable, 4) realistic, and 5) time-sensitive. Tyrion could have used his role as Hand of the King and a similar process to take a small step toward building a functional relationship with Tywin.

The opportunity was there for Tyrion to do a better job at selling his father on his ability to help House Lannister. That isn't what happened. Tyrion reinvented himself in Pentos, and he found his voice to request a leadership role in Meereen. Tyrion's journey is important to the fate of the Known World. He could have done more to manage his dynamic with Tywin, but he used his crucible to find his way forward in leadership.

GET UNSTUCK

The Primer encourages us to remember that "sometimes, even among the truly gifted, *knowing* what you want to be and to achieve is not enough. Despite great ability, motivation, and clarity of purpose, people can simply get stuck."[20] To help you get unstuck, you can follow these steps:

- Do an analysis: Use feedback reports from your team, as well as conversations with colleagues, and self-reflection to gain clarity on your strengths and weaknesses; be sure to identify strengths you can build on and not get lost in emotional reactions; focus on areas to develop.

- Take the time to look deeper at why you have weaknesses or areas that require development; reflect on the context and find any triggers of unwanted behavior that can reveal important insights.

- Figure out why unwanted behaviors keep occurring; focus on behavior, usually a single issue is best, and develop an action plan.

Think of Tyrion's journey, from his mistakes in Westeros to his successes in Essos. Tyrion chose to follow Varys because he understood that to stay in Pentos was to give up. As Varys told Tyrion, "You are many things, my friend, but not a coward."[21] Tyrion is haunted by his murderous actions, but Varys also presents him with an important *why*. Varys suggests Tyrion can choose to die or support a vision of leadership he has always hungered to support.

Develop an action plan, built on analysis that will help prepare you to, in the words of the Primer, "move from a state of bewilderment to one of understanding."[22] If you want to develop as a leader and be an advocate of your potential, you must learn from feedback. You must get unstuck. "As you take your own journey, you'll be asked to do what too few people ever do: solicit critical input from others about your weaknesses as well as your strengths."[23] If you do take the initiative for your personal development as suggested in "A Primer on Personal Development," you will be taking a necessary step in leading yourself to respond to your weaknesses and build on your strengths. This decision will improve how the professional world views your competence and the related capacity to earn trust. This clarity will help decision makers in your professional life choose to provide you with more leadership responsibilities.

SELF-ADVOCACY IN THE SIXTIES

In this section, we will examine how the thirty-fifth president of the United States was able to follow the five principles of authentic leadership, as well as use a method gained from a developmental insight, to navigate a crisis and avoid the risk of nuclear war in what is known in the United States as the Cuban Missile Crisis. Presidents, CEOs, and monarchs may be at the top of the pyramid of their organizations, but they still face situations where they need to advocate for their capacity to be the leader. President John F. Kennedy was in a situation that was fragile. He understood it and he was proactive in solving it.

USE SOMETHING

In 1962, President John F. Kennedy (JFK) had allowed himself to be pushed into the failed covert military action directed at Cuba to instigate a coup against Fidel Castro's government. This failed military action became known as the Bay of Pigs. The Soviet Union placed ballistic missiles in Cuba, ninety miles off the coast of the United States, despite assurances they wouldn't attempt to use Cuba as a military base. On October 15, 1962, President Kennedy and his team were forced to recognize that they faced a crisis. Despite recent assurances from the Soviet leadership that missiles wouldn't be placed on foreign soil, U-2 planes revealed the missiles had arrived on the island and were being prepared to be operational. Just why did the Soviet Union undertake such a reckless move? What objective could the Soviets have had that would have justified a course of action with such a high probability of nuclear confrontation? These questions were the first to be considered by Kennedy's senior advisors when they convened at 11:50 a.m. on Tuesday, October 16. "'We certainly have been wrong about what he's trying to do in Cuba,' Kennedy admitted. 'There isn't any doubt about that.'"[24]

Soviet premier Nikita Khrushchev told his ambassador to the United States, Anatoly Dobrynin, that the primary issue between the USA and the USSR was what would happen with Berlin. The city, under the government of West Germany, was isolated, located firmly in East German territory. "The American belief in their supposed nuclear superiority was making them act, as Khrushchev put it, 'particularly arrogant.' Khrushchev concluded, 'It's high time their long arms were cut shorter.' He liked Kennedy and thought of him as a man of character. Yet, Dobrynin recalls, Khrushchev 'did not conceal his belief that putting pressure on Kennedy might bring us some success.'"[25]

President Kennedy's one meeting with Premier Khrushchev had been rough for the young president. JFK had believed the Soviet assurances to not worry about Cuba; however, after getting the photographic evidence of the missile installation, JFK and his team decided on four hypotheses to explain the Soviet action. It turned out that all four factored into the Soviet decision:

1) The Soviets were invested in defending Cuba, which had been attacked by a US-sponsored rebellion of insurgents that failed dismally at the Bay of Pigs in 1961. Then Kennedy's government had created Project Mongoose, which included low-level sabotage efforts to attack parts of the Cuban economy, including oil and sugarcane production, and had involved discussions of assassinating President Castro.

2) The Soviets wanted to prove USSR global power had shifted in their favor by confronting the United States with a fait accompli—sneaking the missiles into Cuba and then waiting to see if JFK, his administration, and military leaders had the will to respond.

3) The Soviets were making up for an imbalance in their missile arsenal compared to America's. (Nikita Khrushchev told his son that the USSR had nothing to hide when it came to their ability to produce missiles. "We have nothing," Nikita said, "and we must hide it."[26]) Khrushchev was bluffing when he spoke of producing missiles like sausages and he faced the gloomy reality about

the limitations of Soviet ICBMs reaching America from the Soviet bases. "Khrushchev suggested the shortcut of deploying MRBMs and/or IRBMs to Cuba. 'Why not throw a hedgehog at Uncle Sam's pants?'"[27]

4) According to *Essence of Decision: Explaining the Cuban Missile Crisis*, JFK and his team weren't sold on why Khrushchev would care so much about the missile inequality. Why wouldn't he wait for the Soviet technology to get up to speed? They couldn't identify a clear motivation past Khrushchev's own volatile personality. "For Kennedy, at least, a more plausible answer dawned on him shortly afterward. It must be Berlin. Khrushchev would use the missiles to solve the Berlin problem—on his own terms."[28]

JFK's insight about Khrushchev's plan to use missiles in Cuba to leverage Soviet interests in Berlin was complimented by Llewellyn Thompson, who was serving as the State Department's special advisor on the Soviet Union. Thompson had been struggling to understand why Khrushchev and his colleagues, such as Dobrynin and Soviet foreign minister Gromyko, were sending the message they wouldn't raise any issues about the future of Berlin—which the USSR described as a "rotten tooth" in their mouth—until after the upcoming Congressional elections. Once the missiles were discovered, Thompson and President Kennedy came to the realization that, in JFK's words, Khrushchev "played a double game." Kennedy explained, "He said that the weapons were defensive, that they weren't moving any missiles there and all the rest. And obviously he has been building this up in order to face us with a bad situation in November at the time he was going to squeeze us on Berlin."[29]

President Kennedy and his team were dealing with a ticking clock. Their available responses could either increase their vulnerability or contribute to immediate military conflict, which could escalate into nuclear war. If Kennedy and his team chose a military response and acted fast with a sneak air raid to destroy the missiles, the reality is they might not get all the missiles, not to mention the international opinion if the United States, a superpower, initiated an attack on a Caribbean nation. Any exchange of missiles between the two cold war superpowers could trigger catastrophic military conflict. If either side launched missiles and nuclear weapons were released, the results were unthinkable.

If Kennedy and his team chose diplomatic options, they would allow the Soviets more time to establish operational missiles. Since Russia had American missiles pointed at them from Turkey, it was arguable that the United States should just accept the fait accompli of Soviet missiles in Cuba. Kennedy was surrounded with advisors that suggested a first-strike military option to destroy the missiles, followed by a likely invasion of Cuba and removal of the Castro government.

Kennedy had read Barbara Tuchman's *The Guns of August* and was aware of how the European nations had made a series of misguided decisions and triggered World War I. Kennedy had also served in the Pacific during World War II. He had been in conflict and watched Japanese and Americans die. He had been awarded the Purple Heart for his heroism, and had questioned the reasoning behind armies killing one another to defend strategic islands in isolated regions. He understood the suffering and loss of life that could follow questionable military tactics. His skepticism was compounded by his decision two years earlier to allow the US military support of 1,800 CIA-trained Cuban exiles to attempt to spark a coup against Castro's Marxist government. His advisors had assured him that the covert operation would catalyze a popular uprising of anti-Castro civilians, and if it failed, the US-supported rebels had escape options. He realized later the promises were the result of cloudy thinking. The rebels could disappear and become guerrillas in the mountains, but the mountains were eighty miles away from the landing site, separated by swamps.

Arthur M. Schlesinger Jr. was a historian and special assistant to President Kennedy. In the foreword to Robert F. Kennedy's *Thirteen Days: A Memoir of the Cuban Missile Crisis*, Schlesinger describes how JFK "took the greatest care to keep the armed forces on the tightest leash, much to their ill-concealed irritation."[30]

JFK feared what would happen if escalation occurred and resisted signing off on a sneak air attack. "During the missile crisis Kennedy courteously and consistently rejected the Joint Chiefs' bellicose recommendations. 'These brass hats have one great advantage in their favor,' he said. 'If we . . . do what they want us to do, none of us will be alive later to tell them they were wrong.'"[31] But Kennedy had to lead. He had been elected president by the smallest margin at that point in the history of the United States.

He was also the son of Joseph Kennedy, who was criticized for supporting the 1938 signing of the Munich Agreement that had given the

German-speaking part of Czechoslovakia to Nazi Germany and had not attempted to constrain the empire building of Adolf Hitler. Joseph Kennedy was judged as having acted as an appeaser. If his son had agreed to military strikes, it would be an opportunity to stand boldly with the Joint Chiefs and defend the United States, but it would have likely led to the complete destruction of Cuba, and military escalation into a catastrophic nuclear war.

Of the options available on October 22, 1962, President Kennedy decided not to order a surprise air attack, which had been advocated by his national security advisor, McGeorge Bundy, and the Joint Chiefs of Staff. He also initially ruled out the idea of a blockade, followed by negotiations, which had been proposed by his defense secretary Robert McNamara and UN ambassador Adlai Stevenson. He was worried about escalation into nuclear war with the surprise air strike, and he was worried about a loss of US leadership if the nation looked like they were frightened into negotiation and pulled into interminable discussions that resulted in the missiles staying in Cuba. His brother Robert (RFK) was pushing for an invasion, saying an invasion would buy them a little time, but JFK was "becoming convinced that a blockade was the least provocative way to gauge Soviet intentions."[32]

Over the tense days that followed the recognition of the missiles in Cuba, Kennedy and his team debated different views, but Kennedy believed that an effective result would require the United States to remove missiles from Turkey that were trained on the USSR. When his advisor, Thompson, suggested they could pressure Khrushchev to remove the missiles based in Cuba without giving anything up, Kennedy disagreed. "It seems to me that we oughta be reasonable. We're not gonna get these weapons out of Cuba, probably, anyway, but I mean, by negotiation. We're gonna have to take our weapons out of Turkey."[33]

Robert had begun to support a blockade, as had other advisors, including Llewellyn Thompson. President Kennedy chose the blockade, or quarantine of the Caribbean nation, with the threat of air strikes if the Soviet ships crossed the demarcation line.

All through the process, from the first photographs of the missiles being constructed on Cuban soil to the eventual agreements between the two nations that de-escalated the potential of nuclear confrontation, Kennedy was in a situation where he had to lead a complex decision-making process that involved the contradicting opinions of numerous military and political experts. There was no clear path forward and the stakes were inconceivably high.

President Kennedy had needed to pivot after the Bay of Pigs. He had been led into a bad decision that marred his reputation. He had realized he couldn't outsource the leadership, although he did realize he could widen his perspective taking and not rely just on the experts in the room.

Yale psychologist Irving Janis coined the term *groupthink* to capture the psychological group effort for consensus at the cost of suppressing dissent and looking for new alternatives. President Kennedy ordered a review of the decision making that had contributed to the Bay of Pigs. Arthur Schlesinger Jr. had described the process as having an unspoken focus on achieving *assured consensus*.

In the *HBR* reading, "How John F. Kennedy Changed Decision Making for Us All"[34], Morten Hansen describes the four stages in decision making that Kennedy had in place when the missiles were discovered by the aerial reconnaissance photographs:

1) Each participant should function as a "skeptical generalist," focusing on the problem as a whole rather than approaching it from his or her department's standpoint.

2) To stimulate freewheeling discussions, the group should use informal settings, with no formal agenda and protocol, so to avoid the status-laden meetings in the White House.

3) The team should be broken into sub-groups that would work on alternatives and then reconvene.

4) The team should sometimes meet without Kennedy present, so as to avoid people simply following his views.

The whole idea was to solicit diverse viewpoints, stimulate debate, explore options, probe assumptions, and let the best plan win on its merits.[35]

Eighteen months prior to the Cuban Missile Crisis, the young president had accepted the wisdom of his senior advisors, only later recognizing that the language they used to affirm their support of the covert invasion was framed by vague wording that in fact emphasized the likelihood of the mission failing. His experience of trusting the so-called experts in the Bay of Pigs fiasco had damaged his reputation, as well as the reputation of the Democratic Party and the nation. After the rebels who survived the assault were imprisoned, President Kennedy's team, including his brother Robert, negotiated for their release.

The President decided to surreptitiously install a recording system in the offices in the White House, most likely to help with his memoirs, but many believe he also put in the tapes to be able to verify the stance of different members of his team in future decision-making discussions.

At 10:40 a.m. on October 22, President Kennedy got on the phone with the thirty-fourth President of the United States, five-star general in the US Army, and former Supreme Commander of the Allied Expeditionary Forces in World War II, Dwight "Ike" Eisenhower. Ike offered his wisdom, but there was no *wise old man* to step in and solve the crisis. JFK had to make the call. Concerned with the risk of escalation, Kennedy asked, "General, what about if the Soviet Union—Khrushchev—announces tomorrow, which I think he will, that if we attack Cuba that it's going to be nuclear war? And what's your judgment as to the chances they'll fire these things off if we invade Cuba?"[36] Eisenhower told JFK that something might get them to shoot the missiles, even nukes, but he didn't think they would do it over this situation. JFK asked Ike if he himself would take the risk if he was still president. Ike told JFK that if he had something that serious on his flank, and it was going to cause real unease, "you've got to use something."[37]

President Kennedy took responsibility to *use something*: he made the best decision he could make, leveraging the group decision-making process he learned after the failure of the Bay of Pigs.

It turns out that other pieces had to fall into place in order to hold off a nuclear conflagration. Years later, it was acknowledged that second captain of a Soviet B-59 submarine, Vasili Arkhipov, refused to sign off on the release of nuclear torpedoes aimed at the US Navy in the waters outside of Cuba. While the two other captains signed, Arkhipov refused. His decision very likely stopped a horrible military conflict.

President Kennedy also did his part. After his failure of leadership in allowing the clandestine C.I.A. invasion, originally supported by then-President Eisenhower, JFK went and trained himself. He was a firm advocate of his potential after he stumbled. He was part of a team of numerous people, many led by him that were able to follow Ike's advice and find a way in a time of crisis to use something.

As a result of the diverse thinking and effectiveness of that process, JFK made the final decision to order the quarantine and the potential of air strikes. He taught himself and developed his team, while recognizing he had to be the advocate for the correct approach. He had to lead.

Earlier, we mentioned Bill George's five key elements of authentic leadership. Here they are as applied to JFK and the Cuban Missile Crisis:

1) **Pursue purpose with passion**: JFK led his team to confront the issue, recognizing that it would take operating at a very high level to find the best solution.

2) **Practicing solid values**: JFK didn't outsource the decision to his military leaders. This had not worked before and he took responsibility to follow his values and confronted the "brass hats."

3) **Leading with heart**: JFK and his team factored in the various constituents that would be impacted by their decisions, including the people of Cuba, the United States, Berlin, and across the globe.

4) **Establishing connected relationships**: JFK was able to empower his team of direct reports to find alternative possible answers to a volatile solution; this included keeping dialogue open with the Soviet premier and his representatives.

5) **Demonstrated self-discipline**: JFK realized that he needed to leave his team to work without his influence. He also needed to continue to lead the nation, as his team worked to find the best possible solution to the crisis.

Kennedy's leadership contributed to the best possible outcome for two superpowers and one small nation, all poised on the edge of nuclear conflict. Let's now visit a successful entertainer born five years after the resolution of the tense negotiations we know in the United States as the Cuban Missile Crisis. Raised in New Jersey, he decided to interview his heroes in the comedy world and see what he could learn.

SELF-ADVOCACY: WHAT YOU DESERVE

Film director and writer Judd Apatow compiled a series of interviews with professional comedians under the title *Sick in the Head: Conversations about Life and Comedy*. As a teenager, Apatow was fascinated by comedy, all the available platforms in the early eighties, including television, film, and stand-up. In tenth grade, he started to work at his high school's radio station on Long Island in Syosset, New York. A friend at the radio station took the train into New York City and interviewed favorite rock bands, including bands just breaking on the scene, such as R.E.M.

Apatow thought this interview approach might work with comedians. He contacted their agents and requested the interviews. Schedules were arranged for the comedians to be interviewed by a journalist, and then this teenager, Apatow, showed up with his tape recorder. He said the comedians were always respectful and supportive. In 1983 Apatow interviewed talk-show host Steve Allen, comedienne-actress Sandra Bernhard, as well as the first lead writer for *Saturday Night Live* and contributor to *National Lampoon*, Michael O'Donoghue. In 1984 Apatow took his tape recorder and interviewed Jay Leno and Martin Short. Over a two-year period, he interviewed more than forty established and up-and-coming comedians, including Paul Reiser, Weird Al Yankovic, John Candy, and the relatively unknown Jerry Seinfeld. Years later, in the middle of an incredible career in writing, directing, producing shows, and feature films, Apatow kept interviewing creators of comedy. This was a way for young Apatow to develop his knowledge about the art and craft of comedy. This is ambitious self-advocacy from an unproven person who developed as a leader in his field.

SARAH

In 2014 Apatow interviewed the comedienne Sarah Silverman. They talked about the talented people in their industry who haven't managed to develop past their early moments of success. Silverman wanted to help certain people grab the opportunities available and achieve success, "and so you scramble around, trying to get something going for them, and then you come to the realization that they'll never let it happen."[38] You want to see talented people step up and achieve their potential, but you can't *make* them do it. We can support those we believe in. We can take the role of Varys in Pentos and coach Tyrion, but Tyrion must decide he deserves a better future. Each of us must make that decision and persevere with authenticity and the willingness to develop ourselves to achieve our leadership goals. We have to decide to be our best advocate.

Silverman reminds us that when the doors aren't opening and our career is not going well, our success still depends on us. President Kennedy almost destroyed global faith in the United States by accepting the decision that led to the Bay of Pigs. Then he trained himself and succeeded at a leadership moment that could have had a terrible cost in human lives. Despite his doubts, he accepted responsibility to be the right leader at that moment. We can't just hunger to reach our goals; we need to believe we are the right person to make it happen. We need to take the necessary actions.

Silverman encourages us to embrace that responsibility: "You don't get what you want, you get what you think you deserve."[39] To decide we *deserve* success is our choice. Self-advocacy depends on making choices for ourselves. We can find inspiration in the efforts of other people, whether they are colleagues, friends, or public figures. If we choose to identify with people who don't make a real effort and don't succeed, that is also a choice.

Ask yourself, do I believe I deserve the goals I am pursuing? One approach is to reflect on a crucible challenge you faced—a time you were tested. Did you act like someone that believed you deserved to succeed? Tyrion Lannister struggled on many fronts in Westeros, yet he continued to return to the challenges of leadership, even putting his life at risk when he led the King's Landing soldiers out the Mud Gate to defend the city. Tyrion also continued to defend the vulnerable. Leadership mattered to him, and a leader with a similar purpose mattered to him. It made sense that he chose to follow Varys and ride to Meereen.

What purpose is calling you? If a colleague asked you to ride to Meereen to support something that was demanding, dangerous, and important, what would it be? Which *who*, *what*, or *why* will cause you to face your own challenge to win or die? Can you identify the Daenerys Targaryen that will motivate you to ride to Meereen?

SELF-ADVOCACY: FOES AND FRIENDS IN *GAME OF THRONES*

Trust and Friction

In *Friend & Foe*, Professor Adam Galinsky of Columbia Business School and Maurice Schweitzer of the Wharton School write about a necessary component of leadership: *getting other people to trust you*. Tyrion wouldn't have made it out of the Black Cells and escaped his public execution if the Master of Whisperers hadn't trusted him. Varys's trust of Tyrion is not based on the power and wealth he had been born into— his birthright. Rather, it is based on the Imp's integrity, the strong elements of his character, and the intrinsic motivation Varys has been able to define by watching the Halfman in action in King's Landing.

When Tyrion stumbled from the box in Pentos, Varys understands Tyrion is derailed. Varys sees Tyrion drink and vomit and drink again. Varys also believes Tyrion will help him work to improve the political leadership of Westeros . . . *if* they travel across the land to Slaver's Bay and support Daenerys. Varys trusts Tyrion because he observed him in the pressure cooker of the Westeros capital. Varys was patient in King's Landing, aware that one wrong move could result in an order for his own death. He knew he could be sentenced in a heartbeat by King Joffrey or Queen Regent Cersei, "and who will mourn poor Varys then? North or south, they sing no songs for spiders."[40]

Galinsky and Schweitzer point out in *Friend & Foe*, "When trust is low, on the other hand, there is friction in every interaction. We are consumed with minimizing the risk of being exploited. And as a result, we become competitive, even combative. It's tough to be a good friend *or* an effective foe when we're constantly suspicious and fear exploitation."[41] This explains the inability of Ned Stark to leverage the opportunity to recognize Varys as his ally.

Galinsky and Schweitzer co-ran an experiment with Alison Brooks of Harvard in which research assistants approached people and asked if they could use the approached stranger's cell phone. They first ran the experiment with no preface to the request, and then they ran it with a different group but made a polite opening statement, a "superfluous apology." "'I'm sorry about the rain! Can I borrow your phone? I need to make an important call.' This opening statement is, on the face of it, a bit absurd. After all, it doesn't make much sense to apologize for something (like the rain) over which we have no control. However, this 'superfluous apology' demonstrates concern and conveys warmth—and in turn, engenders trust."[42] Warmth matters when you want to build trust. When warmth already exists, based on past connections between family, friends, colleagues, it can trigger quick trust.

Galinsky and Schweitzer say, "We also also build credibility when our deeds match our words."[43] Varys had observed that Ned was loyal to King Robert. Part of the challenge, according to Galinsky and Schweitzer, is that "cues that project credibility in one context may fail to project credibility in another context. What's important is that the cue matches the situation."[44] Varys offers clues, which are a cue to his credibility, but the Spider also works with necessary caution. Ned doesn't ignore Varys, but he doesn't respect Varys and doesn't offer Varys a reason to trust Ned until it's too late. Trusting the wrong person in King's Landing is dangerous. Varys won't step out into thin air and fall to his death. Ned had to trust and he had to read the cues Varys offered.

Friend & Foe explains that "competitive individuals can also become highly cooperative—when they collaborate with members of their group to compete against others."[45] The way to make this happen is to identify the common enemy. The Halfman and the Spider were never combatants, but they become allies when Varys decided to help Tyrion escape and then put his offer on the table: drink yourself to death in Pentos or ride with me to Meereen.

Daenerys, Tyrion, and Jon deliver the wight into the dragon pit in front of Queen Cersei for this exact reason: to build her alliance around a common enemy. The plan doesn't work because Cersei can't imagine the foe descending from the north is more dangerous than the foes that have just dropped an infuriated zombie at her feet.

As *Friend & Foe* points out, "We know that perceived threats promote cooperation within a group and trigger competition between groups. The same principle applies to bringing competing groups together, and to this end there is really nothing that works more effectively than introducing a common enemy. From the diplomatic stage to the boardroom, a common threat can create some truly odd bedfellows as former adversaries shift gears to cooperate with each other."[46]

In Meereen, Tyrion is fortunate that his Lannister name doesn't cause Daenerys to banish, imprison, or execute him, although these options appear likely when Tyrion is first brought in front of the Mother of Dragons. She knows that her father, mother, and siblings were all murdered by the Lannisters, and her heroic brother Rhaegar died on the Trident river, defending the monarchy Tyrion's brother, Jaime the Kingslayer, betrayed.

Daenerys asks Tyrion why she shouldn't kill him and revenge her family. Tyrion points out that he killed his mother the day he was born, and shot his father with a crossbow. "I am the greatest Lannister killer of our time."[47] Tyrion builds an alliance with Dany over their competition with the Lannisters.

Friend & Foe reminds us: "Competence and warmth are the key ingredients for building trust."[48] The authors tell us "one way to build warmth is to demonstrate concern for others or share information about our most important relationships."[49] Tyrion manages to do this in his first intimidating meeting with Daenerys. He confesses that he is someone who was blamed for the death of his mother and admits to killing his father. This is sharing information about important relationships. He also alludes to understanding the pressure she faces in her day-to-day leadership responsibilities.

In his TED talk, "How to Speak Up for Yourself,"[50] Galinsky explains that one effective way to be assertive and still likable, is to *signal flexibility*: provide people with a choice and you can lower their defense. Tyrion uses this technique not by outright attempting to negotiate with Daenerys. She holds all of the power. Tyrion faces a high potential to receive punishment. Tyrion faces the *low-power double bind*. If he doesn't say anything and is too humble and passive, the Mother of Dragons won't notice him and will make her decision regarding his future without any influence from him. If he overreaches, or irritates or enrages her, his offer will be rejected and she will send him to the Fighting Pits to die.

When you lack power, two things are important to implement:

1) appear powerful in your own eyes, and

2) appear powerful in the eyes of others.

Tyrion knows Daenerys can kill him. He doesn't supplicate himself but retains the power of choosing to act brave in the face of a threat. He presents himself as powerful, even if the power is offered through humor . . . and is really the power to not cower and beg. He continues to speak with confidence. He is honest. He presents her with the choice to either kill him or accept him as a brave truth-teller.

Tyrion tells Dany that she will need someone by her side that understands the political, social, and military norms of Westeros. She suggests she won't need his aid in Westeros, due to her army and her dragons. Tyrion says, "Killing and politics aren't always the same thing."[51] He is low on actual *power* but presents himself as high in *expertise*. Galinsky points out that if a person has high power, such as Daenerys Stormborn with her Unsullied army and three dragons, she doesn't necessarily need expertise in leadership, yet it would be helpful, which she recognizes. She has made mistakes before and understands the value of a trustworthy advisor. This is why she evaluates and accepts Tyrion. He manages to follow Galinsky's guideline of being *assertive and likable*. He is serving his interests in self-advocacy by speaking to her with honesty about their shared backgrounds. When Tyrion tried this approach with Tywin, he wasn't assertive about any point relevant to Tywin, and he wasn't likable. Context matters. Tyrion and Daenerys haven't met before, but he understands how to communicate with her.

Tyrion confesses to Daenerys that he has always been a cynic, that despite the requests of various people over his lifetime, he chose not to be a believer in anything, because he saw how belief destroyed people in different ways. "I said no thank you to belief . . . and yet here I am. I believe in you." He jokes in a self-deprecating way that he would swear to her his sword, but he has no sword. Daenerys says, "It's your counsel I need." Tyrion says, "It's yours. Now and always."[52] The Mother of Dragons then places a pin on Tyrion's doublet and names him Hand of the Queen.

Tyrion won't be free of leadership challenges. His road won't be smooth. None of our lives will be free of leadership challenges. Our roads won't be smooth. However, Tyrion did learn how to be his best advocate after his authentic efforts with Tywin were derailed because Tyrion needed more than Tywin could offer. Tyrion was both needy in Westeros and ineffective at being his own advocate. In Meereen, with Daenerys, he is able find a leader with intrinsic values he respects and he is able to turn a foe into a friend. He moves forward on his road and we can learn from his challenges to guide ourselves down the path that waits ahead of us.

THE LEADER'S JOURNEY:
ATONEMENT WITH THE FATHER AND APOTHEOSIS

Joseph Campbell talks about the spiritual metaphors that have served to guide cultures. He talks about gods. When Campbell describes Viracocha, who has a tiara made of the actual sun in the sky, Campbell's god is a *god*: "The mystery of the apparently self-contradictory father is rendered tellingly in the figure of a great divinity of prehistoric Peru."[53] Tywin Lannister is a man. He is fictional, but we understand him as a man like other men we have known. Tywin, despite his demeanor, isn't a divinity. He also, despite rumors, doesn't shit gold. We can choose to identify with Tywin, admire him, or judge him.

Tyrion doesn't have a problem with gods. He has a problem with men, in particular, the man he knows as his father: Tywin. Tyrion doesn't believe in the Many-Faced God, the Drowned God, or the official gods of Westeros—the Seven—or the Old Gods, or R'hllor or any gods. They are no more real than grumkins and snarks to Tyrion. But Tyrion does believe in the reality of the father that has imprisoned him and intends to have him executed. When Tyrion stands up to that father, he is not confronting a god; he is confronting a man that represents the family and culture that have judged him, mocked him, trivialized him since birth. Tyrion wants love and respect. He is angry and he has buried his hurt deep.

"It is in this ordeal that the hero may derive hope and assurance from the helpful female figure."[54] In introducing Atonement with the Father, stage ten of the monomyth, Campbell continues a Navaho tale introduced earlier in his book about two boys who, with the initial guidance of an ally, an old woman known as Spider Woman, make a perilous journey past crushing rocks, slicing reeds, puncturing cactus plants, and across deserts percolating with fiery sands. The boys are searching for their father: the god who puts the sun in the sky.

Spider Woman provides the young men with special incantations that make vicious wild animals crouch in deference. When they arrive at the large, square, turquoise house of their father, the Sun, the two youth, known as the Twin Warriors, use the chosen words to make it past two guard-bears, two threatening serpents, and a combo of unfriendly weather, including wind and lightning. The two journeyers face a variety of gatekeepers, but all that assigned to guard "were readily appeased, however, with the words of the prayer."[55]

When the Twin Warriors enter the house, they are met by a woman. She rolls them up into a blanket, wraps them "in four sky-coverings, and place[s] them on a shelf."[56] When the father returns from his day at work, he hangs the sun on a hook, unrolls the blanket, seizes the boys, and begins the process of trying to destroy them.

The Spider Woman had provided them with "life feathers." They cling to these talismans as the Sun flings them against assorted sharp rocks. Then he attempts to steam them to death in a sauna. He then tricks the youth by accepting them as his sons, only to give them a poisoned pipe to smoke. Fortunately, "a spiny caterpillar warned the boys and gave them something to put into their mouths."[57] The smoke doesn't kill them but tastes sweet. The Twin Warriors survive the series of tests. Their father, the Sun, stops trying to annihilate them. He proudly accepts them as his sons.

Campbell points out one common theme in myths that involve a father: the dad has to be careful before he accepts children as his own. False sons are a danger to the father. The father must protect his legacy and himself. This carefulness often means the father chooses to terrify, rather than welcome. The heroes, the Twin Warriors, must confront their terror before they can reach the possibility of acceptance. They are helped by the Spider Woman to navigate their risks. Tyrion Lannister destroys his father and then needs the help of Varys to move forward from his grief and rage.

Tyrion finds rebirth and liberation. Tyrion's atonement is his ability to accept the humility to let go of his rage. "The hero transcends life with its peculiar blind spot and for a moment rises to a glimpse of the source."[58] Tyrion follows Varys, his mentor, his Spider, who leads them both to their new leader.

All of the previous steps in Tyrion's life, his series of challenges, his successes and failures, have led him to crawling from the wood box with air holes in Pentos. This is the centerpoint of his journey.

Tyrion "The Kinslayer" Lannister navigates past what Campbell describes as "the perennial agony of man, self-torturing, deluded, tangled in the net of his own tenuous delirium."[59] Tyrion yearns for an Atonement with the Father force and he offers his followership to the Mother of Dragons.

In his chapter "Apotheosis," Joseph Campbell writes, "If the God is a tribal, racial, national, or sectarian archetype, we are the warriors of his cause; but if he is a lord of the universe itself, we then go forth as knowers to whom *all* men are brothers."[60] Campbell refers to the Bodhisattva as a god symbolizing the idea of a world full of equals, sharing knowledge and living without tribal aggression. A similar universal brotherhood and sisterhood is what Tyrion, Varys, and Daenerys desire: a world without slaves, where the wheel of power that lifts the spoke of the current racial, national, or sectarian authority is broken.

Unlike the Bodhisattva, neither the Kinslayer, the Master of Whisperers, nor the Mother of Dragons believes this goal can be achieved through peace. They don't believe peace can deliver peace. They rest their chance on dragons, teamwork, and wisdom. Tyrion has found a temporary repose in his followership of Daenerys and his sense of being on a mission that deserves his leadership. The debates of the spiritual world don't interest him. Tyrion is practical as Varys is practical as Daenerys is practical. All three have seen the damage that can occur when a delusional faith in an immoral world runs headlong into a contradictory power.

All three leaders were betrayed at times of vulnerability: Varys, a victim of mayhem; Tyrion lied to and betrayed by his family so he would abandon his first love and wife, and then railroaded in a bogus trial; Daenerys deceived by the vengeful maegi, and betrayed by liars who want her dragons. Our three leaders are not free of the pain of the past, but this pain has contributed to their development, self-advocacy, and ability to build friendships from enemies.

Tyrion achieves a new leadership in Meereen, the Hand of the Queen pin on his chest: "Having surpassed the delusions of his formerly self-assertive, self-defensive, self-concerned ego, he knows without and within the same repose."[61]

If you stumble from the crate in fear and rage, after trembling and vomiting across the Narrow Sea, don't feed your rage. Listen to the voice of an honest mentor, and also listen to your own voice. You are the one that needs to speak and to lead. You must step into the role of your best advocate.

GOING FORWARD

It is important that we advocate for ourselves. We will be blindsided by challenges we didn't expect. We will be asked to agree with decisions that could betray what we believe is important. We must prepare ourselves to learn and develop past our errors. We have to pitch what is authentic about our leadership and not become derailed if the decision makers aren't on our side.

Tyrion almost lost himself during his struggle to prove himself in Westeros. The purgatory of his imprisonment, mock trial, and impending execution were brutal, and he was placed in that environment by his father and sister. Enraged, filled with wroth, his future could have ended in the Red Keep or at the bottom of a bottle in Pentos. The truth is that Tyrion always had options. He followed extrinsic motivations in King's Landing, and waited for his intrinsic motivations to be fulfilled. It is our job to be advocates for ourselves and our colleagues. We must get unstuck and believe we deserve success. We can't outsource our intrinsic motivations. We must take responsibility and be honest about the intrinsic motivations that matter to us. We must confront, and sometimes develop, opportunities with antagonists that could turn to support our leadership.

Our rebirth as the leader we desire to become depends on our capacity to develop in times of need and leverage a world where the difference between friends and foes is fluid. Kingdoms await our ability to make the choice to ride to Meereen!

DON'T WALK, FLY!

HOW TO LEAD WITH ADAPTABILITY

A Game of Thrones begins with a leader, Waymar Royce, who fails to adapt.

On patrol in uncontrolled territory north of the seven-hundred-foot wall of ice, Waymar is informed of the motionless, dead bodies of eight wildlings down in an empty clearing of snow beneath a great sentinel tree. One of the two Rangers suggests they return from the brutal cold to the warmth on the other side of the Wall and report in with their superiors. "Ser Waymar looked him over with open disapproval. 'I am not going back to Castle Black a failure on my first ranging.'"[1] A Ranger suggests they light a fire to ward off certain threats. No fires. Ser Waymar instead wants to confirm the wildlings are dead. He doesn't listen to his experienced direct reports. He has a vision of his success. He sticks to his ideal of bravery and a method for ranging that is thorough, accountable . . . and uninformed about the competition. They arrive at the clearing and the bodies have disappeared.

THE OTHER

Waymar, sticking to his guns, insists, "'We *will* find these men.'"[2] He sends the Ranger Will to climb a tree for a better vantage on the situation. This provides the Ranger a clear view of the duel that ensues when a White Walker confronts Waymar. "The Other slid forward on silent feet. In its hand was a longsword like none that Will had ever seen. No human metal had gone into the forging of that blade. It was alive with moonlight, translucent, a shard of crystal so thin that it seemed almost to vanish when seen edge-on. There was a faint blue shimmer to the thing, a ghost-light that played around its edges, and somehow Will knew it was sharper than any razor."[3] Will climbs down the tree after the Others leave. Will falls into the same trap as Waymar: he believes he understands the competition. He doesn't. New rules. Waymar doesn't adapt. Will doesn't adapt. Waymar rises as a wight with blue eyes.

The third member of their ranging team does attempt to adapt. He escapes the White Walkers by fleeing south of the Wall and out of the reach of the Night's Watch. But he can't outrun Ned Stark, who executes him for abandoning his post, for being an oathbreaker, a deserter. He admits he should have returned to the Night's Watch, but he had seen the truth of the competition and he panicked. His response to the need to adapt was to run. Leaders must be able to adapt . . . and adapt before the terror of the competition causes them to lose control of themselves and their commitments.

Adaptability requires the ability to face risk, handle stress, and support one's effort, and the effort of colleagues, with confidence. The successful leaders in Westeros and Essos have some capacity for adaptability; if not, they would have lost their leadership and, often, their lives. The more challenging the situation, the more an ability to adapt will make the difference. If we can't adapt, we are stuck. We will only succeed if we are faced by challenges and competition we already know. Adaptability is a leadership responsibility to ourselves, our colleagues, our organization, and our community. Embrace it.

CHAOS IS A LADDER

Daniel Goleman's Emotional and Social Intelligence Model (introduced in chapter 4) is structured in two sections—**Emotional** and **Social**—with four subheadings. Each subheading consists of specific competencies listed below.

Emotional:

- **self-awareness:** emotional self-awareness.

- **self-management:** emotional self-control, achievement orientation, positive outlook, and adaptability.

Social:

- **social awareness:** empathy, organizational awareness.

- **relationship management:** influence, coach and mentor, inspirational leadership, conflict management, and teamwork.

Two of the most adaptable characters in Westeros—Cersei Lannister and Petyr Baelish—notice organizational awareness in terms of how it gives them power, but not how it could contribute to build more effective organizations. This limits their capacity to achieve because they are not building adaptive teams. They adapt, but they operate solo. They respond to challenges—both conflict and opportunity—yet, they are subject to their own limitations, both in leadership and emotional and social intelligence. They are both committed to using the skills they have in emotional and social intelligence for their own individual advancement. They are not generous leaders and innovative ideas are not brought to them. Cersei has the minor exception of her maester, Qyburn. He develops weaponry and reanimates Gregor "The Mountain" Clegane, but as a resource, he can't or won't help her past her blind spots. Neither Cersei nor Petyr provide long-term direction or create harmony that builds new ideas with anyone who reports to them. They don't have advisors that coach up and help them develop. If they leverage social skills, such as empathy, they don't expect anyone to benefit except themselves.

Both leaders rely entirely on themselves. Cersei's one mentor, her father, first dismisses her leadership by making Tyrion Hand of the King, then her father is dead. Petyr overevaluates his own capacity to adapt his way to success through threats. They each have triggers that derail them: Cersei lives embroiled in a rage against perceived threats. Red wine and hurting her opponents soothe her. Her list of enemies keeps growing. She hasn't established allies who are sustainable. Her future nuptials with Euron might prove to transform her leadership capabilities, but that seems unlikely. He is a charming, violent Greyjoy, who murdered his own brother to gain his position on the Salt Throne. Euron and Cersei's mutual obsession with sitting in the big chair could get toxic. Her skill at the competencies of self-management aren't balanced with self-awareness. She doesn't understand her triggers and this could make her vulnerable. Petyr's desire for Sansa and the Iron Throne undermines his adaptability competency in Winterfell. He doesn't adjust to being in a dynamic where Sansa has both power and allies and won't be subjugated to constant verbal and physical abuse, which previously had allowed Petyr to present himself as an ally and manipulate Sansa.

Both Petyr and Cersei win when faced with challenges that allow them to continue to do what they already know how to do. Petyr is always manipulative. His leadership style is duplicitous and depends on controlling and disseminating—usually false—information.

Cersei might prove more adaptable than expected. One might give Cersei the benefit of saying she uses a directive leadership style, which is effective when your followers are low on motivation and low on skill. Yet her leadership style, like Tywin's, is command and control. This works in the sense she gains the Iron Throne, but she loses her three children: two die from political assassination and one from suicide. She is pregnant again. Given the death of her previous three children, which were losses to some degree beyond her control, will she embrace a new leadership path motivated by the desire to see her new child succeed and flourish? What she has done up to the present has worked, but she has also faced terrible losses.

Richard J. Davidson describes this type of one-note leadership tendency in Daniel Goleman's *Adaptability: A Primer* as being stuck: "You only react one way and you don't notice that the situation has changed or the context is different. People skilled in the Adaptability Competency are able to make those shifts very seamlessly."[4] Cersei is stuck on protecting and consolidating her power. She has been effective at this process, but the threats to her organization will change. Petyr is stuck on manipulation because he has no greater interest than his narcissistic vision of himself with his trophy, Sansa, at the top of the Seven Kingdoms org-chart.

Despite what they ignore in emotional and social intelligence, Cersei and Petyr were masterful in a self-serving way at operating within Goleman's first three categories of self-management: 1) emotional self-control, 2) achievement orientation, and 3) positive outlook. Their blind spots were in: 4) adaptability. As George Kohlrieser contributes in the *Adaptability* primer: "Adaptable people see change as positive."[5] Littlefinger famously said, "Chaos is a ladder."[6] Petyr has a point, but Petyr slips.

As Richard Boyatzis writes in *Adaptability*: "Adaptability is where you are on a path toward something and it's not working."[7] Things worked for Petyr Baelish, until they didn't. The Master of Coin had become Lord Protector of the Vale, but his manipulative leadership style becomes transparent to Sansa. By the time things aren't working for Baelish, he doesn't have a chance to react.

Queen Cersei discusses her leadership challenges with her brother in the King's Landing courtyard. Jaime and Cersei stand on a map as it is being painted by an artisan on his knees. The map reveals their strategic peril. They are surrounded by enemies. Jaime tells Cersei they need allies. She asks him, sarcastically, if he thinks she never learned anything from their father. Cersei has partnered on the sly with Euron Greyjoy. He delivers to Cersei her enemies from Dorne. Things are working for Cersei, but her father is dead and she doesn't invite or pursue other mentors. Her ability to self-manage is not supported by other competencies that can contribute to her ability to adapt. The Night King and winter will descend on the capital of Westeros. She may have Euron, Qyburn, and the Mountain, but she has not developed skill in relationship management. She doesn't inspire, manage conflict, influence, mentor, or work in teams. She doesn't completely control. Will she adapt?

DON'T GET STUCK

Bran Stark, despite his adept climbing skills, has to adapt.

After being pushed off a high window ledge in Winterfell, Bran awakes, paralyzed. He dreams of a raven with three eyes. The bird guides him into the crypts of Winterfell. Bran dreams he sees his father, Lord Stark, in the crypt at the time Ned Stark is beheaded in King's Landing.

Bran recognizes that he is being called to a task, but he doesn't want to face it. He doesn't want a life without the use of his legs. He is a nine-year-old boy that wants to run, ride, shoot arrows, and train with wood swords. He doesn't want to lead. He wants to live. He wants to grow to be a man like his brother and father.

It takes the Crannogmen, Jojen, and his sister Meera to teach him. Jojen has greensight and helps Bran understand that his dreams can be a form of messaging, also a method to learn about the past, present, and future. Bran begins to warg into his direwolf, Summer. It is liberating to be free of his constraints and fulfill the sigil of the Stark clan. "He was strong and swift and fierce, and all that lived in the good green world went in fear of him."[8]

This offers Bran an incredible chance to adapt to his injury, but it is not sustainable. He wargs into his direwolf and doesn't want to return. He can hunt, eat meat, and live with the power of mobility and fierceness. He can avoid seeing himself as Bran the Broken, a boy carried in a basket on the back of a giant man.

But he needs to be Brandon Stark, Prince of Winterfell. He needs to be brave enough to go beyond the Wall.

Jojen impresses upon Bran that he has a choice to make and the results could go either way: "I dreamed of a winged wolf bound to earth by chains of stone, and came to Winterfell to free him. The chains are off you now, yet still you do not fly."[9]

Bran ends up facing his fear. He is frightened for understandable reasons, but he also decides he doesn't want to be limited by the injuries that happened to his body when he was pushed from the castle-window ledge. Despite his immobility and vulnerability, the youthful warrior in Bran is still very alive and he commits himself to adapting to the challenge thrust upon him. "He balled his hands into fists. 'I want to fly,' he told them. 'Please. Take me to the crow.'"[10]

ADAPTABILITY

Adaptability can be an advantage to us both individually and organizationally. If an organization fails to operate with adaptability, the leadership can create blind spots that cause the organization to react slowly, or not at all. This can mean the end of the organization. If we can't adapt as individuals, we will find our leadership limited to what we already know and understand. We can miss the chance to lead ourselves and shift to what the challenge requires from us.

Adaptability happens when a leader stays in control of themselves and their team while facing the unknown. They don't derail or lose emotional control because of events that were unexpected. The adaptable leader looks to find solutions. They have the capacity to keep moving forward. They can meet new challenges and respond to the unpredictability of events. "The Adaptability Competency means having flexibility in handling change, being able to juggle multiple demands, and adapting to new situations with fresh ideas or innovative approaches. It means you can stay focused on your goals, but easily adjust how you achieve them."[11]

Goleman writes, "It's no surprise that, in a constantly changing world, the data shows that adaptability is an asset in leadership. It is also at the heart of innovation."[12] Goleman references a study that followed up on a group of MBA students five to nineteen years after they graduated, which showed "a strength in adaptability predicted their life satisfaction, their career satisfaction, and, in fact, their career success."[13]

Adaptability does not come easy. Other cognitive biases, such as loss aversion and denial work against it.

Research in Motion (RIM), for instance, were the makers of the Blackberry, an early market leader in smart phones. My wife, a finance professional, insisted she would never leave her Blackberry keyboard for the flat-screen of an iPhone. RIM bet on the belief that the majority of their customers would make a similar choice, and stay loyal to the device that had been pleasing them. Many customers were unshakable in their verbal commitment to the Blackberry keyboard. Except this loyalty didn't happen. While the top leadership at RIM understood the customer appeal of touchscreens and other elements, such as apps that were available on the iPhone and Androids, they were blinded by an overarching assumption that touchscreen smart phones would be consumer devices and that business users would stay loyal to their keyboard-enabled phones. RIM had a poorly diversified portfolio. They were locked into one vision of their product, overly confident in their customers' commitment to the value that product provided against possible competition.

RIM didn't move to apply touchscreen technology on their phones until it became clear that a new "bring your own device" era was being ushered into business, and customers were bringing their beloved iPhones and Androids to the office. Precious time had elapsed due to a bias that slowed down the adaptability of RIM. The company had been overly confident in the tech naysayers who said battery life and wireless technology challenges would hinder the success of the Apple and Samsung products.[14]

Rita McGrath at Columbia Business School reminds senior executives: "Don't get blindsided by customers finding a new way to get their needs met."[15] In other words, adapt before your customers adapt away from following you.

Product advantages have life cycles. RIM mismanaged the "transient competitive advantage" that was provided for a time by the success of their product. The organization's leadership blinded themselves because they failed to revisit the assumptions they made about what users wanted in their products. By the time the market told RIM the cost of their error, it was too late for their portable phone business to recover.

Rita McGrath describes the cost of not adapting to the competitor's challenge: "Finally, of course, you can consult your numbers. The first thing that usually happens is a small decline in the sales growth rate. Then a flattening out. Then eventually declining sales. Unfortunately, by the time a decline shows up in your performance numbers, it is usually too late to muster a proactive response, and you find yourself clambering back in a weaker position than you had been in."[16] Organizations won't be adaptable without adaptable leadership.

One of the reasons this adaptability is a challenge for business leaders is that near-term performance will almost inevitably decrease as the organization manages the transition and attempts to transform. McGrath makes the point that if a person pursues a graduate degree to build their knowledge and capabilities for a specific profession, they need to commit to a period of time where they are just learning and haven't seen the benefit in action. We talked about this in chapter 3 with Josh Waitzkin's concept about the importance of "investment in loss." Waitzkin emphasizes the importance of those periods during development when performance must coexist with the opportunities to grow new skills. This is true in chess and martial arts and it is true in business. McGrath references the management development author, speaker, and advisor, Geoffrey Moore's point that the reason organizations don't jump from one S curve to the next S curve is the difficulty being able to tolerate the J curve—that intersection between two "S" curves when performance declines.

Adobe, on the other hand, successfully adapted to changing circumstances. The company was started in 1982. When cloud technology arrived, it would have been easy for Adobe to follow the RIM assumption that the technological problems and challenges of redesigning their business model wouldn't be worth the effort, and would mean giving up their competitive advantage. They could have done what Bran Stark debated doing and stayed south of the Wall and avoid the challenge of looking for wisdom and guidance from the Three-Eyed Raven. But as Adam Lashinsky writes in *Fortune*, Adobe "changed course dramatically, painfully converting its product offering to a subscription model and aggressively attacking new areas like analytics, marketing software, and e-commerce tools. The reinvention worked. Adobe's stock is up nearly six-fold in half a decade, and the company is worth a cool $127 billion."[17]—with Adobe's net worth listed at this writing (October 26, 2018) at $119.98 billion.

The challenges that will disrupt your business come from the outside. Leadership requires creating awareness and this requires adaptability. Digital McKinsey's Kara Sprague interviewed Adobe's Chief Financial Officer Mark Garrett and Vice President of Business Operations Dan Cohen about what triggered the organization to make the move from their traditional perpetual-licensing model to the subscription model. Inside the company was a belief that Adobe could reach a broader market. The perpetual-licensing model, as Garrett pointed out, "delivered product updates only every 18 or 24 months, but our customers' content-creation requirements were changing much faster than that, with advances in devices, browsers, mobile apps, and screen sizes."[18]

Adobe leadership was also motivated by the fact their perpetual-licensing model was slow to generate recurring revenue. In the downturns of 2008–2009, they had very little financial buffer. Companies with high recurring revenue were more resilient in terms of their growth rates and valuations. Dan Cohen explains the other reason they needed to adapt: "We had extremely high customer-satisfaction rates for our products, but when we drilled down into the numbers, we saw that people were saying things like, 'I'm happy with what I have, I don't see the need to ever buy another one again.'"[19] The new software companies that were successful were using the cloud model. Adobe decided to adapt.

Adobe did the research and also ran their old perpetual-licensing system side-by-side with the subscription model. They realized the new model would bring in new subscribers and encourage current customers to upgrade. They were confident that a move to the cloud would modernize the business and face the company in the right direction to keep growing. This was the moment equivalent to Bran Stark's decision to head north of the Wall. It was risky, but as Dan Cohen said, "Executives in every industry need to read the tea leaves and look at changes that are happening in their own or adjacent industries. Don't wait until someone is disrupting your business to start moving to the cloud or, for that matter, making any kind of necessary transformation. It will already be too late."[20] Cohen goes on to point out that once you see where the market is going, you have no choice. To put this into the language of Jojen Reed, Bran Stark, and the Three-Eyed Raven: you have to forget about walking; you have to learn to fly.

EXERCISE #1: RITA MCGRATH'S SEVEN QUESTIONS

Part of this challenge is to recognize what is going on before it's too late.

Bran Stark was pushed out of a tower before he understood what he was seeing. Then his home was taken out from under him before he could resist. Finally he had to escape Winterfell. If Bran had ignored what was going on at the edges of the kingdom, no one could blame him. He was young and should have been focused on the challenges of growing up as a normal son of the Starks. But this urge for a different present wouldn't have changed reality. In the Known World and in our world, winter won't wait. Threat is heading toward Westeros, just as threat is heading toward each of our organizations. Our enemies may be more civilized than the White Walkers, but competition gathers in the woods. Competition arms up and watches our territory.

Leaders must anticipate. What is happening Beyond the Wall? How must the change be confronted? Brandon Stark has the ability to greensee: to dream the past, present, and future. Recognizing the future will require our own version of greensight. The effort Adobe put into working to understand what was happening and what they could do to confront their challenges allowed them to adapt before it was too late. Adobe didn't have a seer living in the roots at the base of an ancient tree, but they were able to understand where the past and the present were intersecting with challenges and opportunities, and then predict the best moves to secure a successful future.

Rita McGrath references former Intel CEO, Andy Grove, from his book *Only the Paranoid Survive*, about the challenge of being able to adapt. You have to evaluate what is happening at the edges of your business. Grove uses a snow metaphor where spring represents change: "When spring comes, snow melts first at the periphery, because that's where it's most exposed."[21] The Adobe team did research and were able to identify where the snow was melting. Their perpetual-licensing system wasn't providing enough financial buffer and wasn't motivating customers to upgrade. The organization was not in the middle of an avalanche, but the snowmelt was significant at the perimeter.

McGrath asks seven questions with seven examples aimed at helping business leaders keep an eye on the snow at the perimeters. Ask yourself these questions, and write down where you and your organization have responded, and where you need to respond in order to see clearly and prepare your leadership to take the organization where it can adapt and fly.

1) Do I have mechanisms to come in direct contact with the "edges"?

Facebook (FB) was caught off guard in the 2016 U.S. presidential election. They were either unaware or disinterested in the costs to their organization's credibility and business model if dishonest customers weaponized the FB platform. This is what happened. Bad actors falsified accounts to spread malicious information to achieve political and criminal ends. Facebook leadership made an assumption their customers were collegial and well-intentioned. Facebook didn't work to get an understanding of how customers would try to leverage their platform for nonbenign ends. Facebook didn't understand the customers at the edges working with malicious intent.

Bran Stark allows himself to be carried in a basket, on a man's back, and dragged through the snow on a litter, in his effort to reach the mentor that will help him see what the nonbenign forces will do to achieve their goals. He puts himself at risk to understand the edges.

2) Am I regularly gaining exposure to diverse perspectives?

The start-up LinkNYC attempted to repurpose New York City phone booths as public spaces for a variety of productive Internet uses, supporting the project with advertising dollars. The concept was to offer a useful service to people traveling around the city who needed to scout out local businesses and recharge their devices. This is a forward thinking idea, but its developers didn't take into account how it could be misused. The high-speed wireless in public locations was accessed for porn. In addition to misusing the access to wireless, people unfortunately without places to live began to set up around the kiosks. Homelessness in New York City is an obvious issue. Diverse perspectives could have identified how LinkNYC could be misused. The unpredicted ways LinkNYC was misused greatly impacted the effectiveness of the business opportunity.

Bran Stark was born a prince in the royal house of Winterfell. After his escape from Winterfell, he could have chosen to travel to one of the Houses that had sworn their banners to House Stark. He was on the verge of making this choice when Jojen and Meera argued for him to cross Beyond the Wall and search for the Three-Eyed Raven. He listens to the perspective of the Reed siblings and chooses the dangerous path: he travels into harm's way to meet a mentor who might offer him the necessary skills to confront an enemy he barely understands. Bran accepts the recommendations of the Reed siblings. Jojen and Meera's people are disparagingly called mudmen, frog-eaters, and bog devils. Bran trusts diverse perspectives, confronts risks, and also avoided the dire fate that confronted Rickon and Osha, who both went south under the belief it was the safe choice.

3) Am I trusting and empowering small, agile teams?

Trusting and empowering small, agile teams to support adaptability requires senior leaders to use their emotional and social intelligence. In *Fast Company*, Rachel Gillett writes that small teams are "believed to help diminish various innovation killers like groupthink and social loafing."[22] Dr. Adrian Furnham, writing in *Psychology Today*, emphasizes rigor and clarity on the meeting agenda in advance. "Take charge of the agenda and the outcomes."[23] Be specific about the topics of the agenda in advance, as well as the time; recognizing small teams only have agility if their processes are structured to be efficient. Amazon

CEO Jeff Bezos has a two-pizza rule. No team should be any bigger than can be fed on two pizzas.[24]

In George R. R. Martin's Known World, small teams bring necessary perspective to the leadership at the top of organizations. Think of Varys and Tyrion deciding to travel to Meereen, or the Brotherhood without Banners. This group of outlaws represents commitment to a mission despite the political winds. They were sent to arrest Ser Gregor "The Mountain" Clegane by Ned Stark when he served as Hand of the King. This small team has defied the political direction of Westeros and have stayed devoted to resist Lannister rule.

Bran's team comprises of four people, each with a distinct role: 1) Bran is the person with the recognized expert skill in being able to warg and greensee. The purpose of the team is to deliver Bran safely to the Three-Eyed Raven for the training that will prepare him to assume that leadership role. 2) Jojen is the person with the vision for delivering Bran to the Three-Eyed Raven. He also has a rudimentary level of skill in greenseeing and understands why it's important for Bran to train and take the new role. 3) Meera is the hunter who provides them with the resources to survive. 4) Hodor provides them with the strength, complementing their cognitive abilities. Osha and Rickon could have provided additional help, but Osha wouldn't commit to the journey. She took what appeared to be the safe path and both Osha and Rickon died at the hands of Ramsay Bolton.

The teammates that did commit to join Bran were 100 percent present for what they believed needed to be done in order to achieve a necessary goal. They could have decided this wasn't their battle but they didn't. As Meera says, "Some people will always need help. That doesn't mean they're not worth helping."[25] Bran's agile team had all the resources the team required.

4) Do I have a mechanism for fostering "little bets"?

McGrath references Adobe's Kickbox, a process designed to mobilize and accelerate employee innovation. Employees are provided with red boxes that contain guides on how to move forward with ideas they have to benefit the company. It shows them how to test their ideas and see if they have value. The box also contains prepaid credit cards with $1,000 limits. Employees are provided that seed money to pursue their individual ideas. The assumption is that no idea is exactly right when you start. It's about putting it out and testing it, getting feedback, iterating that idea. The goal, as Adobe VP of Creativity Mark Randall explains, is to fail fast.[26]

McGrath points out that you don't want to have every new concept go through the same long corporate-approved process; rather, make limited resources available and let people test ideas. You want a mechanism in place that helps people evaluate viable options.

Bran wargs into his direwolf, Summer, building skill at transferring into another living creature. The challenge is to disengage without becoming locked into the excitements and rewards of the visceral escape.

This prepares Bran to respond in a crisis and warg into Hodor. The act of warging also prepares Bran to engage in viewing the past, as he does with the Three-Eyed Raven. The act of becoming the next seer— a conduit to the historical information of Westeros—is demanding. It can't be achieved in one unprepared leap but, like the Adobe Kickbox concept, requires iterative learning, and, hopefully, small failure to develop new capabilities. After Bran's first experiences traveling to the past, the Three-Eyed Raven warns him: "It is beautiful beneath the sea, but if you stay too long, you'll drown."[27]

Bran takes small steps and prepares himself for the leap into a transformational existence and a new set of leadership responsibilities.

5) Do I regularly get out of the building to see what is going on?

In our professional lives, it is very easy to be too inwardly focused, responding to e-mail and meetings, as opposed to figuring out what is going on in the marketplace. Leaders benefit from turning their point-of-view away from their minute-by-minute obligations. Entrepreneurs need to get out and do what serial entrepreneur, Steve Blank, calls *Customer Discovery*. This isn't to be confused with sales. This is figuring out if the solution you are offering with your entrepreneurial business idea is relevant to your customers.

Blank suggests you start talking to people without worrying about having the perfect conversation with the top person in the organization. Find people that might benefit from your solution. After talking to them, ask them who else you should talk to. Ask them for a quick referral to other contacts. Ask them what questions you should have asked that maybe didn't occur to you. Collect the data points and discover if your idea is viable to potential customers.

In *Game of Thrones*, Cersei operates with little understanding of what is relevant outside of the Red Keep, much less what is relevant outside the capital. Her forced humiliation by the High Sparrow's requirement that she walk naked through the streets of King's Landing doesn't help improve her nonexistent interest in the citizenry.

Bran has *stepped out of the building* both by leaving the semisafe protection of being south of the Wall but, more important, by recognizing and accepting the responsibility to step outside of the confines of his previous individual experience as "Bran." He will become the Three-Eyed Raven. Leadership almost always requires that certain elements of our personality be put to the side, or accessed less, due to what is needed to fulfill our goals. Leaders must decide where to focus their effort. Bran realizes he must make the choice to let go of a part of himself and embrace the new role.

For Bran, this focus requires him to step out of the building of himself. Meera loses her temper with him before she leaves him at Winterfell. She angrily tells him that "Bran" died in that cave Beyond the Wall with Hodor, Summer, and Leaf. The "Bran" that sits in front of her, Meera argues, is someone different.

Bran's leadership commitment has required him to leave much of his old self behind to be able to fulfill the expectation that he become the source of wisdom—the visionary Three-Eyed Raven 2.0. The young man Bran is still a part of him, but he has become a centralized repository for a massive amount of historical data. Hopefully that data can be interpreted into useful decisions. His fate was to either accept or deny the opportunity to take on this new role.

The actor that plays Brandon Stark, Isaac Hempstead Wright, was asked if Meera was right to say Bran died in the cave. "Sadly, I think in many ways she was right. It's just this whole idea that Bran has become a much smaller part of the character's brain."[28]

McGrath's recommendation could be compared to taking a moment to "Be Bran" and step away from all that consumes us and keeps our nose pointed at a screen. Be an adventurer willing to receive learning from the world outside the walls of your office. It may be overwhelming, as it is for Bran, but it takes courage to try to see, while the rest of your community is too busy fighting to look up and understand. Allow yourself to remember that you can choose to leave the building to gain insights about your organization, the competition, and your leadership opportunities.

6) Are incentives aligned with gaining uncomfortable news?

Upton Sinclair was a Pulitzer Prize–winning novelist who wrote a hundred books, including ones that had a transforming impact on industry standards in businesses such as food production, the coal, oil, automotive industries, and journalism. *Time* magazine wrote that Sinclair was "a man who had every gift except humor and silence."[29] His novels were an effort to bring uncomfortable news to public awareness. He recognized the challenge people faced in hearing negative news about their business. He once said, "It is difficult to get a man to understand something, when his salary depends upon his not understanding it!"[30] McGrath reminds us that we need to construct a method to make sure we receive uncomfortable news, even if it means negative personal consequences. The more senior you are, the more you must implement a conscious plan to get this feedback. As a professor and colleague of mine says: "The higher you move up in the organization, the better looking you get and the funnier your jokes get."[31]

No one in King's Landing wants to tell King Robert that he will be allowed to win the melee as he does not take getting bad news very well. Conversely, Bran Stark accepts the self-sacrifice to put himself in harm's way to understand the bad news that faces Westeros.

7) Am I making sure I'm not in denial?

McGrath writes, "I see a lot of denial in organizations whose main business models are shifting underneath them, and yet their executives simply don't want to be exposed to this information."[32] The examples of RIM and Adobe provide two contrasting stories of senior leadership approaches to transforming, competitive change.

The entertainment industry is fundamentally volatile in terms of the unpredictable success of content, due to the enormous number of variables that interconnect in the development and creation of fictional and nonfictional visual narratives: series and limited series and the variety of shows now available, including cinematic film releases. Yet, despite this volatility, there are strategic choices being made on what projects to support.

Successful organizations have benefitted from *not* denying the reality of their industry. Television experienced a competitive opportunity when cable channels saw they could reach a niche of customers with edgier, complex storylines. HBO put in the order for *The Sopranos* in 1997 and the show premiered in 1999. The success of the dramatic series catalyzed the creation of a variety of dramas on different channels. Based on the recognition that the cable business model could benefit from rethinking previous constraints on story structure and content, television narratives were able to carve into the story territory previously controlled by feature films.

Amanda Lotz, Professor of Communication Studies at the University of Michigan, describes how Netflix, when it launched in the late nineties by distributing DVDs by mail, disrupted the film rental industry.

Broadcast networks and cable channels made their money, as Lotz explains, "by selling audiences to advertisers." *The Sopranos* and other shows that followed on HBO and similar cable channels transformed the way television entertainment was perceived. "Because many of these channels earned revenue from both subscribers and advertisers, they could be successful even if these programs didn't reach a mass audience."[33]

The production of edgy dramatic and comedic programming grew in the new century. "Then, during the early 2000s, advances in compression technology—coupled with more homes gaining access to high-speed internet services—allowed large video files to be easily streamed over the internet."[34] Netflix CEO Reed Hastings had said for years that Netflix recognized that streaming was the future. Netflix made the move away from mailing DVDs to streaming their product in 2007. Creating product to appeal to this new market and leverage a competitive advantage over network television became the new normal, and HBO had been at it a long time, adapting and leading. Their senior leaders might have chosen to keep making shows set in urban locations, such as *The Wire*, or on simple, one-location sets, such as *Deadwood*, but they didn't deny the competition. They recognized the volatility in the industry. It was a risky time, but a time of opportunity. HBO went all in for a new show and authorized not just a huge, multi-location show that demanded costumes, sets, and special effects but backed up their decision when the two showrunners of the epic fantasy, after some negative feedback, asked to reshoot the pilot episode. This was a critical moment of confronting the danger of denial. The pilot to be reshot was titled "Winter Is Coming." The series on HBO: *Game of Thrones*.

Making films and shows is a daunting, collaborative process. Imagine the prospective showrunners—Dan Weiss and David Benioff—of *Game of Thrones* facing the variety of challenges involved in creating a successful show. If they fell into McGrath's trap of denial, the show would have failed. It is difficult to overcome a pilot that doesn't work. The network would likely not support a show with a pilot that left the audience scratching their heads instead of intrigued, curious, and ready for more episodes.

Before being in the position to write and film the pilot, Weiss and Benioff had a meeting with George R. R. Martin, author of the series of epic fantasy narratives A Song of Ice and Fire. They needed his support to move forward with the adaptation and creation of the show. Martin tested their understanding of his storyline by asking who they believed was Jon Snow's mother. After succeeding at what Benioff called "the Wonka test," Benioff and Weiss had to lead the creation of the pilot, funded by HBO. This would present an unpredicted, demoralizing challenge that had to be confronted with the skill of adaptability. They had to face reality and not deny the feedback of trusted colleagues.

After the show was a success, Weiss recounted when the pilot was first screened to trusted friends for critical advice, including the screen-writer Craig Mazin. Remembering the experience on the podcast *Script-notes*, Weiss said: "Watching them watch that original pilot was one of the most painful experiences of my life. As soon as it finished, Craig [Mazin] said, 'You guys have a massive problem.'"[35]

Weiss and Benioff decided to go back to HBO and request more money and a reshoot. They were able to fight past the temptation to deny the feedback. They could have chosen to disregard the critical acuity of the friends that provided the feedback. They chose instead to fix their mistakes. It was a moment to win and not die. According to Benioff, "None of [our friends] realized that Jaime and Cersei were brother and sister, which is a major, major plot point that we had somehow failed to establish."[36]

"'I was taking notes,' Benioff says, 'and I had this yellow legal pad, and I just remembered writing in all caps, 'MASSIVE PROBLEM,' and it's all I could think about the rest of the night.'" The partners brought in a new director, adjusted the script, changed one casting decision, and it worked. After the reshoot premiered, Mazin recounts: "I very specifically remember walking out and I said to [Weiss and Benioff], 'That is the biggest rescue in Hollywood history.' Because it wasn't just that they had saved something bad and turned it really good. You had saved a complete piece of sh*t and turned it into something brilliant. That never happens!"[37]

Bran Stark could have decided to deny the threat of the Night King.

He could have denied the encouragements of Jojen and Meera. He tried to deny the dream visits of the Three-Eyed Raven, but when it came time to accept responsibility or walk away from it, when it was time to adapt and work for success, Bran answered Rita McGrath's seventh question by heading north Beyond the Wall to confirm what he needed to learn from the Three-Eyed Raven.

Weiss and Benioff faced the same challenge. They would need to reshoot the pilot. The message arrived to them, not in a dream of a three-eyed raven, but in a critical note from an ally: "You have a massive problem."

EXERCISE #2: LEAD YOUR ADAPTABILITY

Organizational theorist Richard Boyatzis writes: "Adaptability is very often practiced by thinking of what other things can be done in various situations."[38] This doesn't mean simply practicing a different choice, but developing the awareness to step back when in the middle of doing something. Is it working? Are you doing the right thing in the right way? Is it possible that you are stuck in advocating the wrong approach and should adapt? The risk of continuing to push is that you inadvertently build resistance. Boyatzis recommends that when you see resistance—whether you are in a business meeting or a discussion with a colleague, friend, or family member—that you attempt to lead yourself. Ask the following:

1) Is there another way to approach this conversation?

2) Am I clear on the other person's position, including what they might need?

3) Rather than continuing to state my position, can I offer questions or communicate with the intent of finding areas where we can agree?

The goal is to practice self-management and not trap yourself in trying to confirm the correctness of your original position.

The clinical psychologist and founder of *compassion focused therapy* (CFT), Paul Gilbert, and his cowriter Choden (Sean McGovern), a meditation teacher and honorary fellow at the University of Aberdeen, wrote *Mindful Compassion*, a book on the science of compassion and our emotions. "We all tend to have strong ideas about what we want and what we do not want, but reality seldom accords with our preferences."[39] Think of adaptability as an opportunity to redirect your effort from what you believe you want toward solutions. Reality won't often provide what we want, but we can choose to adapt.

Adaptability could be the difference between success on a project or failure. In terms of interacting with colleagues who hold a different perspective from you, one approach is to practice looking at their effort not as a form of resistance to your goals but as an effort to find the best solution. You can choose to be grateful for their effort. This approach isn't always applicable, but when your evaluation of the situation suggests it is appropriate, be grateful. The colleague that is arguing with you, or not accepting your analysis of a solution, could be the reason you find the right answer to a difficult challenge.

In his book, *Just One Thing*, Rick Hanson offers simple practices aimed to help the brain adapt. The goal is to train the brain to get past the reptilian, instinctive reactions that were an important part of our evolution. For example, if we build our brain's awareness of gratitude, the training can help the brain be more proactive and less reactive. Hanson writes: "We experience gratitude when we are freely given something good."[40] These exercises leverage *experience-dependent neuroplasticity* to guide our brains to not act in limiting ways. His exercises offer us the chance to adapt, not just react.

Hanson recommends that we prepare ourselves to feel grateful by thinking of people in our past that have offered us reasons to be grateful. We can also look around at the things in our life that cause a sense of gratefulness in us. These things can involve nature, sports, family, food, entertainment—or anything that triggers a positive reaction in yourself. They can also involve people that have helped us professionally. The boss that caused you to persevere through a challenge . . . or the colleague that defended your abilities and helped you secure an opportunity to flourish. The idea, in Hanson's words, is to *prime the pump.* "Gratitude does not mean ignoring difficulties, losses, or injustice. It just means *also* paying attention to the offerings that have come your way. Especially the little ones of everyday life."[41] Putting ourselves in a place to experience gratitude that has happened in our past, and is currently available to be appreciated in our life, can also help us be prepared to see how a situation that appears contentious could be a way forward to a new solution.

BUSINESS LEADERSHIP INSIGHTS
FOR THE KNOWN WORLD

After accepting the role of the Three-Eyed Raven, Bran returns to Westeros, joined by his remaining siblings—Sansa and Arya. The Stark family is part of a team that faces a competitor that can overwhelm their resources and defeat them. This will not be like the Blackberry error in leadership: a small decline in sales that RIM recognized before the flattening out that led to too-late efforts to redesign their offer to customers, followed in turn by recognition their game was over and it was time to move into other products and services. Failure in Westeros will mean the annihilation of all the people and their organizations. There will be no human survivors.

Adobe changed course dramatically and converted to a new model of business. They adapted. They understood they needed as much buffer as they could to have the resources to compete, but as much as they needed resources, they also required the right plan and strategy. They recognized that risk was part of the equation. As their CFO Mark Garrett said after they had won: "A lot of people didn't buy into the idea at the beginning. . . . And we knew it was going to be a long, hard road."[42] Dan Cohen, the VP of Business Operations and Strategy, said, "One aspect of the strategy was that we were being more aggressive in shifting our Creative Suite (CS) business to the Creative Cloud. Another aspect was that we were doubling down on our cloud-based digital-marketing business."[43] What will Team Stark and Team Targaryen double down on?

If Bran's organization fails, the nightmares once told by septons at bedtime to scare children will become reality. The competitive threat of the White Walkers is the reason Bran has become a vehicle of massive data. The data in Bran's mind must be leveraged to provide necessary knowledge for his team to adapt, compete, and win.

His team will include his cousin. Jon (or Aegon) understands the competitive terrain is shifting. He has been brought back from death. He also understands that the sorcery of the Red Woman is only one weapon, and a dangerous one . . . "Sorcery was a sword without a hilt. There is no safe way to grasp it."[44] Jon as King in the North, Daenerys as the Mother of Dragons, and their team of direct reports will need to be resourceful and adapt. The team will include those who can survive and keep contributing, including Brienne, Sam, Gilly, Ser Davos,

Jaime Lannister, Theon, Melisandre, Jorah, Varys, Tyrion, and possibly Cersei and Euron. They can't approach the challenge of the White Walkers with a predictable plan and strategy or with moderate commitment. Their team can't *walk*. They must find a method to fly, not just on dragons but as an organization with inventive solutions and adaptable leadership.

Goleman tells us that adaptability is "an asset in leadership" and "at the heart of innovation." Both of these skills will be required.

Here are other takeaways for Team Targaryen/Stark drawn from Goleman's primer *Adaptability*:

1) Skill in adaptability means shifting to the context and not being stuck in your one way of resolving a challenge. Use positive input—*contemplative aerobics*—to be mentally ready to adapt (from Richard J. Davidson's chapter "Training Your Brain to Be Flexible").

2) See change as positive (from George Kohlrieser's "A Mindset of Adaptability").

3) Collective wisdom is the advantage of working on a team. The leader doesn't need to predict the solution (from Vanessa Druskat's "Teams and Adaptability").

4) Adaptability involves the practice of leading yourself to think of the other ways a solution can be achieved (from Richard Boyatzis's "Adaptability and Leadership").

5) Strength in adaptability offers a prediction of success (from Daniel Goleman "Adaptability: An Introduction").

THE LEADER'S JOURNEY: THE ULTIMATE BOON

The Ultimate Boon is the achievement of the quest. The prior stage—
Apotheosis—found Tyrion Lannister in Meereen, the Hand of the Queen symbol representing his new leadership role. The Mother of Dragons has turned to him as her advisor. This road will continue to be difficult for Tyrion. He did not find the balance that Campbell writes about when Campbell describes how the mighty Bodhisattva achieves a perfect peace and boundless love. The Bodhisattva can see "the

delicate wings of an insect, broken in the passage of time"[45] and can appreciate both the perfection of that moment and the disintegration represented.

This may be your leadership ideal. I identify with the desire to find that serenity, and I also identify with Tyrion's human struggle to win and not die. Tyrion has been "self-torturing, deluded, tangled in the net of his own tenuous delirium"[46] and also has the capability to achieve that serenity. We all do. It may help each of us to remember Campbell's guidance about our own capacity to ignite our inner abilities to see the truth of perfection and disintegration and how they coexist in our world. To be okay with our mortality and with the struggle of existence and to see the beauty in it. Whether your god is the Bodhisattva or another of the primary candidates in either our world or the Known World, Campbell writes: "The sufferer within us is that divine being. We and that protecting father are one." As Campbell writes with confidence: "This is the redeeming insight."[47]

Tyrion experienced Campbell's apotheosis when he crawled from the box with air holes in Pentos, and he may achieve a greater spiritual apotheosis, but reporting to the Mother of Dragons on Dragonstone is a time to lead and fight. Fighting and leadership will require adaptability.

Bran closed in on the Ultimate Boon, but he needed to learn from the father figure seated on a root-throne under the weirwood. The Three-Eyed Raven spoke to him in a dream: "Look for me beneath the tree . . . North!"[48] After the culmination of the impending war between Lightness and Darkness, Bran may achieve a subsequent boon. He may find a capacity to transform back to the young man who fate called to the north. He may find an ability to be both the vehicle of comprehensive knowledge—seeing past, present, and future—and not have to abandon his humanity. Or, Bran may find himself walking further down the path he has been following.

Campbell writes: "Those who know, not only that the Everlasting lives in them, but that what they, and all things, really are *is* the Everlasting, dwell in the groves of the wish-fulfilling trees, drink the brew of immortality, and listen everywhere to the unheard music of eternal concord. These are the immortals."[49] Will Bran move closer toward immortality or return to a youthful innocence?

Campbell's eleventh stage involves the hero being able to step into the role that waits. There is a transcendent moment where an elixir or something akin to the Holy Grail is achieved in the myth. A powerful gain happens to the elect on their journey. Once the elect have reached a certain moment on their path, the powerful thing is achieved. "Such ease distinguishes numerous fairy tales and all legends of the deeds of incarnate gods. Where the usual hero would face a test, the elect encounters no delaying obstacle and makes no mistake."[50] Bran has followed the Three-Eyed Raven in journeys back through time. He has made small errors, and he *does* make a big mistake when he wargs through the heart tree and joins the Night King's army, not knowing the Night King can see him. He is marked and the sacred, protected place in the cave is now a target. But Bran survives because his colleagues— Leaf, Summer, Hodor—sacrifice themselves to protect him. With no further delay, Bran becomes the Three-Eyed Raven.

The Ultimate Boon was not yet Bran's because he had to move through Atonement with the Father and Apotheosis. Often the Ultimate Boon is not handed easily: "The gods may be oversevere, overcautious, in which case the hero must trick them of their treasure."[51] This is what the Polynesian god Maui must do when he confronts the guardian of fire, Mahuka.

Bran doesn't connive his way into stealing the boon from the gods; rather the Three-Eyed Raven reaches out to Bran and calls him to the service of a good cause: protect humanity. Bran is still a young man and he stumbles, takes a weirwood trip without his mentor and calls down the wrath of the enemy, but he course-corrects and escapes the cave, his ally, Hodor, sacrificing his life to the wights, guiding his final efforts by repeating "Hold the door! Hold the door!"[52]

There is an element of immortality to this boon handed to Bran Stark. The Three-Eyed Raven had encouraged Bran that he must learn *everything*. Before succumbing to the attack of the White Walkers and wights, the Three-Eyed Raven had also told Bran that he was not yet ready but he must move forward. "The time has come. Leave me."[53]

Campbell writes, "To this very day, the possibility of physical immortality charms the heart of man."[54] As A Song of Ice and Fire shows us: immortality comes with a price. The heroes and heroines in *Game of Thrones* are the people driven to achieve a purpose that helps others. They are not above self-interest. They care about their own achievements. Yet, those achievements have the goal of helping individuals and communities. The heroes and heroines that earn our greatest concern and respect play the game of thrones, by fighting for a cause bigger than themselves.

Bran Stark achieves the ultimate boon by becoming the Three-Eyed Raven. Campbell writes, "The boon bestowed on the worshiper is always scaled to his stature. [. . .] The agony of breaking through personal limitations is the agony of spiritual growth."[55] Bran Stark is given a choice and commits to find the Ultimate Boon that his family and community need from him. He has accepted a difficult, almost terrible, sacrifice of himself in order to learn *everything*. The price he has paid reminds us that we are fortunate to live our mortal lives without being asked to abandon every experience for an all-seeing wisdom. The Everlasting lives in him. He has broken through physical limitations. He went on a dangerous journey Beyond the Wall to meet a mentor and gain a necessary power to bring back to help his community. The Known World must thank him. He could have chosen to continue to feel sorry for himself. Instead, he accepts that his delicate wings were broken. He finds new, powerful wings that fly him to the past and will help him confront the challenge swarming through the melted Wall.

GOING FORWARD

Adaptability impacts effective leadership. "Whatever your professional role, it can help you respond to an ever-changing world and take advantage of new opportunities as they arise."[56]

Remember to use the Seven Questions from Rita McGrath to understand if change is happening at the perimeters and what it can mean for your leadership challenges. Flexibility in handling change is what adaptability is all about. It is important to seek out clarity about what is changing in order to apply an adaptable response to the challenge. The purpose of practicing adaptability as a leadership competency, as Daniel Goleman points out, is to not get stunned into inaction by resistance to change.

This capability to confront the challenges means confronting fear of change. It means being comfortable with leadership uncertainty. RIM didn't respond in this way, Adobe did. Dan Cohen at Adobe said the "market trends that we saw toward recurring-revenue models and cloud computing, made us confident."[57] They saw a future where Adobe was modernized and set up for future growth. This wouldn't have happened without a willingness to confront the fear and take risk.

Littlefinger was right about one lesson for all of us to remember: *Chaos is not a pit, chaos is a ladder.* Lead yourself and your team through chaos together. It might be hard to walk, but you can learn to fly.

DON'T GET ASSASSINATED!

HOW PERSUASION DRIVES STRATEGY

Lord Commander Jon Snow faces a classic leadership dilemma: *he must make a decision that has no easy solution.* Should he risk alienating the men of the Night's Watch by letting the wildlings through the Wall or should he close the gate to wildlings, let the blue-eyed Others slaughter the Free Folk, and strengthen their army of undead wights? To understand the best choice for Jon Snow, we need to recognize the relationship between strategy and persuasion.

LORD COMMANDER SNOW

Robert E. Quinn at Harvard Business School, and his son Ryan W. Quinn, write in *Lift*: "Many scholars agree that leadership does not depend on position. They define leadership as a process of social influence that involves determining collective goals, motivating goal pursuit, and developing or maintaining the group and culture."[1] The Quinns go on to explain that leadership is often intentional and often not intentional. They also make a point that leadership can occur "when people *choose to follow* someone who *deviates* from at least one accepted cultural norm or social convention."[2] Jon Snow makes a decision that goes against the norms of Castle Black culture. He has followers and he has assassins.

In order to determine the collective goals, motivate goal pursuit, and develop and maintain the group and culture, leadership requires making strategic choices and aligning individuals around a common purpose. This alignment of individuals to pursue the strategy depends on the effective art of persuasion. Leadership requires persuasion to drive strategy. This has never been more necessary than when Jon Snow decides he must create a partnership with the wildlings and bring them to the safe side of the Wall as allies in the fight against the Night King.

"WHAT ARE THE WILDLINGS, IF NOT MEN?"

Jon Snow's values are: *Truth*, *Community*, *Empathy*, and *Courage*. Jon exemplifies *courage* on a daily level, both in his abilities as a warrior and his willingness to confront false assumptions about the wildlings. His commitment to *empathy* is noticeable in his ability to see past Westerosi biases about the wildlings, as well as Night's Watch biases about people that don't fit the warrior norms, such as Samwell Tarly. Jon's commitment to his *community* is the result of always being an outsider in House Stark. He understands the importance of a community that embraces diversity and is inclusive. Jon has the *courage* and *empathy* to see his community from a wider perspective. It doesn't just include his family, or his friends, or even the members of the Night's Watch. Jon puts himself in harm's way to support the benefit of the Seven Kingdoms. His *community* is the entire continent of humanity from north of the Fist of the First Men to the hot sand dunes of Dorne. He is driven by *truth*. He has had to live with not knowing who his parents were . . . which has cost him, placing him in the category of "bastard" in Westeros.

Jon pursues his leadership challenges as Lord Commander as he once worked to live up to the expectations of being a Stark. His own adopted mother, Catelyn, avoided ever communicating with him or showing him motherly affection. He was accepted but as a permanent outsider. Jon has been driven by an outsider's desire to be accepted.

Jon Snow understands that truth isn't just a talking point; the truth has impact. The truth matters. The truth can't be talked around and adjusted to suit a particular leadership agenda. Jon believes he suffered because the truth of his parentage was hidden from him, and that his interests were disregarded by the man and woman who created him. Jon takes a leadership responsibility to be truthful and accountable; his belief his own parents abandoned by leaving him parentless and without a family name is what drives him.

Jon has to make a choice regarding the White Walkers. If he pretends the White Walkers don't exist, that is a choice. Lord Commander Snow faces tension in his leadership role. His strategic insight catalyzes a plan to confront the White Walkers. His plan triggers resistance from his followers. Jon decides to use his authority as the new Lord Commander to invite *all* the self-professed Free Folk—known on the warm side of the Wall as wildlings—to cross into Westeros. His plan is to let the wildlings make their homes in the Seven Kingdoms. His strategy is to have the wildlings: 1) help guard the Wall and 2) not get killed and turned into weaponized zombies.

In exchange, the wildlings will promise to abandon their nomadic warrior habits of rape, reave, and murder. The wildlings will give up any items they own that can be sold for food. They will also allow their children to be placed into Westerosi homes as assurance the wildlings won't go rogue and start slaughtering the Westerosi. The Westerosi have a term: *wards*. This term is used when children from one family are placed with another family in a sort of hostage situation, as a guarantee to control the parents of the ward. Some of the Free Folk will even join the Night's Watch and take the oath to protect civilization from the blue-eyed threat to humanity that builds an army Beyond the Wall.

Jon Snow's purpose is to be an effective leader: this means not just following rules or tradition; this means leading the Night's Watch to fulfill their task: protect humanity.

Lord Commander Snow and Tormund Giantsbane are both aware of time constraints. Both men understand the White Walkers are attempting to surround the wildlings north of the Wall. Jon knows this wight army and the White Walkers won't be satisfied to stay in the cold lands north of the Wall. Winter is coming.

Jon and Tormund negotiate the new partnership. Jon agrees to allow the Free Folk to cross the Wall. Tormund agrees to accept all of Jon's demands. The most difficult part for Tormund is the commitment to submit wildling children to become wards of Westerosi families. Tormund knows it will be hard for the Free Folk to hand their children over to the people they call *The Kneelers*. Tormund has no choice. He accepts and agrees to convince the Free Folk to Jon's nego-tiation terms.

Jon knows that selling the wildlings' belongings for food to help both wildlings and Westerosi survive the winter is of limited value, but this is the only sellable resource Jon can identify. Jon needs a plan to de-liver on his strategy. If strategy is about doing the *right things*, as Pro-fessor Willie Pietersen writes in *Strategic Learning*, planning is about doing *things right*. Jon needs a "how we will get this done" to support his "what needs to get done." Jon knows he needs to get the Free Folk to relative safety and have them help defend the Wall. This requires a plan to house and feed them. If Jon Snow can lead the execution of his strategy, humanity north and south of the Wall might stand a slim chance of surviving the strategy of the Night King.

The Others had been gone so long, they were considered a myth to the Night's Watch. This changed when the White Walkers and wights assaulted and killed a large percentage of Lord Commander Mormont's soldiers at the Fist of the First Men during the catastrophic Great Rang-ing Beyond the Wall. The Old Bear led his men Beyond the Wall to gain knowledge about what was causing movement in the wildlings clans. The Rangers considered the main threat to Westeros to be the wildlings, but the intel gained from their journey into enemy terrain was a game changer: White Walkers and wights.

The wildlings were not the cause for the ancient creation of the Wall. The Wall was built eight thousand years earlier as a way to pro-tect humanity against the White Walkers. The wildlings are the tribes that lived north of the Wall when the barrier of the three-hundred-mile-long, roughly seven-hundred-foot-high perimeter of ice was cre-ated. Tribes such as the Thenns, the Frozen Shore tribes, the wildlings that dressed in bones from the Frostfangs, and the King Beyond the Wall, Mance Rayder's, own chosen tribe from the Haunted Forest, were isolated on the cold side of the Wall, blocked from developing with Westeros, engaging only in violent interactions. The wildlings, like the Starks and northern families with the blood of the First Men in their veins, still worshiped the Old Gods. The wildlings have different cultural norms, but the two peoples are not that different.

Despite the wildlings isolation Beyond the Wall; despite their com-mitment to a nomadic life and disinterest in building cities, farming, industry, and trade; despite their rejection of a hierarchical society of servants and masters, the wildlings are driven by values. They are a democratic meritocracy of warriors, and are unwilling to sign away the individual's right of free choice. These wildling cultural values have been in conflict with the values of the Westerosi for generations. Still, both wildlings and Westerosi are human. They need each other if they are to confront the two-pronged assault of the global climate change of winter and the blue-eyed killers. Lord Commander Snow must persuade his direct reports to follow his strategy and his plan to support that strategy. If he fails at his leadership task, the fate of the wildlings and the Westerosi will be grievous.

Legend says the Children of the Forest called themselves *"those who sing the song of earth"*[3] and spoke the True Tongue. The Children had welcomed the First Men to Westeros, after the immigrants crossed from Essos on the ancient land bridge now known as the Broken Arm of Dorne. The Children's generosity was based on a belief there was land enough for all. But when the First Men started to cut down the trees where the Children made their home in "the vast primeval forest that once stretched from Cape Wrath to Cape Kraken, north of the Iron Islands,"[4] the two different cultures clashed. They attempted to coexist in the stormlands of what later became known as Westeros. This effort failed.

The Children were driven north of the demarcation where the Wall would be built. They were few in number but lived for many thousands of years. The two groups shared the Old Gods but struggled over resources. Tensions continued: the First Men wanted to build forts, keeps, walls, and vehicles with the weirwood and other trees that were the temple and home of the Children. The First Men had superior iron weapons and slaughtered the ageless Children. The twelve-thousand-year-old Leaf tells Bran: "The direwolves will outlast us all, but their time will come as well. In the world that men have made, there is no room for them, or us."[5]

Attacked by the First Men in the days before the Seven Kingdoms, the Children needed a weapon and created the first Other—the first White Walker—by piercing a dragonglass blade into a captured Ranger's heart. The Night King was not a strategic success for the Children of the Forest.

During the Age of Heroes, the Others turned on the Children, who chose to ally with their former oppressors, the First Men, at the Battle for the Dawn. It is said the Wall was created by the early Starks, including Brandon the Builder, with the help of the magic of the Children of the Forest. The Children stayed North of the Wall, sharing territory with the wildlings and the Giants, who called the Children *woh dak hag gram*, which translates as *little squirrel people*. The strategy of the Wall was to stop a dire enemy, to isolate the White Walkers from humanity that lived south of the demarcation line of the mammoth barrier of ice.

On Lord Commander Mormont's Great Ranging, the Night's Watch army discovers the existence of the White Walkers. In addition, Jon and Sam realize the Others have an arrangement with Craster, allowing him sanctuary in exchange for his inbred baby sons. The wildlings are not just a nomadic enemy that wants to kill Rangers; they are a resource for the White Walkers. Alive and north of the Wall, the wildlings are a much greater threat to Westeros because they become a *how* to the White Walkers *what* . . . a plan to carry out the Night King's hegemonic strategy, which appears to be to annihilate humanity.

The fact that the reanimated weapon-wielding undead wildling wights are a huge risk to the Rangers doesn't register with the irate Night's Watch. These direct reports haven't bought into Jon's vision and they present a threat to Jon's leadership. "Marsh flushed a deeper shade of red. 'The lord commander must pardon my bluntness, but I have no softer way to say this. What you propose is nothing less than treason.'"[6]

Jon points out that their mutual purpose should be the defense of humanity. "*I am the shield that guards the realms of men.* Those are the words. So tell me, my lord—what are the wildlings, if not men?"[7]

Jon Snow doesn't understand—or won't accept—that he is in a situation where the successful execution of his strategy and plan requires persuasion. He has completed his negotiations with Tormund and he delivers his orders to his direct reports but he misses out on the opportunity to persuade them. His strategy is necessary; his plan to support the strategy is the best one available. He fails at persuasion.

Persuasion takes time and Jon doesn't believe he has time. He resorts to commands. He expects his followers to see the truth of the situation. He expects truth to win, but this is a judgment decision. Jon must persuade them of his judgment.

Persuasion is the method for Jon to help his followers choose to follow him. Jon needs to find a way to carve out time and slow down the process that escalates the rage of his direct reports. Unfortunately, Commander Snow doesn't give them the communication and time to resolve their doubt and choose to follow him. Jon delivers his strategy without the benefit of his practicing the art of persuasion. This is a critical mistake in any leadership environment. It is worse at Castle Black. Jon leads in an environment that is not generous to leaders that make mistakes. Lord Commander Snow's angry team of Night's Watch choose the exact opposite of following him. They choose to assassinate him.

WINNING PROPOSITION

Strategy is the act of putting organizational purpose into action. Jon Snow's purpose is to be a successful leader, which requires him to protect humanity; that means confronting the grievous threat of the Night King's army of White Walkers and wights. Strategy is about making competitive decisions in a volatile environment in order to raise the chances the organization's purpose will succeed.

Columbia Business School professor Bill Duggan explains, in the opening of his book *Napoleon's Glance*, how the term *strategy* entered the English language. *Strategia* was the post for an army general in ancient Greece. Over time, the term "came to mean the craft of generalship instead of just the job. *Strategia* spread to French as *stratégie*, and then to English as 'strategy' in 1810."[8]

Strategy is a selection of choices that will drive the successful achievement of organizational purpose by creating the ability to win. Strategy guru Michael Porter said, "Competitive strategy is about being different. It means deliberately choosing a different set of activities to deliver a unique mix of value."[9]

Willie Pietersen insists this unique mix of value must result in a competitive advantage. Pietersen is a former Rhodes Scholar, raised in South Africa, who served as CEO for multibillion-dollar businesses, including Seagram USA and Tropicana. In addition to his advising roles for numerous global companies such as Boeing, ExxonMobil, Novartis, and the Girl Scouts of America, he has served as a professor of the Practice of Management at the Columbia Business School for over twenty years. Pietersen writes, "If you had unlimited resources, there would be no requirement for a strategy because there would be no need to decide what *not* to do."[10]

If Lord Commander Jon Snow could keep throwing an inexhaustible number of Night's Watch soldiers at the oncoming horde of White Walkers and wights, the death toll would be incomprehensible, but the enemy wouldn't progress and Commander Snow wouldn't need to think strategically. But he doesn't have an inexhaustible resource of men to sacrifice to the enemy. The situation is exacerbated by a truth captured in *The World of Ice & Fire: The Untold History of Westeros and the Game of Thrones*: "Sadly, the most important truth about the Night's Watch today is its decline."[11] Lord Commander Snow is not leading a healthy organization. After the slaughtering of the Night's Watch on the Fist of the First Men, and after the bloody mutiny that resulted in the murder of Lord Commander Mormont, the Night's Watch is decimated.

Strategy drives the choices the organization makes to define and achieve success. This involves deciding where it will compete, how it will create value for its customers, and how it will create superior returns to those invested in the organization. As Pietersen says, "The first and most crucial point is that a strategy must define how you will win."[12] Organizations need to think strategically because they don't have unlimited resources and they must make choices that focus their effort to answer where they will compete in order to achieve a specific aim that will lead to competitive victory. The organization's success in business will be measured by the value they add to their customers, which will bring superior profit to the organization. This is Pietersen's definition of the *Essence of Strategy*.[13]

Jon's purpose is to be a worthy leader, which means protecting Westeros, which requires him to stop the real threat in the north: the undead army. He identifies a strategy that provides the best chance for his team, the Night's Watch, to win. Jon will remove a resource from the Night King, taking potential wights—the living wildlings—to a safer environment, protected by the Wall.

Jon must align a variety of individuals and their specific understanding of their purposes with Jon's vision of how to move forward with an effective strategy and plan. In military leadership—which is Jon Snow's challenge—Pietersen points out: "War is a matter of life and death, and wars are typically zero-sum encounters."[14] There are different possible aims from going to war. Winning an armed conflict might mean disarmament, regime change, or nation-building. In Jon Snow's case, winning means the survival of humanity. In a business context, as Pietersen explains, *"Winning in business means winning at value."*[15] Strategy must answer four key questions: Where will we compete? What do we want to achieve? How will we win? What are our key priorities?[16]

Lord Commander Snow, facing the ominous competitor that had created a technological game changer with the ability of turning dead enemies into killing units, might have written his prospective answers to Pietersen's four questions on a scrap of scroll from Maester Aemon's study in the following way:

1) Where will we compete? *We will compete at the Wall.*

2) What do we want to achieve? *Defend the border and not allow the Others to cross.*

3) How will we win? *No clue how, but winning means annihilating the White Walkers.*

4) What are our key priorities? *Guard the Wall and hinder creation of wights, while searching for a solution to destroy the Night King and his army.*

Strategy and *planning* are not the same thing. Willie Pietersen says, "One of the most mischievous terms is strategic planning."[17] The development of a strategy is very different from the development of the plans related to that strategy.

Strategy is deciding where you will put down the railroad tracks. Planning involves the steps you need to take to guarantee the trains run on time. Strategic planning is a problematic term because it conflates two ideas and muddies the fact they are distinct steps in an interconnected process. Strategy requires determining where to compete and how to win. It is about making the best choices. It requires an intense focus on key efforts. Planning provides orderliness and discipline. It is about putting strategy into action, not creating that strategy. It involves the structure of actions that support the strategy, such as forecasting, logistics, and budgeting.

Lord Commander Snow doesn't succeed at delivering clarity to his direct reports about the difference between strategy and planning. A group of his men become violent with rage at the plan. These men don't understand, or accept, the strategy.

The strategy of Brandon the Builder was to work with the Children of the Forest and create a barrier to keep the White Walkers from entering Westeros; this involved using the Children's capacity for magic to create an ice wall that extended three hundred miles on the northern border of the Seven Kingdoms, with the Nightfort the original home of the Night's Watch and Eastwatch-by-the-Sea as the port on the eastern end at the Bay of Seals to the Shadow Tower at the Gorge on the western end near the Bay of Ice.

The planning required sustaining the forts, as well as managing a steady supply of food for the border warriors. The Stark family donated fertile land south of the Wall, known as "The Gift." Planning to defend the Wall changed over generations. The heroic volunteers willing to take the black eventually became groups of prisoners and disenfranchised men with little options for professional success. The strategy that led to the building of the Wall was effective for a thousand years. The planning eroded as the Night's Watch dwindled to roughly one thousand men under Commander Snow, and the reality of a new competitor with a game-changing military tactic arrived on the scene.

In *Strategic Learning*, Pietersen writes, "Because their outputs are so different, combining strategy and planning into one process is a toxic mixture."[18] Pietersen argues for being very clear about developing your strategy first, and the plans to support the strategy second. Don't mix the two. Jon Snow's misstep on this challenge is magnified in Westeros because Jon's disgruntled colleagues get tangled in their emotional reaction to Jon's plan to invite the former enemy—the wildlings—into their country, welcoming them as neighbors, colleagues, and potential citizens. The Night's Watch's apprehension is understandable. Jon Snow can't select only certain wildlings. He must allow them all, including the Weeper, who would carve out the eyeballs of captured Rangers. Jon Snow is faced with a tough task, but he must stop the weaponizing of dead wildlings. He didn't recognize he had to sell his strategy and plan.

Lord Commander Snow struggles with executing his strategy and his plan because he isn't clear on the difference. His irate followers only grasp the plan. They don't understand how the plan drives a strategy that fulfills a purpose that aligns with their professed purpose as

Rangers. Jon is focused on his strategic insight to help improve humanity's chance to win. This requires difficult choices. He makes the choice but doesn't deliver his decision in a way that gains followership.

As Willie Pietersen also likes to say, "Strategy isn't horse-trading."[19] Strategy isn't a question of swapping various resources, naming metrics to be hit, or juggling people up and down the org-chart. Strategy is what you do to define how you will win. The critical step in making this decision is figuring out how you will extend the gap between the cost to your organization and the value you can offer to your customers.

Strategy must support and deliver a value that results in competitive success. "An organization's Winning Proposition encapsulates measurable competitive advantage and defines how an organization will win the competition for value creation."[20] Pietersen says that identifying the winning proposition requires understanding what unique benefits the organization will offer to the customer that will cause the customer to choose the organization over the competition, and how these benefits will translate into customer value.

Pietersen recommends his strategic learning cycle as a process to help define the winning proposition. In *Strategic Learning*, he points out that all effective winning propositions "focus on superior benefits customers will receive, not just the internal actions these organizations will take."[21]

I asked Elby Stewart, a recent participant in our Advanced Management Program, if she could provide the winning proposition for Ross Stores. One of the superior benefits she shared resonated with me. Since childhood and throughout my adult life, I have been a fan of yard sales and thrift stores. Ross's slogan is "Dress for Less." This appeals to anyone that respects a budget and looks for value, but their winning proposition as Elby shared in her e-mail to me dated August 28, 2018, includes "creating a 'treasure hunt' bricks-and-mortar experience, incentivizing shoppers to physically visit a Ross store to capitalize on low prices not available elsewhere."

That idea that Ross is focused on a "treasure hunt bricks-and-mortar experience" is the focus that reaches this customer, and many others. The experience of thrift-store shopping and yard-sale hunting is the experience of searching for a treasure that appeals to you and that you have earned through your search. The search is part of the experience; without the search, the treasure would have remained buried.

This is a different winning proposition from a company such as Zappos that says their number one core value is "to deliver WOW through service."[22] Zappos and Ross are both marketplaces for a variety of products, but one commits to impress their customers with service and one commits to the treasure-hunt experience, complemented by branded apparel priced 20 to 60 percent below most department store prices. Both organizations have winning propositions that offer unique benefits and will cause targeted customers to choose the organization over the competition.

I imagine Lord Commander Snow's winning proposition to be: *The Night's Watch will maximize all potential resources available inside and outside the Seven Kingdoms to protect the safety of the people of Westeros.*

Zappos was able to transform online purchases by allowing the customer to return items conveniently with no penalty. This was a winning proposition: purchase products with fast, guaranteed delivery and an easy return process . . . create WOW. It became more convenient to order clothes from a device in one's home than travel to a store. I know because the Cabazon discount malls are only a twenty-minute drive from my house in the Coachella Valley. I didn't mind the drive, or the process of shopping in the malls, but Zappos made the effort inefficient. My one motivation for the drive would be the "treasure hunt" experience that Ross put into their winning proposition, but often there was the pragmatic need to be efficient, select the necessary products, and buy them at a good cost.

Zappos CEO Tony Hsieh titled his book *Delivering Happiness: A Path to Profits, Passion, and Purpose.* The Zappos winning proposition contributed to happiness through their strategy and planning around service. A few years back, 75 percent of purchasers at Zappos were returning customers and their most profitable customers also had the highest product return rate.[23] The return process was not impacting their sales but in fact was supporting it.

Zappos created a clear value that positively impacted the organization's ability to compete. This value was built on doing something important in a unique way. Competitors followed. As an organization, they managed to offer value, while keeping their costs in a place where they could make profit. Their volume of sales expanded as word spread of their unique value. Zappos decided how to lay down the tracks of that railroad, and they planned and managed the process in a way that built market share.

Pietersen argues that the focus can't just be on a *value proposition*; the focus must be on a *winning proposition*. The distinction between a winning proposition and a value proposition is crucial. "This always concerns me. Pursuing value is obviously the right thing to do, but this is plainly not a competitive statement. It ignores the most important question of all: How much value? In a competitive marketplace, absolutes have no meaning. It's the margin of difference—the gap—that counts. All value is relative, and customers have choices."[24] Your strategy must be centered on how you will win the competition for value creation. In which areas will you compete, which customers will you serve, and what will you offer them? Once you understand how you will compete for value creation, you can focus on the key priorities that will make the biggest difference. You must approach those key priorities with relentless focus, which also means subtracting what is not important. You must ask: What are we going to do? What are we not going to do? In that process you must do two things: reinvest the learning and focus.

In the executive education classroom, Pietersen discusses the British Royal Air Force acronym **OODA: Observe + Orient + Decide + Act**. This acronym captures a cycle similar in structure to Willie's learning cycle: **Learn + Focus + Align + Execute**. The key point is that these are cycles. Once you reach the *Act* or *Execute* stage, you need to go around the cycle again, and keep going around it. Your deliberate practice of the cycle will fine-tune your knowledge and skill at identifying and supporting the winning proposition.

"Focus is what you get when you have defined your Winning Proposition and Key Priorities and are utterly clear about what you are not going to do."[25] Success is about subtracting the distractions and going around the learning cycle from: Learn to Focus to Align to Execute. We use his learning cycle as an organizing principle to the educational journey of the senior executives in our four-week Columbia Business School Advanced Management Program. Our executives take the model back and apply it to confront their strategic challenges. The aim is to keep your knowledge growing exponentially. Willie calls this exponential learning that one extracts from the cycle *compounding*: **Focus x Compounding = Excellence**.

PERSUASION

Bob Bontempo is a significant teaching presence across the portfolio in the executive education department of the Columbia Business School. His session on *persuasion* offers the executive audience a take-away and a challenge. The takeaway is his model on how to achieve persuasion. The challenge is to admit how difficult it is to lead oneself to apply the model. Part of the difficulty is because the model requires restraint, perspective, and vision. Bontempo makes the point that persuasion is a discipline that takes time. He uses the image of planting a grain of sand in the oyster to create a pearl. The grain of sand is an idea the persuadee can accept. This idea is not a challenge or a confrontation but more a suggestion or a question. The grain of sand over time will result in the pearl: persuasion. The grain of sand can be looked at as an invitation to consider a possibility. Once the person who has heard this invitation reflects upon the idea and decides to own it, they have been involved in the process of persuasion. Bontempo's concept is based on the idea that intelligent adults aren't convinced by argument. They are convinced by themselves, when they take time to reflect on a question and make an eventual, considered decision. Persuasion takes time.

As strategy is not an act of horse-trading, neither is persuasion an act of negotiation. One expects to negotiate under time pressure. When Jon Snow and Tormund Giantsbane discuss wildling children serving as wards to Westerosi, Jon and Tormund are in a negotiation. Either Tormund sold his part of the deal to the wildlings or they would have to stay on the cold side of the Wall. "*It was that, or watch his people die. 'My blood price, he called it,'* said Jon Snow, but he will pay."[26] This is negotiation. Persuasion is a different process meant for a different challenge.

Bontempo points out that we often approach a persuasion challenge and make a big mistake. We act like we are in a negotiation. If negotiation is required, negotiate. Persuasion is what we do when we need someone to buy into an idea and make it his or her own. Persuasion aims at helping people take full ownership of an idea. The *persuader* must let go of control. The *persuadee* must make their own decision to take on the idea and change their thinking on that subject.

Persuasion isn't about stating a demonstrably correct answer. When we are involved in an act of persuasion, we don't present a perfect truth and then sit back and wait for agreement. If the listener hears a perfect truth presented as a demonstrably correct answer to a question, what follows is a eureka moment. The listener has been shown the truth. It is irrefutable. The truth can be proven to be correct. Persuasion is not about revealing a provable truth. In certain situations, the facts might not all be available to absolutely prove the idea correct, but the idea is compelling and intuitively sounds correct. In both cases, *truth wins*.

In *truth wins* cases, the specific facts are on the side of the argument being presented. Jon Snow doesn't need to persuade Tormund Giantsbane to accept the idea the White Walkers are an immediate threat to the existence of the Free Folk. Tormund has seen the horror of the White Walkers and their capacity to bring dead wildlings and their animals back into military action, fighting on the side of the Night King. Tormund and Jon must work together to negotiate the terms of their partnership, but Tormund has fully bought into the need to build an alliance with the Night's Watch. The truth is irrefutable to Tormund.

On the other hand, Jon does need to persuade his own Night's Watch followers to understand both his strategy and corresponding plan to put his strategy into action. Jon's strategy is not an irrefutable truth. They may believe the White Walkers are real, but that doesn't prove the wildlings need to be invited to cross the Wall and join the Night's Watch. Jon needs to persuade his followers to trust his judgment.

If you face a communication challenge where the facts are on your side, the most effective approach is to lead with the correct point of view, present the data, be charismatic and charming (if inclined), and convince the listener.

However, many of our communication challenges are resolved by the judgment of the listener. An objective answer isn't available. These are not *truth wins* situations. These are *judgment wins* situations. This is when persuasion is necessary.

If you are in the Night's Watch and report to Lord Commander Snow, you might agree with your leader that the existence of the White Walkers supports allowing the wildlings across the Wall. You might decide it is a eureka situation: 1) demonstrably correct, 2) intuitively compelling, and 3) truth wins.

However, this depends on a belief that the Wall won't keep the White Walkers on the north side, slaughtering your current enemy the wildlings. If you believe in the efficacy of the Wall, which has held for thousands of years, then Lord Commander Snow's argument isn't close to a eureka situation. If the White Walkers can't get across the Wall, let the wildlings and White Walkers slaughter one another. Why should the Rangers care? The Wall could hold for a thousand more years. Lord Commander Snow's decision is really a judgment decision. His logic depends on variables open to debate. It might be safer to embrace the potential danger of partnering with an ancient enemy—the wildlings—to increase the odds of confronting a more ancient enemy that could find their way across the Wall: the White Walkers.

Jon Snow's angry followers believe the White Walkers are a distant threat with no capacity to cross the Wall. Let them slaughter the wildlings. Let them all stay north of the Wall. The threat is vague at best; in fact, this might take care of two challenges: let them wipe each other out.

Jon Snow is confronted with a situation where an objective answer is not available. The majority view wins . . . and for Jon Snow, the majority agree with him. However, if the minority have weapons and will consider using them in a mutiny, the situation requires Jon to find a way to unlock the frozen perspective of his angry direct reports. The idea is for Jon to get that grain of sand inside the locked shell of their biased, angry, resistant minds. His armed direct reports need persuading on his strategy and corresponding plan. The way to make persuasion happen is to do the following:

1) Identify the continuum of possible beliefs.
2) Select a message right at the edge of the listeners' latitude of acceptance.
3) Accept that it is a gradual process of small movements that require the persuader to plant the idea and then wait for the idea to catch and develop in the mind of the persuadee.

If we are confronted with a challenge based on judgment where objective answers are unavailable, we need to plant that grain of sand. We should not hammer at people with our opinions. We are involved in a communication challenge and it demands persuasion. We should not continue to present our argument as if it is a eureka moment of objective truth, when it's not. We should not keep negotiating our point if it only makes our direct reports reach for their blades. It should be written on the wall of our office or workspace that our opinions don't change other people's opinions. Only the grain of sand, placed with discretion and allowed to grow, will turn into the pearl.

The time pressure Jon Snow faced was real. His inclination to muscle his idea forward makes sense. Except it was the wrong leadership approach and he failed. Even with the time constraints, Jon needed to work the craft of persuasion and try to guide his resistant followers in his direction.

When Alan Mulally, former CEO of Boeing, took over as CEO for Ford Motor Company at the end of 2006, the organization was in serious trouble. Ford's stock price had fallen, with a low at $1.01 a share in 2008. Its debt was at junk status, and 2006 would be the worst year in the company's history. Ford would end the year with a $12.7 billion loss. The expectation was that Ford would file for bankruptcy.[27]

He rallied followers across the global organization to recognize the challenge: they needed to feel dissatisfaction. He told them, "We have been going out of business for 40 years."[28] The statement resonated with people in the Ford Motor Company. The mutual urge to save the company motivated people to support Mulally's four key points.

These four key points became known as Mulally's One Ford plan. The organization's winning proposition would depend on its capacity to work together, to be *One Ford*.

Mulally said, "Ford has become a house of brands."[29] There was no specific Ford identity. What did the famous round Ford logo actually represent? It was revealing to Mulally that when he walked around the executive garage at Ford headquarters, he couldn't find a single Ford vehicle.

One of Mulally's key points was to focus on financing. He restructured Ford by mortgaging assets to the tune of $23.6 billion dollars in 2006, right before the Great Recession. This was prescient leadership, allowing Ford to focus on technological advances while competitors in the industry struggled to stay solvent during the recession.

Mulally also focused the organization on leveraging Ford's automotive assets and knowledge, and building cars and trucks that people wanted and valued. It's significant that of his four strategic targets, the point at the top of the list was to bring all Ford employees together as a global team. Success would require building trust.

As with Jon Snow at Castle Black, this was a persuasion moment for the CEO. Both Jon Snow at the Wall and Alan Mulally in Detroit were committed to building a team whose success depended on different groups working together. Mulally knew he had to break down the silos and stop the turf battles. One Ford was the grain of sand he placed in the oyster.

The clear facts were that the organization was in trouble, but that reality didn't gain buy-in on the best way to succeed, any more than the Rangers agreed with Jon Snow just because their fellow Rangers had been slaughtered Beyond the Wall by White Walkers and wights. Mulally's One Ford presented a future that people could all see themselves working to achieve. It was a future they could imagine, placed within their continuum of beliefs; it was aspirational, but also a goal people would accept. His four key points could work, but his followers needed to make that decision. It wasn't a *truth wins* decision. It was a judgment decision.

Mulally's intention was to bring personnel around the world together to network, share ideas, and support the whole Ford Motor Company effort, not just support their specific brands in their specific regions. The networking could be mandated, but for the trust to stick, to be put into practice and be more than just talk, the behavior needed to be accepted by individuals. It was a judgment decision. If it was going to work, Mulally's people needed to buy into accepting One Ford. This was Mulally's equivalent to Jon's challenge to persuade the Rangers to accept the wildlings.

Mulally needed trust for the One Ford plan to create the pearl. "'Never make a joke or try for humor at someone else's expense,' Mulally said. 'In a high-stakes environment, everyone needs to feel safe.'"[30] In the past, no executives wanted to admit failure, as they would risk losing their job. When Mulally took over, he literally applauded the first executive that had the courage to admit internal problems and not just present predictions of a rosy future.[31] In a "house of brands," Mulally persuaded the Rangers to work with the wildlings.

He convinced his global organization of the threat of the White Walkers, not by a mandate but by declaring his strategy and also recognizing his followers needed to buy into the fact they were at the brink of cataclysmic failure. His followers responded. One Ford succeeded at helping Ford employees work together to achieve success.

When competing automotive companies took government bailouts due to the financial pressures of the Great Recession, Ford didn't.

While competitors struggled, Ford was on the path of developing innovative advantages and operating profitably. Mulally's strategy was effective, and part of the success was because he had used persuasion to lead.

Exercise: Practicing Persuasion

Think of a specific communication challenge that involves encouraging someone to change their mind and agree with you.

Explain the challenge:

What does the person currently believe?

What would you like them to believe?

1) Does this communication challenge involve persuading the person of a/an:

a. Eureka decision?

i. Demonstrably correct

ii. Intuitively compelling

iii. Truth wins

  b. Intellective decision?

    i. Demonstrably correct

    ii. Not intuitively compelling

    iii. Truth wins

  c. Judgment decision?

    i. Objective answer unavailable

    ii. Majority wins

2) Identify your persuadee's:

  a. Latitude of acceptance (zone of positions he or she accepts)

    i. Where do you estimate they stand in terms of their current belief on the related subject?

  b. Latitude of noncommitment (zone of positions she or he neither accepts nor rejects)

    i. Where do you think they don't have a firm commitment of belief on the related subject?

  c. Latitude of rejection (zone of positions he or she rejects)

    i. What do you think they firmly don't believe and will resist on the related subject?

Brainstorm a suggestion you can make to the persuadee that will be on the edge of their latitude of agreement and noncommitment:

How to win a judgment challenge:

1) Identify the continuum of possible beliefs.

2) Select a message right on the edge of the audience's latitude of acceptance.

3) Accept that for smart adults, persuasion is a gradual process consisting of small movements.

4) Recognize persuasion must involve a decision where the *persuadee* accepts an idea without you insisting it is your idea.

DO YOU FACE A TRUTH
OR JUDGMENT DECISION?

Castle Black has filled with Free Folk. The wildlings in the know warn the Night's Watch that harm is heading south. Shut the gates. The wildling skinchanger, Borroq, tells the Night's Watch: "You close it good and tight. They're coming, crow."[32]

Jon unclasps his cloak when Clydas hands him a parchment from Cotter Pyke in Hardhome. There are *"dead things in the woods. . . . Dead things in the water."*[33] The situation is grievous. Humanity will face a collapse of climate, an onslaught of murder, and Jon knows the Rangers that report to him and the leadership of Westeros have no idea of the true threat. *"Night falls,* he thought, *and now my war begins."*[34]

Jon's blind spot was his unwillingness to use persuasion to respond to the tension from his direct reports. The anger and disagreement from his men initiated sharp pushback from Snow, as opposed to listening, responsive leadership, and persuasion. On the day of his assassination, confident in rightness of his strategy and plan, Jon attempts to control the crowd of knights, wildlings, Watch, and various armed people that congregate at the sound of horrific screaming. The wildling giant, Wun Wun, holds the dismembered body of one of Queen Selyse's knights. The useless, arrogant knight threatened the giant and Wun Wun slammed the man into dead, human putty. Even at Castle Black, where violence is commonplace, the giant slamming the remains of human sludge against a stone turret is an ugly image.

Jon yells at everyone to put away their blades. Jon doesn't want the giant to smash another human against Hardin's Tower. Jon sees Wick Whittlestick holding a blade. "'No blades!' he screamed. 'Wick, put that knife . . .'"[35] But Jon can't get out the word "away" before he is slashed by Wick. Jon, in response to a slashed throat, can't manage his sword, his fingers, body, and mind stunned. He drops to his knees in the snow, engulfed with pain. He whispers the name of his direwolf: *Ghost*.

"When the third dagger took him between the shoulder blades, he gave a grunt and fell face-first into the snow. He never felt the fourth knife. Only the cold . . ."[36]

Jon wasn't wrong in his decision to allow the wildlings to cross safely into Westeros, but the Lord Commander failed at persuading his resistant followers. Bowen Marsh, Alliser Thorne, Wick Whittlestick, and the rest of the assassins were locked into what Bob Bontempo calls the *Latitude of Rejection*. They had fought in bloody battles against the wildlings, and had seen their friends die at their hands. Jon Snow's negotiation with the wildlings was not a leadership decision the angry Night's Watch would accept. Their hatred blinded them to their human need for a pact of peace with the wildlings. Both sides needed to align against the true threat.

Jon fell into the leadership trap of assuming his decision would be clear. Jon didn't recognize he was presenting a judgment decision that required the buy-in of his team. Jon thought the answer was simple. He felt it was a decision where, in Bontempo's words, *truth wins*.

Lord Commander Snow was wrong. This was not a leadership decision with a demonstrably correct answer, where truth wins. Young Olly, who ends up knifing Snow in the heart, watched his parents get murdered by Ygritte's crew of marauding wildlings. The mutinous Night's Watch doesn't accept the assumptions behind Jon Snow's decision. They haven't bought into the need to create an alliance with their sworn enemy. *Truth* is neither demonstrably correct nor intuitively compelling.

Jon Snow thought he was in an argument where he could state his position, outline the reasons, assert the data, rely on the logic, and convince. Jon Snow thought he was in an argument where the facts resulted in only one conclusion: partner with wildlings. Instead, he was involved in a judgment debate, where he needed to support his projected truth because it was not intuitively compelling and there wasn't an objective truth.

Jon could have surfaced the level of anger and rebellion triggered by his decision. He might have been able to either 1) imprison or constrain his potential assassins, or 2) persuade them with his *judgment argument*, supported over time by a real agreement on the risk of the army led by the Night King. Persuasion takes time. Negotiations can often be done quickly, particularly if both sides are motivated and one side doesn't use time to leverage a decision from the other party. Jon and Tormund both understood the impending risk of the White Walkers and neither of them used time to the disadvantage of the other person. Persuasion depends on those being persuaded: they have to take ownership of the idea. It can't be forced on them.

Under the extreme pressure and time constraints Jon faced as Lord Commander of the Night's Watch, Jon needed to 1) better understand the breadth of potential beliefs on his team, 2) select a message right at the edge of the disgruntled Rangers' latitude of acceptance, and 3) recognize that he was involved in an act of persuasion, not a negotiation. In the end, Jon could have surfaced the tension, still failed at persuasion, but at least understood the depth of resistance he faced with his team. Jon could have tried reframing the conversation and focused on what the Rangers could accept about the real threat presented by the White Walkers and wights, as opposed to allowing the angry cohort to focus on the wildlings.

In order for Lord Commander Snow to have succeeded at shifting the opinions of his recalcitrant direct reports at Castle Black, he had to choose persuasion. If that didn't work, he needed to arm himself and his close allies on the Watch against insurrection. The Red Woman, Melisandre, told him to keep his direwolf close, but Jon was consumed by his responsibilities and miscalculated the resistance to his strategy and plan.

The goal of a judgment decision is to get a message right where the listener can't reject it. Jon could have said, "When we had dead Rangers brought to Castle Black from across the Wall, they reanimated as wights and attempted to kill the Old Bear, Jeor Mormont. We can kill them if we burn them, but otherwise, they stay animated, even if sliced with swords. Would an army of wight wildlings be an issue?" This would have been one useful grain of sand.

Jon has to get his message out of their *Latitude of Rejection* and into their *Latitude of Acceptance*, or, at least, into their *Latitude of Noncommitment*, where they can reflect on the options without instant rejection. Jon stumbles in a critical leadership moment because he underestimates the potential backlash of resistance on his team. Jon assumes his argument is based on truth and truth wins. His direct reports don't buy it. Jon's *Eureka Argument* is a *Judgment Argument*. Professionally, we are often like Jon Snow. We believe it's time to win through facts when we need to win through persuasion.

THE LEADER'S JOURNEY: REFUSAL OF RETURN

In Westeros, crucible follows crucible for Jon Snow. He falls in love with Ygritte on the cold side of the Wall, forsakes his vows, in part to gain buy-in to the people sworn to destroy his country, in part out of obvious passion and emotional connection. Jon rejoins the Night's Watch, unable to choose Ygritte over duty to the Westeros border patrol. Ygritte dies in his arms in the Battle for Castle Black. Jon follows this trauma by stepping up to lead through crisis, working with Tormund Giantsbane to create a partnership with the wildlings. He is rewarded not only with his own assassination but a return to mortality. He recognizes his effort was rewarded by getting knifed to death in the snow.

Jon faced the trial of an assassination by his own men. This was, hopefully, his last crucible experience. Campbell states at the beginning of the Refusal of Return phase of the Hero's Journey: "The adventurer still must return with his life-transmuting trophy"[37]

Jon Snow doesn't want to return from his death and face leadership. He demands Melisandre let him stay dead next time. "Returning from death" is not a pass to a carefree, no-stress life. "Returning from death" is a challenge to face more of what got one killed in the first place. Jon Snow would be forgiven if he said he'd had enough of Westeros leadership responsibilities, paid passage on a Braavosi trade galley, and left for the Summer Islands.

Jon Snow offered everything and he was killed. Melisandre has found, to her surprise, that calling Snow back with her Asshai spells, *worked*. In Joseph Campbell's language: "The full round, the norm of the monomyth, requires that the hero shall now begin the labor of bringing the runes of wisdom," where the wisdom, the boon, can contribute "to the renewing of the community, the nation, the planet, or the ten thousand worlds."[38] Jon gave everything and suffered death, and now he needs to return to the world the knowledge he has earned from his courage and suffering.

Snow gasps back onto this mortal coil only to be slammed with shame and rage. Luckily he is coached by one of the most courageous and emotionally intelligent leaders in Westeros: the Onion Knight. Entangled in the guilt and anger he feels after the brutal, negative feedback of being knifed to death by his colleagues on the Night's Watch, Snow tells Ser Davos: "They stabbed me. Olly . . . he put a knife in my heart."[39] Ser Davos watches the disheartened leader say, "I failed." Davos replies, "Good. Now go fail again." Davos tells Jon: "You clean up as much of the shit as you can."[40]

Todd Jick at the Columbia Business School says, "Leaders take organizations to places that they would not otherwise have gone to."[41] This is true. This is what Lord Commander Jon Snow attempted to do by treating with the wildlings. He aimed for a necessary path forward for his organization. He paid for it, but that doesn't mean he was misguided. His strategy was on target, but he was thrust into a crucible. He was tested, and could benefit from the suffering. Bill George at Harvard Business School writes, "A crucible can be triggered by events such as confronting a difficult situation at work, receiving critical feedback, or losing your job. Or it may result from a painful personal experience such as divorce, illness, or the death of a loved one."[42]

Warren Bennis writes in the classic *On Becoming a Leader* that he and his writing partner, Bob Thomas, discovered the importance in leadership development of "some rite of passage, often a stressful one."[43] He references former first lady, Abigail Adams, telling her son, John Quincy Adams in 1780 that the crucible is how leadership is forged. "'It is not in the still calm of life or the repose of a pacific station that great characters are formed,' she counseled. 'The habits of a vigorous mind are formed in contending with difficulty. Great necessities call out great virtues.'"[44]

We all face crucible experiences when our aspirations run head-on into failure, into a test where we are delivered into a bright, hot heat of confusion, frustration, exhaustion, criticism, and pain.

In George R. R. Martin's Known World of Westeros and Essos, resurrection is a crucible that other characters face. Jon is not the first character to be reanimated. The walking, disfigured, vengeful corpse of Catelyn Stark, now known as Lady Stoneheart, approves the hanging of Merrett Frey as retaliation for his part in the Red Wedding. We also have Lord Beric Dondarrion, known, due to his flaming sword, as *the Lightning Lord*. Beric is a follower of the Lord of Light and is brought back six times from death by the self-professed failure and drunk, the Red Priest: Thoros.

Beric is brutalized by each death, but he is driven to not refuse to return and pursue his purpose. George R. R. Martin is quoted in *Vanity Fair*: "Each time Beric's revived he loses a little more of himself. He was sent on a mission before his first death. He was sent on a mission to do something, and it's like, that's what he's clinging to. . . . His flesh is falling away from him, but this one thing, this purpose that he had is part of what's animating him."[45] Beric loses bits of his humanity after each return to life, but he doesn't lose his sense of mission.

Ygritte's death, the destruction of Winterfell and death of siblings and adopted parents, and Jon's own death were not the first crucibles Jon Snow had faced. His childhood was protected by membership in the powerful Stark clan, but he was not accepted by Catelyn Stark.

He referred to Robb, Bran, Sansa, and Arya as "Starks." He wasn't a Stark. His security had emotional limits. Before leaving on his journey to Castle Black, Jon went to visit Bran after Bran's terrible fall from the tower window, and Catelyn called to him as he was leaving the room.

"He was at the door when she called out to him. 'Jon,' she said. He should have kept going, but she had never called him by his name before. He turned to find her looking at his face, as if she were seeing it for the first time.

'Yes?' he said.

'It should have been you,' she told him. Then she turned back to Bran and began to weep, her whole body shaking with the sobs. Jon had never seen her cry before."[46]

Despite his opportunities and learned skills, growing up as an illegitimate child in the Stark clan, Jon knew people could harbor unfair judgments. Jon wasn't naive on the dynamics of emotion. This is why he supported the outsiders that fell under his leadership. His purpose was to protect humanity and lead with the integrity of a Stark, while not misjudging people with potential. Jon had to bear the knowledge that Theon Turncloak had betrayed Winterfell and executed their trusty aid and mentor Ser Rodrik Cassel. "The great stronghold of House Stark was a scorched desolation. *All my memories are poisoned*."[47]

Jon takes his first gasps of breath after death. He has returned to life, but that doesn't mean he will choose to return to leadership. His emotional reaction is the twelfth stage of Campbell's monomyth: Refusal of Return. Jon wants to do something we haven't seen in him. He wants to quit. He doesn't want to face again what he has already faced, and failed.

When Jon left Winterfell to join the Night's Watch, he said his good-byes to Robb, Sansa, and Arya, gifting her the sword Needle. Jon had the sword made special in the Braavosi style: thin, perfect for punching deadly holes in an opponent. Jon gives Arya the reminder she will never forget about using the "pointy end." Sad at saying farewell to Arya, Jon says, "Different roads sometimes lead to the same castle."[48]

He travels to Dragonstone to address Daenerys and when word arrives that Arya and Bran are alive, his decision is immediate. He must return and protect them. This is a reborn version of his original purpose and he is reanimated by the realization he can protect immediate family. Daenerys reminds Jon Snow that he hasn't asked if he can leave Dragonstone and her presence. "I don't need your permission. I am a king."[49]

After being resurrected, Jon Snow's confidence is crushed, but in Dragonstone, he finds his purpose in the defense of his family. He may still believe he was brought into the family out of an obligation that faced Ned Stark, but he will soon understand his love for his siblings coexists with a surprising insight about his true parents. Jon Snow chooses to return. He will soon learn his true name is Aegon Targaryen.

GOING FORWARD

Our strategy is a process that will benefit from the cycle: **Learn + Focus + Align + Execute**. Repeat this cycle in order to build on your learning and develop clarity on your *winning proposition*. It's not enough to compete on improving your organization's value proposition. We must look at value as an element of how we compete and the value our organization provides only matters if it leads to our customers making the decision to choose us over the competition.

Leaders take organizations to places that they would not otherwise have gone to. This is risky. Leaders must separate planning from strategy. Leaders must not confuse negotiation with persuasion.

When the Red Woman reanimated Jon Snow, he told Davos Seaworth, "I did what I thought was right. And I got murdered for it."[50] We need to remember that even when we have pursued our Leader's Journey into new territory and achieved success, we may still stumble. Our strategy may deliver the winning proposition. Our planning will be necessary to support our strategy. Our leadership decisions are on target to provide the value needed to confront the challenge of competition, but we may need the art of persuasion. If our followers are anchored in the Latitude of Rejection, we have to find time to communicate and place the grain of sand into the oyster. Leadership under pressure requires followership. Jon Snow attempted to order his men to follow his solution. Many were willing, but he didn't confront the challenge he faced with followers who hadn't accepted his message.

Frustrated by the resistance in his team, Jon let the simmering anger continue to simmer, angry at Bowen Marsh for not seeing the obvious wisdom in Jon's strategy and plan. "Jon wheeled his horse around. 'Enough talk. Away.'"[51] From Jon's perspective, "Bowen was a good man in his way, but the wound he had taken at the Bridge of Skulls had hardened his attitudes, and the only song he ever sang now was his familiar refrain about sealing the gates."[52] Lord Commander Snow allows Bowen Marsh to stay locked in his bias that all wildlings must be kept on the other side of the gate of the Wall.

Jon knew the Wall was the best place to stop the White Walkers. Jon knew the Night's Watch needed the support of the wildlings. He confronted Ranger resistance with a message he believed would solve the argument. When it didn't, he just stopped trying.

Jon understood the challenge that faced him was daunting. He didn't take it lightly. He thought of Sam Tarly: *"Sam, you sweet fat fool, you played me a cruel jape when you made me lord commander. A lord commander has no friends."*[53] But Jon confuses the hard realities of leadership as an excuse to push his order across the team without gaining their understanding of the judgment behind his strategy and plan.

"'Winter is coming,' Jon said at last, breaking the awkward silence, 'and with it the white walkers. The Wall is where we stop them. The Wall was *made* to stop them . . . but the Wall must be manned. This discussion is at an end.'"[54]

Lord Commander Snow's decision to stop trying to persuade his angry men is understandable, but it doesn't succeed. His attempt at the execution of his command results in his assassination.

Lead with the strategic wisdom of Jon Snow but don't get assassinated. If your followers, colleagues, and stakeholders are looking for answers from you, identify the communication challenge. If the decision is demonstrably correct and truth wins, find the demonstrable answer and deliver it. But if, like Jon Snow, you face a judgment decision where an objective answer isn't available and the majority is needed to confirm your decision wins, don't fall into negotiation. You face a judgment decision.

Remember to identify the continuum of possible beliefs for your followers; select a message that is right on the edge of your followers' latitude of acceptance; and recognize that smart adults will be persuaded through a gradual, slow process.

Lord Commander Snow had options to plant the grain of sand in the oyster and create an idea that his whole team would accept as a pearl. Jon Snow could have planted the idea that the White Walkers would breach the Wall at one of the weak spots where the forts were unoccupied. He could have empowered his more experienced Rangers, such as Bowen Marsh to think through options and join Jon in evaluating the options. Jon fell into the trap of believing he was limited by time. What limited Jon, and cost him his life, was that he didn't make a leadership commitment, under pressure, to practice persuasion.

8

FIND DRAGONGLASS!

HOW DO YOU GET THE BIG IDEA?

Jon Snow's life is impacted by two big ideas. One he doesn't recognize as a big idea at first, but it turns out better than he ever could have expected. The other he does recognize, but it turns out far worse.

TAKE THE BLACK

At Castle Black, the new recruits train in combat under the severe gaze of Ser Alliser Thorne, the Master of Arms. Jon Snow is skilled. Samwell Tarly is not. Thorne dubs the overweight, not very strong young man from Horn Hill as *Ser Piggy* and the *Lord of Ham*. Thorne pits Sam against the muscular, skilled bruiser, Halder. Sam is promptly hammered to the ground. He doesn't fight back. When others are set against him, Jon comes to his defense, then tells Sam he will do better tomorrow. Sam "looked mournfully back over one shoulder. 'No I won't,' he said, blinking back tears. 'I never do better.'"[1] When Sam walks off, the other two recruits, Grenn and Pyp, stare at him, shocked that Sam didn't try to defend himself. Jon sees something different.

FACE THE HARD TRUTHS

On the road to Castle Black, Tyrion Lannister tells Jon that taking the black isn't the noble journey Jon believes it to be. Jon is signing away his freedom to a false brand, choosing to die with criminals and losers. When Jon admits he understands and can accept the reality of his new situation, Tyrion smiles. "That's good, bastard. Most men would rather deny a hard truth than face it."[2] Jon recognizes in Sam a similar capacity to see the truth and have the courage to accept it.

Jon's first big idea is to support Sam. This appears generous, maybe even suggesting softness on Jon's part, but Sam brings resources to the challenges Jon faces, offering both leadership to Jon and skills to Jon's team. He contributes to Jon's promotion to Lord Commander. He contributes in a significant way to battling the threat of the Night King.

When Jon Snow and Samwell Tarly serve as new recruits to the Night's Watch, they believe the challenge that confronts Castle Black is to keep the wildlings on the colder side of the Wall.

After Lord Commander Jeor Mormont takes over a third of his men on the misguided Great Ranging Beyond the Wall, this reality changes. Sam and Jon go on different paths and discover a threat worse than vicious nomadic tribes. They learn about the murderous army of non-human Others and undead zombie wights. The Others, or White Walkers, long described as fantastical and nonexistent, are real. Their leader is the Night King. He has the ability to raise his dead enemies back as undead warriors to support his strategic goals. Jon and Sam realize the Night King plans to lead his frozen warriors south past the Wall. The undead army wants to destroy humanity.

As a result, after Jon is promoted to the top of the Night's Watch org-chart, he has his other big idea: invite the wildlings to join the Night's Watch and defend the Wall. This idea doesn't result as Jon hoped, but it was the right call.

Jon achieves these two moments of *strategic insight*—the first supporting the development of his team, the second transforming the resources of the Night's Watch—by accessing what Prussian general and military theorist Carl von Clausewitz called *coup d'oeil*.

Jon needs these two ideas for the same reason all leaders need big ideas: he faces challenges in his available resources and can benefit from the opportunities created by the big ideas.

In his early days as a recruit, the challenge to his resources—which he is unaware of—are the limits to his personal leadership. Sam helps him. When Jon is voted Lord Commander of the Night's Watch, he faces the expected competition of internecine conflict with the wildlings but soon recognizes he also faces a barely understood and potentially insurmountable competitor in the Night King and White Walkers.

The question is, how can we recognize our own big ideas?

STRATEGIC INSIGHT

In *Napoleon's Glance*, Professor William Duggan from Columbia Business School describes how von Clausewitz in his classic on military strategy, *On War*, describes *coup d'oeil* as the "rapid discovery of a truth which to the ordinary mind is not visible at all or only becomes so after long examination and reflection."[3]

What Clausewitz saw as a flash of insight, William Duggan breaks into four steps: 1) examples from history; 2) presence of mind; 3) the flash of insight itself; and, 4) resolution.[4] This is the process necessary to achieve what Duggan calls *strategic intuition*. It is possible to have an expert intuition based on years of proficiency in a specific area, but to gain the big idea in strategy, the solution is to catalyze a flash of insight. This won't be achieved through willpower, but the process can be nurtured. Strategic insight is what results from the coup d'oeil.

In *The Art of What Works*, Duggan encourages the reader: "You do what you can, not what you want."[5] This is the gift of coup d'oeil. We can prepare ourselves for that glance, that flash of what is possible.

Jon's analysis of Sam is an example of strategic intuition. Jon makes the decision to talk to Maester Aemon and encourage him to find a more useful role for Sam. Jon uses *"examples from history"* to make the point that Sam's father, Randyll, tried to beat and shame Sam into becoming a warrior. It didn't work when Randyll did it, and it won't work if Ser Alliser Thorne does it. History has proven this won't work and a resource in the Night's Watch—Sam—will be destroyed in the process.

Jon is able to have the strategic insight, in part because he leads himself past one of the most difficult obstacles to achieving the second stage: *presence of mind*. "The first obstacle is the simplest: too much focus."[6] *Presence of mind* is based on the idea of finding the calm center in the mind, similar to the meditative yet attentive state achieved in martial arts or in the practice of sitting meditation. Focus is a good thing, but constant focus prohibits the mind from moving into the stage of presence of mind, which is critical to the arrival of a flash of insight.

Howard Schultz needed the ability to let go of all the things he was focusing on early in the development of Starbucks in order for the insight of a Milan coffee bar to arrive. Duggan points out that figuring out what to do is *straight strategy*. "And the goal of this strategy is simple: free yourself from negative emotions to achieve presence of mind."[7] The goal is to turn stress into strategy. This is what Jon is able to do when confronted with the challenge of Sam. He could have focused on training Sam to fight or build his courage to confront battle. This would make logical sense, but Jon found a strategic option because his mind was not too focused on the logical. This results in the third stage of the method: *flash of insight*.

Jon decides to talk to Maester Aemon. The fourth stage, *resolution*, is intimidating for a young recruit. He has no problem persuading— either cajoling or intimidating—the recruits, convincing them to be kind to Sam in the training fights, but Jon also faces a late night conversation with Maester Aemon. Jon convinces the Maester to consider assigning Sam to his own office, suggesting using Sam's ability with reading and writing to benefit the old maester.

It would be easy in the brutal, organizational culture of Castle Black for the Bastard of Winterfell, already an outsider, and himself a newbie, to disregard Sam. The fat boy doesn't want to defend himself and appears to have nothing to contribute. Jon and Sam build trust and support each other, both aware they are in a competitive, dangerous environment. Both young men have the courage to see their reality and face it; plus, both men are open to learning. Jon Snow helps Sam, who is disregarded by the senior leadership at Castle Black.

Jon also benefits from Sam's guidance: Sam helps Jon recognize an opportunity and not derail when Jon is placed in the role of Steward to Lord Commander Mormont. Jon can't believe that a recruit with his sword and riding ability isn't put into the category of Ranger. He is very upset and starts to derail. Jon sees the decision as a plot by Ser Alliser. Samwell points out that when he was young, Sam's father wanted Sam at all public events, until he didn't. Then he wanted Sam's younger brother, Dickon, by his side. Sam points out to Jon that Lord

Commander Mormont wants Jon by his side because he might be preparing Jon to replace him as Commander. "You'll be as close to him as his shadow. You'll know everything, be a part of everything . . . and the Lord Steward said Mormont asked for you *himself!*"[8]

Sam helps Jon understand the context of a decision Jon was eager to assign to Ser Alliser's manipulation. Sam helps Jon understand the compliment, as well as the leadership opportunity, at being assigned to steward the Lord Commander. Without Sam's help, Jon would have simmered in resentment and not understood the potential of his new position. Sam is Jon's big idea. Jon defends him and gains in numerous ways. The insight Sam offers to Jon, helping him understand the context, builds a capacity in Jon to get past his emotions and understand what is going on. Sam's moment of coaching helps Jon *see true*. This prepares Jon for leadership and for strategic intuition.

Jon saw the value in a direct report who triggered disdain in peers and a boss. Jon defended Sam and built an ally. Jon would have preferred if Sam had stood up from the dirt, defended himself, and committed to building his skill as a warrior. Yet when Sam didn't fight back, Jon didn't give up on his colleague. A Duggan phrase—"You do what you can, not what you want"—offers a powerful insight that applies to the first interactions between Jon and Sam. Jon developed a key resource when he defended Sam, rather than standing to the side and watching that resource be destroyed.

The mantra I repeat to myself when I'm teaching supports Jon's coup d'oeil, and has supported the development of many allies: "meet people where they are." Jon Snow meets Samwell Tarly where he is, accepts him, defends him, and builds a resource, builds an ally. Lord Commander Snow meets the Free Folk where they are, and builds a resource, builds allies. But Lord Commander Snow also stumbles with his resistant direct reports: Alliser Thorne, Bowen Marsh, and the rest. He does what Duggan reminds us we can't do without peril: he ignores what he *can* do, which is work to persuade them, and he insists on choosing what he *wants* to do, which is ignore them and expect them to fall in line. He fails to meet them where they are. Coup d'oeil offers advantages, yet still requires leadership—even Napoleon lost.

STRATEGIC INTUITION

Strategic analysis leads to the opportunity of strategic intuition—the catalyst that creates the big idea—which will be followed by how you put the details in place (planning). Strategic intuition isn't a concept you draw out of thin air in an act of mystical inspiration. "You do not imagine the unknown. You discover it and make it known. And it turns out to be different from what you imagined."[9] Duggan suggests that numerous great achievements in the sciences and the arts do not develop due to "a leap of thought to a new theory, but rather from combining specific achievements that lead to a theory, which explains them. It's an act of combination, not imagination. Specifically, it's the selective recombination of previous elements into a new whole."[10]

A person operating with strategic intuition doesn't start from setting the goal first, and working to achieve it but rather from recognizing opportunities that are available, often opportunities that no one else has recognized. This is the *strike of the eye* moment. This is *the glance* where experiences combine in a new pattern to offer a solution to a challenge. This is coup d'oeil.

During the siege of Toulon in September 1783, the army of the French Revolution surrounds the strategically important port city, which had been invaded by the British forces. The senior French general plans to retake the city with a direct assault of soldiers using guns and bayonets. Napoleon was provided a chance to respond to his strategic intuition. "Napoleon put his strategy together over several days and talked with other junior officers about it."[11]

Napoleon believes if the French army would concentrate their efforts and take a key fort, the British will leave the city. Napoleon was given his chance when General Jacques Dugommier decided to put the young military officer in command.[12]

As Duggan writes, "Military historians know the elements that Napoleon put together to make his winning idea: contour maps, plus the light cannon, plus the American Revolutionary War, plus Joan of Arc."[13] Napoleon was able to bring together specific knowledge about the instruments of his trade, the contour maps and small cannons, recognizing their usefulness in gaining the high ground and taking the fort. Napoleon was also able to go further afield and draw on historical examples from the American Revolutionary War, when the British abandoned military locations in order to avoid being separated from their navy. He also drew on the historical example of Joan of Arc. She saved France in 1429 by taking small forts around the fortress of Orleans, then liberating the central fortress. "Napoleon had never fought a battle like Toulon, but he was able to find on the shelves of his mind a set of elements that solved in previous battles different pieces of the Toulon problem. The combination was new, but the elements that made up the combination were not."[14]

Napoleon faced three options: 1) the general's plan would work, 2) no plan would work, or 3) a new plan would work better. It is important in strategic intuition to be able to calm the mind to be open to possibilities, to not get derailed or develop tunnel vision focusing on one specific option. Napoleon's commanding superior was locked into the idea of using soldiers to assault the city and drive the British from Toulon with military force. Napoleon was able to see another option: if the French army could create the correct pressures, the British would choose to leave.

THE METHOD

Strategic intuition is not necessary 99 percent of the time, but 1 percent of the time it can make the difference between mediocrity, failure, or success. "You cannot force *coup d'oeil*. It comes or it doesn't."[15] But you can lead yourself to create an environment that makes the insight more likely to arrive. Remind yourself to do the following:

Step #1: Build your knowledge of historical examples and draw from disparate categories of disciplines. Your big idea may be the result of knowledge that arrives from connecting insights from different areas. For example, the design company IDEO uses a process of being divergent in their search for ideas, reaching beyond the industry of the product they are developing; they implement a process of convergence, of bringing the ideas together. You want to be accessible to creative combination, and that requires looking in a variety of areas, not pre-judging their relevance. The trick is to stay open to resources that will contribute to transforming creative combinations.

Step #2: Build your ability to achieve presence of mind. If you are always down in the weeds, you may not be mentally ready to look for opportunities other people haven't seen. If you are locked into a predetermined version of the way forward, you will also miss opportunities. It is important to prepare your mind in order to avoid pushing for an idea that won't work. Remember the maxim: "You do what you can, not what you want."[16] This is a core principle to put into action. It is liberating, empowering, and guiding. Napoleon refers to similar ideas in his memoirs, pointing out how he was not driven by ideas or trying to control the situation. "I was not so insane as to attempt to bend events to conform to my policies. On the contrary, I bent my policies to accord with the unforeseen shape of events."[17]

Step #3: When the flash of insight hits, recognize it and act on it! Examples of leaders having their eyes closed to coup d'oeil often end badly for their organizations. Kodak developed a digital film camera in 1975, but the product was dropped because it was considered to be in direct conflict with the company's film business. In the eighties, Kodak was blind to the potential threat of Fuji and allowed Fuji to become the official film of the 1984 Olympics. Even in the nineties, Kodak executives were unable to envision a world where their cherished film product didn't hold a top position against all competition. Kodak's top leadership didn't look outside their industry for historical examples of technological transformation. They failed at recognizing opportunity. They didn't acknowledge that some elements of their future were out of their control. Customers had choice. Kodak focused on what they decided was important, what they wanted. They were blind to the flash of strategic insight.

Step #4: Put your resolve into motion and understand that execution will be exhausting yet critical to your success. The flash of insight has to be leveraged with energy to move forward. The reaction that follows the verbalizing of a strategic insight is often disdain and skeptical laughter. Picasso exercised creative combination when he put together the visual influence of African sculpture, staged on the canvas with a nod to the bucolic serenity of Matisse's *Joy of Life*. This juxtaposition of the surprising and the traditional in Picasso's painting *Les Demoiselles d'Avignon* resulted first in ridicule and shock, and eventually, in praise. He was mocked by his friends and professional peers when he first revealed the painting, including by Matisse, who had loaned him the African mask that triggered Picasso's coup d'oeil. He also faced pushback from the artist Georges Braque, who later joined him in contributing to the Cubist movement.

BE READY FOR THE BLUE EYES

The strategic insight concept encourages exploration, often outside of expected and authorized areas, for the purpose of finding new options and gaining competitive advantage. Your next major rival can appear from anywhere, and likely won't present itself in a way you can predict. This is what happens to the Night's Watch when they first see their own dead reanimated as murderous wights. This is the threat of the Night King and his army. The snarks and grumkins that Tyrion teased Jon Snow about on the road to Castle Black turn out to be real.

Lord Commander Mormont, Jon, Sam, and the Rangers, with the help of Jon's direwolf, Ghost, find the dead bodies of Othor and Jafer Flowers, two of their colleagues, in the forest Beyond the Wall. Sam points out that the dead men have dried blood. They were not freshly killed. The living men try to figure out how the dead men could have been dead long enough that their blood is calcified, dried, yet their bodies haven't decomposed. Someone whispers they should burn the bodies, but Mormont wants to bring them back for evaluation. As they prepare to bring the bodies back to Castle Black, they notice that both dead men have one thing they didn't have during life: blue eyes. This is the way the competition will arrive: difficult to evaluate, slightly changed, transformed by a new big idea—in this case, the Night King's big idea. Don't ignore the opportunity of strategic intuition. Also, don't forget the big idea is also available to your competition.

Every industry in the twenty-first century faces the fact that blue-eyed wights will arrive.

STRATEGIC INTUITION IN THE 1970S

It is not easy to transform an industry. Most days are a success when the right tasks are ticked off the To-Do list. Leadership is a daily, exhausting grind, but some wins transcend the humble checkmarks on the To-Do list. Some wins have the sweet taste of real victory. When completing an important project and recognizing that challenges were met with a quality effort and the goal was achieved . . . that's a great feeling. The client might be an external customer or internal client, but the win is a win. Success might not have changed the world, but it took all we had to give in order to do a solid job and live up to all the expectations. We achieved our goal and can acknowledge it, and feel good about it.

But sometimes coup d'oeil happens. Sometimes strategic intuition comes into play and as leaders we see a big idea and work to achieve it. Our knowledge of what has failed or succeeded triggers the coup d'oeil. It might not be realistic to expect to change the world with our vision, strategic decisions, and leadership skill, but on the other hand we can still choose to pursue a big idea and see where our journey takes us. That's what George Lucas did when he and his producer partner, Gary Kurtz, decided to follow his successful movie *American Graffiti* with a completely different kind of film project.

George Lucas transformed an industry. In addition to the success of the film *Star Wars*, Lucas had the foresight to negotiate for the serial rights and merchandising. This was unheard of in the seventies. Lucas could have demanded more upfront compensation, but went for what was considered a lower-tier bargaining request. As Brian Jay Jones writes in his biography on Lucas, "And no one, not even Lucas, appreciated that by securing sequel and merchandising rights, he had just negotiated for himself a billion-dollar clause. Decades later, Fox executive Gareth Wigan would shake his head in wonder at Lucas's instincts and audacity. 'George was enormously far-sighted, and the studio wasn't, because they didn't know the world was changing,' said Wigan. 'George *did* know the world was changing. I mean, *he changed it.*'"[18]

Lucas couldn't have predicted either the future success of *Star Wars* or the financial benefits of getting the merchandising and serial rights, but he knew he was on the right track. A film director, writer, and friend of Lucas's, John Milius remembered Lucas saying how he was going to make so much money on those "science fiction toys."[19]

The project that achieved this transformation in the industry, *Star Wars*, was entirely unlike the successful film that preceded it: *American Graffiti*. Lucas had a coup d'oeil, a strike of the eye, a flash of insight. He followed that strategic intuition against incredible odds, and almost inevitable failure. He was laughed at many times, yet his effectiveness in the fourth stage—resolution—is impressive. He faced continual strategic choices about his limited resources and was responsible not just for the success of his film, including the merchandising and sequel rights, but also for the creation and success of the special effects company launched during the production of *Star Wars*—

Industrial Light & Magic. How did strategic intuition help George Lucas achieve the dream of his space opera?

Universal Pictures was making a second edit to George Lucas's film *American Graffiti*. The situation was tense. Lucas didn't agree to the edits but was under a signed contract and Ned Tanen at Universal put his foot down. Lucas was also in debt. He gave a handwritten fourteen-page outline for a film project to his agent. Jeff Berg said he was a bit confused by the idea and didn't know how to pitch it. The scribbled pages were bound in a black leather binder with "The Star Wars" in gold lettering on the cover. Lucas compared the project to Buck Rogers and Flash Gordon. He called it a "space opera." "It's James Bond and *2001* combined—super fantasy, capes and swords and laser guns and spaceships shooting each other, and all that sort of stuff. But it's not camp."[20] It was definitely not "camp." It was not ironic. Lucas was in the mix to direct Francis Ford Coppola's *Apocalypse Now*—a film based on Joseph Conrad's novella *Heart of Darkness*—set during the American military conflict with Vietnam. Years later, Lucas and others would mention that *Star Wars* was both influenced by, and a reaction to, the Vietnam War.

Lucas's agent, Jeff Berg, negotiated a deal with 20th Century Fox for *Star Wars*. Alan Ladd Jr. was the studio's new vice president of creative affairs. Berg smuggled him a cut of *American Graffiti*. Ladd loved it, predicted a hit, despite word on the street and Universal Pictures's own doubts about the film. Lucas signed the deal memo with Alan Ladd Jr., or "Laddie" as he was known. "'It was a gamble,' said Ladd, 'and I was betting on Lucas.'"[21]

American Graffiti was a home run and Lucas was pointed in the direction necessary to try to deliver the resolve to get *Star Wars* on the screen.

The production was in constant peril. Actors in the film claimed years later that they were convinced the movie would be rubbish. Filming in Tunisia was difficult, particularly if you were English actor Anthony Daniels, stumbling around in a sweltering C-3PO metal costume. In London, the English crew didn't have a positive, working relationship with Lucas and were heard to refer to Chewbacca as "the dog." They showed little respect for the young director with the weird habit of wearing a baseball cap inside and outside of the studio.

Harrison Ford refused to wear the costume created for him in wardrobe for his role as Han Solo. It involved a high-necked pink collar. He voiced frustration at the convoluted dialogue, telling Lucas that the dialogue might look good on the page, but it was incapable of being spoken out loud for the camera. The film had issues with the budget, locations, acting, script, editing, and most important, the development of the special effects.

Lucas held a private screening of the rough cut for Ladd and a few other Fox executives, including Gareth Wigan. It went well. Wigan, who had supported the project, wept in his seat. He returned home and told his wife, "The most extraordinary day of my life has just taken place."[22]

Then Lucas held a private screening in San Anselmo of the incomplete film for his close friends and professional colleagues, including Martin Scorsese, Brian De Palma, Steven Spielberg, the journalist Jay Cocks, and Alan Ladd Jr. George's wife, the film editor, Marcia Lucas, wept, saying it was terrible. Director Brian De Palma was "carping about everything from Leia's hair to Vader's nondramatic entrance in the opening scene. 'What's all the Force shit?' De Palma thundered. 'Where's the blood when they shoot people?'"[23] Lucas did receive support, but the majority of the feedback, as remembered by people at the private screening of the rough cut, was negative. On the positive side was Spielberg, "I loved it because I loved the story and the characters."[24] Granted, the rough cut was *rough*. With the exception of a few shots, the special effects were still in the process of development by Industrial Light & Magic. The company would succeed beyond anyone's wildest dreams, but at this point, George and Marcia Lucas had intercut footage he had previously recorded from his television of World War II feature films with dogfights between the Axis and Allied powers.

The crawl (the words on the screen providing context to the opening action) and the concept of the Force are both now iconic elements of the movie and of subsequent films in the *Star Wars* series. They were harshly criticized. Lucas faced the idea that he might be making a film that was sophomoric, a failed Disney effort comparable to *The Computer Wore Tennis Shoes*. He worried that adult audiences wouldn't take the film seriously. Director Brian De Palma, referring to Carrie Fisher's coiled braids wrapped at the side of her head in her role as Princess Leia, asked Lucas if they were Danish pastries. He snorted after seeing Darth Vader. "That's your villain? That's the best you can do?"[25]

Despite the naysayers, Spielberg insisted Lucas was on the path to greatness and would achieve it. He just had to execute on his vision. Lucas didn't lose his resolve. He carried his team and project forward in a tense journey that left him physically exhausted, yet professionally successful.

The odds were against Lucas, but his coup d'oeil after the unexpected success of his low-budget film, *American Graffiti*, was to make a movie that reached back to the innocence he remembered as a boy. Lucas was born and raised in Modesto, California. He fondly remembered watching movies and television shows with heroes that fought to succeed against the evil forces conspiring against them. In creating *Star Wars* Lucas lifted ideas from the shows that had inspired him during his youth, with characters such as Buck Rogers and Tarzan. His idea for the film was triggered at the beginning by those same World War II dogfight scenes from his childhood. "One of the key visions I had of the film when I started was of a dogfight in space with spaceships."[26]

As Picasso had lifted from Matisse, Lucas also lifted right at the beginning from Japanese film auteur Kurosawa. From *The Hidden Fortress*, he lifted ideas for his plot, building on the idea of a princess being escorted through dangerous territory by a wise, battle-scarred general. Lucas also used the plot device of two comic foils. With Kurosawa, they were bumbling bureaucrats while with Lucas they were robots; one he even described as looking like the robot in Fritz Lang's 1927 art deco classic *Metropolis*.

Shortly before the film opened on May 25, 1977, Fox began removing the trailers from theaters. The studio was deeply skeptical that the film would find an audience, despite the assurances of Alan Ladd Jr. The general criticism from Fox was that adults weren't responding with positive comments to the trailers. Actor Mark Hamill had a different experience. He saw the trailer with a primarily young audience and they cheered.

Charles Lippincott, who was on the marketing team, said, "Adults hated the trailer and the kids loved it. And I knew then that we were right on target. We had the kids."[27] The prediction was that the top science-fiction film of that year would be 20th Century Fox's one other film in that genre: *Damnation Alley*. What happened instead is that *Star Wars* transformed the film industry. When the lines formed outside of the Westwood theater where *Star Wars* opened, the energy was incredible. (I remember being one of those audiences in Los Angeles as a teenager when the film opened with a theater-shaking rumble and the spaceships filled the screen.) Executives from other studios, driving by the long lines of patient customers viewing and re-viewing the movie, recognized the success of their competitor and bought stock in Fox. The studio stock shot up 1,400 percent and, as Jude Brennan reported in *Forbes* (May 2014), saved the company.

Let's apply the strategic intuition method to the *Star Wars* story:

1) EXAMPLES FROM HISTORY

<u>Learning from what someone did before you and combining those insights in a new way.</u>

Lucas drew on numerous influences in cinematic history when it was time to write, and then direct *Star Wars*. He recorded the dog-fights on WWII movies, cutting twenty hours of film down to eight minutes and studying the movement on the screen. He acknowledged the influence of Joseph Campbell's *The Hero with a Thousand Faces* as a guide, in particular with triggering the concept of a spiritual element in his film: the Force. He has acknowledged the influence of different film genres, including westerns, sci-fi, fantasy, samurai, and war films. He even pursued the possibility of Toshiro Mifune taking the role of Obi-Wan Kenobi, prior to Sir Alec Guinness accepting the role.

2) PRESENCE OF MIND

<u>Having the mental calm to be available for the big idea.</u>

Lucas, who had worked closely with Francis Ford Coppola, had expected the director's role in Coppola's project addressing the horror of Vietnam, *Apocalypse Now*. When that opportunity evaporated for Lucas, he was able to redirect his focus and not be derailed by the loss of a project. He could look in different directions and not be incapacitated over an expectation that had become impossible. Lucas moved on from one desired goal that wasn't available and had the presence of mind to consider new options, while still keeping the Vietnam concept accessible for motivation. "'Most people,' said one associate later, 'have no realization that part of [*Star Wars*] is about a Vietnam situation.'"[28]

3) FLASH OF INSIGHT

<u>Based on applying the first two steps, this is the ability to recognize the big idea.</u>

Lucas was completing work on *American Graffiti*, based on his youth in the Central Valley of California. The film is set in 1962 as a group of high school students graduate and prepare to embark into their adult lives. Filmed on a small budget, the movie made money and was nominated for a number of Academy Awards, including Best Director, Best Screenplay, and Best Picture. Lucas would have been financed by Universal to make similar movies. Instead of taking the approved path, Lucas saw an opportunity to transform the struggles of the conflict in Vietnam—the idea that had intrigued him with Coppola's project—and add an uplifting heroic saga that would match the experiences he had enjoyed as a boy, watching films where the hero wins against evil.

When Universal turned down their option to support *Star Wars*, Lucas pitched the idea to Ladd, focusing primarily on the heroic; it appealed to Ladd who became his chief ally at the studio. Ladd and Lucas shared a similar low-key style in a dramatic industry, and they connected over similar cinematic influences.

Lucas's big idea was to direct his anger at the Vietnam War, with a recognition that the customer didn't need any more dark films with dysfunctional protagonists who confront the enemy and fail. Instead, Lucas would bring spaceships onto the big screen in dogfights; his characters would confront evil in his "space opera" . . . and they would win, not die. This big idea, this coup d'oeil moment, was initially met with disdain and skepticism.

In the late sixties and seventies, there were very few studio films in the sci-fi genre. The films making money almost all had tragic plots driven by antiheroes who failed against powerful forces and/or were driven by internal demons. The successful sci-fi films were dystopian, such as the original *Planet of the Apes* series, *Silent Running*, and, Kubrick's *2001: A Space Odyssey*. They were not films that left the audience cheering. These were not films where a heroic team of overachievers defy the Orwellian control of an evil empire, achieve victory, and are honored by the princess at a grand ceremony.

Lucas wasn't interested in creating a film that was camp . . . or a bubble-gum romp aimed at kids. The film couldn't succeed as a Hero's Journey if there wasn't real danger. When Luke Skywalker returns to his stepparents' farm to find them murdered by stormtroopers, Lucas gives a nod to John Ford's *The Searchers*, lifting from it a brutal moment necessary to send the hero forward. The characters faced real threat.

When it came out in 1977, *Star Wars* was heroic but also edgy and filled with adrenaline. I remember reading an article in *Time* magazine before seeing the movie. The article talked about the gritty world Lucas had created. The future was mechanized, grubby, oil-stained, and violent. The future had metal edges and real people. I wanted to see that future, and it required standing in a long line in Westwood. The adventure was visceral, exciting, and cathartic. Part of Lucas's big idea was that his film merged a gritty sci-fi world with a heroic story.

4) RESOLUTION

<u>Calling on resolve to put the flash of insight into action.</u>

After the success of *American Graffiti*, Lucas put $300,000 aside for working capital. This began the journey of creating the film. In addition to coproducing, writing, and directing the film, Lucas chose to partner in starting the special-effects company that would create the effects necessary for the success of the film: Industrial Light & Magic. If that company hadn't been created and hadn't succeeded at their task, there would have been no way for Lucas to complete the film. When *American Graffiti* was a success, Lucas could have negotiated for more money or points; instead he focused on control of his project and had the resolve to negotiate for serial and merchandising rights, both which turned out to be incredibly lucrative.

Lucas was committed to his project. He ticked off tasks and worked himself to exhaustion. He also followed his coup d'oeil and made his space opera. He was in debt and helped build relationships with a few key allies who supported him, even if they didn't fully grasp his project. Part of Lucas's commitment to himself was to do everything in his power to control the project in order to help himself see his vision fulfilled and to control future versions of that vision he believed would be successful and deliver more opportunities. "I was very careful to say, 'I don't want more money,' Lucas explained later . . . 'I don't want anything financial, but I do want the rights to make these sequels.'"[29]

When coup d'oeil arrived, Lucas followed it, leading himself with strategic intuition. He transformed an industry.

MAKE A DENT IN THE UNIVERSE

Using an approach similar to Lucas's, Steve Jobs transformed another industry.

About a year and a half after the first lines formed outside of theaters for *Star Wars*, he took his small Apple team to Xerox PARC in December 1979. Jobs saw something that revised the way he understood future possibilities. As Walter Isaacson in *Steve Jobs* describes it: "By the fall of 1979 Apple was breeding three ponies to be potential successors to the Apple II workhorse. There was the ill-fated Apple III. There was the Lisa project, which was beginning to disappoint Jobs. And somewhere off Job's radar screen, at least for the moment, there was a small skunkworks project for a low-cost machine that was being developed by a colorful employee named Jef Raskin, a former professor."[30] Raskin wanted to get Jobs to find a way to review what was being done at Xerox PARC, the research center established to create a space to develop new digital ideas. Jobs didn't like Raskin but did approve of another Apple employee, Raskin's former student Bill Atkinson.

Jobs worked out a deal where Xerox could invest in Apple, but it would require Xerox showing Apple what was being developed at Xerox PARC. On their first visit, Jobs, Raskin, and the Lisa team leader, John Couch, were given a presentation of the Xerox Alto. One of the Xerox briefers, Adele Goldberg, wasn't pleased that Xerox was revealing their secrets to a competitor. She tried not to let the Apple team see too much. Jobs and his team were not satisfied. Jobs's team had read up on published papers by Xerox PARC and could tell more was available for them to view. Jobs called Xerox HQ in Connecticut and demanded to see everything. The senior leaders at Xerox HQ insisted that Goldberg and her team provide Jobs with full access to their projects-in-development. The Apple team saw three features, all incredible. "'It was like a veil being lifted from my eyes,' Jobs recalled. 'I could see what the future of computing was destined to be.'"[31]

The Xerox team showed the Apple team that 1) computers could be networked, 2) how object-oriented programming worked, and 3) how graphical user interface (GUI or "gooey") could work with a bitmapped screen. The *gooey* part was the veil that lifted for Jobs. He saw the future. Xerox had tried to commercialize it but had missed the mark, creating a machine that cost $16,595 at retail stores and targeted a networked office model. Jobs, Atkinson, and the Apple team were able to see the new future—to grasp an intuitive insight that was strategic.

Part of the new future they intuited required the solving of a challenge: delivering on the idea of folders nesting within folders graphically on the screen. "Atkinson made it possible to move these windows around, just like shuffling papers on a desk, with those below becoming visible or hidden as you moved the top ones. . . . To create the illusion of overlapping windows requires complex coding that involves what are called 'regions.'"[32] Atkinson believed he had seen the regions capability in place on the screen at Xerox PARC, so he pushed himself hard to re-create it at Apple. "'I got a feeling for the empowering aspect of naïveté,' Atkinson said. 'Because I didn't know it couldn't be done, I was enabled to do it.'"[33] Atkinson had imagined his own coup d'oeil, believing he saw what didn't yet exist. Another element that supported Atkinson's resolve to create what he believed he had seen was Jobs's commitment to the idea that his team could make what he described as "a dent in the universe."

In *Napoleon's Glance*, Duggan references the American philosopher George Santayana, and the idea that "Civilization is cumulative." History is a series of stories and these stories create a narrative of what humanity has experienced. "History is the sum of human experience. In Napoleon's glance, you draw from it 'combinations' to suit the new situation."[34] Napoleon's coup d'oeil describes exactly what Jobs was able to experience after negotiating and blustering his way into Xerox PARC. Jobs and his team didn't want to create the $16,595.00 Xerox Star (which failed). They weren't even on the same page with each other. John Couch wanted to focus on the networked corporate idea; Raskin wanted a small, economic, low-tech device. Jobs wanted to put *a dent into the universe* . . . and create a machine that would transform the industry.

They were one team yet were all looking at different possible combinations and committing to conflicting visions. Their individual coup d'oeils had catalyzed different interpretations. "There was also a clash of visions. Jobs wanted to build a VolksLisa, a simple and inexpensive product for the masses."[35] But even Jobs's vision of an inexpensive product was driven by his expectation of a high-quality, unique product and went against the more humble vision of Jef Raskin. Within time, Raskin was out and Jobs drove the Macintosh to success.

Jobs transformed personal computing. He and his team did what he had insisted they do: make a dent in the universe. Atkinson put it this way: "When Steve turned the Mac into a compact version of the Lisa, it made it into a computing platform instead of a consumer electronic device."[36]

In Robert Cringely's 1996 film about the computer revolution, Jobs talks about how he was "blinded." He saw the graphical user interface and instantly connected the technology with a new possibility. In Cringely's film, Jobs uses the phrase: "It was obvious." He saw the future in a way he hadn't seen it only minutes before. "Xerox's graphical user interface (GUI) came with a mouse to move the cursor around. The GUI combined in Jobs's mind with Apple's small machines. The Xerox machine was the size of a refrigerator, and Xerox had no plans to make a small one. So Jobs set out to make a small one himself. The result was the MacIntosh, the first PC with a GUI."[37] Jobs uses the language of coup d'oeil . . . the strike of the eye. Jobs described this process in a 1996 *Wired* magazine interview excerpted in Duggan's book: "Creativity is just connecting things. When you ask creative people how they did something, they feel a little guilty because they didn't really *do* it, they just *saw* something. It seemed obvious to them after a while. That's because they were able to connect experiences they've had and synthesize new things."[38]

Let's apply the strategic intuition method to the story in Cupertino:

1) EXAMPLES FROM HISTORY

<u>Learning from what someone did before you and combining those insights in a new way.</u>

In terms of Jobs's team at Apple, they attempted to learn from history by understanding their industry, which was in a constant state of change. They had read up on papers relating to Xerox's technological advances, and this prepared them to ask the right questions when they visited Xerox PARC.

2) PRESENCE OF MIND

Having the mental calm to be available for the big idea.

In terms of Steve Jobs, his behavior wasn't calm, but that doesn't mean he didn't have presence of mind. At one point, as he and his team listened to an engineer attempting to entertain them with a word-processing program, he snapped, "Let's stop this bullshit!"[39] and pushed for further information. This presence of mind happened when Jobs called Xerox HQ and insisted on seeing everything. He was not distracted and he accessed what was needed.

3) FLASH OF INSIGHT

Based on applying the first two steps, this is the ability to recognize the big idea.

In terms of Jobs and his team, when Jobs saw the three features revealed, and when the veil lifted for him, he excitedly insisted they move ahead. He demanded to hear how long it would take to implement.

4) RESOLUTION

Calling on the resolve to put the flash of insight into action.

In terms of Jobs, there are many examples of the resolve to get it done. The story above of Atkinson pursuing the "region" concept under the misbelief he had seen it at Xerox PARC captures this stage in action. A related example is how Jobs's direct reports would talk about his "reality distortion field"—the ability to turn reality in his direction by his strong belief. Bud Tribble, a software design engineer, took the phrase from the *Star Trek* episode "Menagerie." The aliens create a new world through the power of their mental capabilities. Tribble used the term for Jobs as both complimentary and cautionary. "It was dangerous to get caught in Steve's distortion field, but it was what led him to actually be able to change reality."[40]

EXECUTION MATTERS

Related to the fourth stage—Resolution—what can be lost in the examples of the creation of the Macintosh and *Star Wars* is how much success depended on execution. The flash of insight hit Steve Jobs and George Lucas. This was the one-percent gift that is delivered with coup d'oeil. But the first three steps only take the leader to the beginning of the journey.

Jobs enlisted a then relatively unknown design company called IDEO, tasking them with figuring out how to make the $400 mouse work significantly better for $15, and move as smoothly on Steve Jobs's jeans as on Formica. (IDEO famously succeeded by using the roller ball from an underarm deodorant can.) As mentioned earlier, Bill Atkinson, the gooey wizard, was motivated to find a way to make the graphical user interface achieve the potential he believed he saw at Xerox PARC succeed. He worked hard and was lucky to survive a car accident. He drove his Corvette into a parked truck. When Jobs visited him at the hospital, Atkinson told him, "Don't worry, I still remember regions."[41]

George Lucas returned from filming in North Africa and realized that Industrial Light & Magic hadn't filmed any of the special effects. He also realized that the film editor provided by Fox Studios had edited the film in a traditional and ineffective series of shots. He later said, "I thought, 'This is it. I really got myself into a mess I'll never get myself out of.'"[42] Lucas was worried that the ship had sunk; he just didn't know it yet. He didn't quit.

Both Jobs and Lucas faced numerous moments where their Resolution to deliver on their coup d'oeil was the difference between success and failure. The energy they found in their resolve to succeed fueled their effective ability to execute on their strategic intuition.

Strategic Intuition doesn't provide a guarantee of success. It does provide a conceptual structure to help leaders prepare themselves for identifying the big idea. When the big idea is available, leadership requires understanding the potential opportunity and the personal responsibility to guide the team to achieve that potential.

STRATEGIC INTUITION AT THE WALL

In Westeros, Lord Commander Snow recognizes that he's faced with an irreconcilable challenge: the Night's Watch will fail if they attempt to defeat both the wildlings and the White Walkers in combat either Beyond the Wall or at the Wall. The Night's Watch doesn't have enough soldiers to provide protection against the great expanse of territory covered by the Wall. If they attempt to guard the Wall and keep the wildlings on the other side, the Free Folk will be slaughtered by White Walkers and will reanimate as wights, with the mission of destroying the Night's Watch and the citizenry of Westeros. Jon Snow understands the future will arrive and it will have blue eyes and be dead and murderous. He also understands that with the right motivation the wildlings will choose to stop fighting the Night's Watch due to the blue-eyed threat. The Free Folk are courageous and committed to their independence, but they don't want to see their friends and families transformed into wights.

As we discussed in chapter 7, Jon negotiates with Tormund Giantsbane, and then orders his direct reports at the Night's Watch to accept the deal. The negotiation will require the wildlings to abandon a cultural history of aggression against the Westerosi. Jon faces many obstacles in the execution of his coup d'oeil and brings an admirable resolve to achieve it. His effort and commitment parallel the efforts of Lucas and Jobs. Lord Commander Snow almost makes it, but stumbles.

Let's apply the strategic intuition model to Lord Commander Jon Snow at the Wall in 302 AC.

1) EXAMPLES FROM HISTORY

Jon Snow has lived with the wildlings and understands their culture. Despite years of conflict against the Night's Watch, the wildlings are human and share human concerns for their families and communities. The differences between the Westerosi and the Free Folk are the results of their different environments—living in Westeros versus living in the badlands Beyond the Wall. The Westerosi expect hierarchical power, including deference to positions of authority, whereas the Free Folk value their independence from authority. Both groups respect courage, both groups are comprised of families and individuals who are both honorable, less honorable, even repellant. Both groups are *human*.

Jon understands that the wildlings are different due to their historical isolation on the north side of the Wall. He also realizes the Free Folk are less of a threat than the White Walkers and the wights. Jon understands the Wall was initially created by Bran the Builder, with the magical help of the Children of the Forest, in order to protect humanity from the White Walkers. Over thousands of years of border tensions, norms developed that the Wall was created to defend Westeros from the wildlings, but the historical purpose of the Wall is to defend humanity. Jon realizes through his *strike of the eye* strategic insight that it is his leadership responsibility to save humanity. Part of him wishes this task had fallen in the hands of Lord Commander Mormont, or Qhorin Halfhand, or his Uncle Benjen, but he acknowledges that it is his job and he will do everything to fulfill it.

2) PRESENCE OF MIND

Jon's time with the Free Folk, including his romantic relationship with Ygritte and the mentorship he receives from Mance Rayder, have opened his thinking to the possibility of alternatives. The sworn oath of the Night's Watch is to protect humanity. The understanding of most of the brothers of the Night's Watch is that they must fight the wildlings. Jon is able to step back and realize the need to follow the advice in the chapter "Warrior Buddha" of Duggan's *Strategic Intuition*— "You find your Way by sorting out what exactly is within your control and what is not, and then finding the particular thoughts and actions within your control that best fit what is beyond your control rather than what you most desire. You do what you can, not what you want."[43] It would be much easier for Lord Commander Snow if he could order a continuation of the strategy of defending the Wall against the wildlings, but he has the presence of mind to recognize what he can't control: the White Walkers and the wights. The wildlings are less of a threat; they are also a potential ally.

Jon can see this option because he can calm his mind regarding the wildlings. He can remove the generational hatred of the wildlings from his point of view. He has lived with them, learned from them, and loved one of them.

3) FLASH OF INSIGHT

"Winterfell is burned and broken and there are no more safe places."[44]
Jon recognizes that the world has changed dramatically, and that he
must use the ideas that work. He takes a loan from the Iron Bank of
Braavos, not liking the interest but understanding that *"when the
choice is debt or death, best borrow."*[45] Jon is leading in crisis. Confronted
by the White Walkers, the choice is either death, or a financial debt to
the Bank of Braavos—and partnering with the wildlings. Lord Commander Snow sees his strategic insight and chooses to act on it. The
debts are worth it.

4) RESOLUTION

As the plan goes into action for the wildlings to cross the Wall, Jon recognizes the difficult leadership path he has chosen. "Every choice had its
risks, every choice its consequences. He would play the game to its conclusion."[46] Jon has the resolution, the courage to carry his strategic insight forward. He stumbles in the execution, which has a high cost.

RESOLUTION, EXECUTION,
AND RESISTANT FOLLOWERS

Execution, including his inability to persuade his followers, is what
takes down Jon Snow at Castle Black. He had the resolve to achieve
his goal, but resolve needs to translate into effective execution.

Jon Snow knows the White Walkers created some kind of bargain
with Craster and are eager for infant male children. Jon knows the
wildlings are a military resource for the White Walkers. The wildlings
understand this, too. Bowen Marsh insists to Jon Snow that they all
swore an oath. The Bastard from Winterfell flips the script and tells his
angry colleagues that the logic behind inviting the wildlings across the
Wall is to support the intention of the Night's Watch's oath. The purpose of the Watch is not to protect Westerosi, but to protect humanity.

This moment is one of Lord Commander Snow's great phrases delivered in misjudgment. He offers his insight to his direct reports as if
he provides a key that will unlock the resistance of his followers—

Marsh, Thorne, and the rest—and connect them to his vision. Snow doesn't understand, or won't accept, that he is in a situation that can't be solved by orders, or even by a quick flourish of argument. As discussed in chapter 7, this situation needs the benefit of persuasion.

Commands worked for Steve Jobs and George Lucas, but the stakes weren't quite as high for the personal computer and film teams as they were for the brothers of the Night's Watch. Jon Snow needed to do more to offer his followers the chance to align themselves with his vision.

Strategic intuition almost delivered success for Jon Snow, the Free Folk, and the Night's Watch. Fortunately for Snow and the Known World, he and his team will expand and they will get another chance.

THE LEADER'S JOURNEY: MAGIC FLIGHT

Sam Tarly was recognized for his unique skills by Jon Snow, who successfully pitched for Sam to be taken into the service of Maester Aemon and removed from the sadistic training of Ser Alliser Thorne. When Jon is asked if he wants to swear to the Old Gods in taking his oath to the Night's Watch, Sam decides to join him and swear his faith to the Old Gods, too. Sam recognizes that he needs to pivot, and swearing in as a brother at the Wall, including selecting a new religion, will be that moment.

The past has to be the past and Sam must leave the past, including his father's judgment, behind. Sam must move forward. On his flight back to the Wall with Gilly and her baby, exhausted and lost, Sam drops to his knees and prays to the Old Gods, the gods he chose over the Seven. "The dusk was deepening, the leaves of the weirwood rustling softly, waving like a thousand blood-red hands."[47] In a short amount of time, Sam has learned that his team faces a threat far beyond his initial fear of the wildlings. Sam has also seen that dragonglass can kill a White Walker.

The thirteenth stage of Joseph Campbell's cycle is known as Magic Flight. This stage recognizes that the hero is a regular person facing great odds. Sam returns against such odds, with Gilly, her baby, and the boon of the dragonglass. The obsidian offers something vital to the survival of humanity against the White Walkers. Campbell argues that the arrival of the boon, if the story is to inspire us, can't be delivered by superhuman ability—by some power beyond our individual abilities—and it can't be delivered by our failure. Sam has to build the strength and resources Beyond the Wall, to return with the boon, the magical gift, the power, to Castle Black. "If the monomyth is to fulfill its promise, not human failure or superhuman success but human success is what we shall have to be shown."[48]

Sam Tarly and Jon Snow go on separate journeys Beyond the Wall. Jon joins Qhorin Halfhand's team to search the Skirlings for wildling lookouts. Sam returns to a Castle Black organization that has been decimated by the attack of the Night King's army at the Fist of the First Men, and by the Mutiny at Craster's Keep. When the two friends are reunited, they will face the very real challenge of finding a solution to the threat of the White Walkers.

Jon Snow generates the big idea of inviting the wildlings to join the Night's Watch. He stumbles in his efforts, but his strategic intuition is put into action and survives even his death.

As Samwell Tarly returns with the dragonglass and lives the stage of Magic Flight, Jon Snow also returns from his time with the wildlings, aware of their humanity. He attempts to put his strategic insight into action against the terrible reality of the dead horde marching toward their community and their country.

Both Sam and Jon have brought boons back to their community at the Wall. They have survived Magic Flight, and their journeys will continue.

GOING FORWARD

Ninety-nine percent of the time, our leadership doesn't require a big idea. Most of leadership is a process of executing on the plan developed based on the strategic analysis and conclusions on what needs to get done. But one percent of the time a big idea arrives, either as an insight to solve an irreconcilable challenge or as a transforming opportunity. The former is what happened when Jon Snow realized he could bring the Free Folk to join the Night's Watch. The latter is what happened when Picasso held the African mask Matisse showed him and saw an idea for a new painting. Picasso and Snow were both struck with a glance, a strike of the eye, a flash of insight, a coup d'oeil.

Both Picasso and Snow received ideas based on historical knowledge of the situation, combined with the presence of mind to allow the idea to arrive and not be ignored. Both men, the Spanish painter and the Westerosi border commander, acknowledged the flash of insight and had the resolution to do the work to carry that flash of insight forward. In the seventies, George Lucas and Steve Jobs saw a path forward that they hadn't seen before. They followed it with tenacity, transforming their industries, making two big dents in the universe.

There is a method to elicit this flash of insight. Keep yourself accessible to the method. Recognize when the moment arrives. Allow the possibility that you may have a chance to make a dent in the universe. Don't focus so hard you become blind to strategic intuition. Allow your eyes to see what others may be too busy and blind to notice. Invite the big idea. Find dragonglass.

KILL THE WHITE WALKER!

HOW TO DO BETTER

Horn Hill is a hard place to grow up if you are overweight and prefer books and music to hunting. But Horn Hill is no harder than the environment north of the Wall, where Sam reinvents himself, or the Citadel where Sam is tasked with cleaning bedpans and sweeping and mopping up blood-soaked body organs. After his first day in the Castle Black training yard, Sam tells Jon he won't improve. "I never do better." The reader can relate. We have all faced fear, and almost all of us have confronted some level of disrespect in pursuit of a paycheck. Each of us has faced our own Ser Alliser Thorne: the person in charge of the resources who isn't our fan.

THE LORD OF HAM

How then does Samwell get from "I never do better" to killing a White Walker, defending a wildling woman and her infant, taking her as his lover, and traveling to the distant Citadel to heal Jorah Mormont of the incurable greyscale? How does Sam change and do better?

Sam was not raised with an overabundance of what ethologists call *secure attachment*—the strength that results from being loved. When Samwell returns to Horn Hill with Gilly and the baby, he is met with genuine warmth by his mother, Lady Melessa, and by his sister, Talla, but there is no secure attachment from his father, Lord Randyll.

Gilly explodes at Lord Tarly's disrespect of Sam, pointing out that he killed a White Walker and a Thenn warg and is a greater warrior than either Randyll or the chosen son, Dickon. Gilly is correct. Sam has developed and performed in crisis at great risk to himself and in support of those around him. He has come a long way from cowering in the dirt of Castle Black.

Sam doesn't see himself as courageous, compared to his father and younger brother, but he does see himself as having a mission. He can assess his flaws realistically and still stay focused on a positive future for Westeros, despite what he knows about the White Walkers. He is driven to support the survival of his community. He doesn't want to see civilization die on a luminescent White Walker blade.

Martin E. P. Seligman, professor of psychology at the University of Pennsylvania and a past president of the American Psychological Association, is a leading motivational expert and an authority on the concept of "learned helplessness." In *Authentic Happiness: Using the New Positive Psychology to Realize Your Potential for Lasting Fulfillment*, Seligman refers to Barbara Fredrickson's work on positive emotions and evolution. "Fredrickson claims that positive emotions have a grand purpose in evolution. They broaden our abiding intellectual, physical, and social resources, building up reserves we can draw upon when a threat or opportunity presents itself."[1] People like us are better when we are in a positive mood, which sounds reasonable. "Friendship, love, and coalitions are more likely to cement."[2] All three of these will happen for Samwell Tarly.

Positive emotions help us expand our resources—intellectual, physical, and social—and build up strength for confronting threats. Happiness can make us more adaptable and it can make us more altruistic. *"A positive mood jolts us into an entirely different way of thinking from a negative mood."*[3] If we are negative, we focus on what is wrong and try to eliminate it. This is Sam's perspective when he arrives at Castle Black. He expects to be shamed and hurt. He tries to avoid it, but he doesn't try *that* hard. Part of him has quit inside and accepts the pain and shame. Beyond the Wall, he learns to see past his short-term suffering. His view expands to focus on Gilly, Little Sam, the brotherhood of the Night's Watch, Westeros, and the fate of humanity.

Sam doesn't fight back when battered on his first day on the training ground, but in his first days as a recruit, he takes steps that prepare him for his future success, which depends on his capacity to see past his fear. His first smart move is that he is honest with Jon Snow. He is not positive, but his honesty gives Jon the motivation to help Sam. This positive emotion from Jon is returned when Sam points out to him the advantages of his new role as direct report to Lord Commander Mormont.

Sam gains a small amount of secure attachment from Jon. Jon orders, persuades, and threatens the Night's Watch within his influence to take it easy on Sam in upcoming training classes. Ser Alliser Thorne rages, but the young men don't crush Sam's spirit. They don't beat him each day into a bloody pulp. They protect him by pulling their punches and their strikes. Sam doesn't reject this positivity but accepts it and is energized by it. Sam finds Jon one night and tells him that he knows Jon did something to protect him. Sam calls Jon his first friend. Jon offers Sam something beyond simple friendship: partnership in a brotherhood.

Prior to his arrival at Castle Black, there was a brutal, soul-crushing day when Sam's father, Randyll, told Sam he wasn't worthy of their Valyrian blade, Heartsbane. Sam managed to listen to his father's hatred and not let it destroy him. Scared and pessimistic at Castle Black, can Sam's pessimism be changed to optimism? As Seligman writes when asking if a pessimist can change to an optimist: "The answer to that question is yes."[4]

When Sam journeys Beyond the Wall, he finds a way to transform his pessimism and balance it with optimism. Seligman writes about *depressive realism* and how people who are depressed are "accurate judges of how much skill they have, whereas happy people think they are much more skillful than others judge them to be."[5] Bloody and bruised in the sparring session at Castle Black, Sam is a depressed and accurate evaluator of his lack of fighting skill and courage, but he also can't see past his pessimism and depression to imagine a situation where his strengths would be valuable to the Night's Watch. This changes as Sam's purpose becomes clear to him.

Sam's accuracy at evaluating his limitations fades, along with his depression, when he decides to help Gilly and her newborn infant flee Craster's Keep, when he takes on the challenge of healing Jorah Mormont of greyscale at the Citadel, and when he attempts to persuade the Conclave to believe Bran's letter. Sam transforms from a depressive realist to an engaged optimist.

In the preface to *Authentic Happiness*, Martin Seligman writes how psychology has been focused on mental illness, and it is time for a science that can "understand positive emotion, build strength and virtue, and provide guideposts for finding what Aristotle called the 'good life.'"[6] He makes the point that people don't want to just fix weaknesses: "They want lives imbued with meaning, and not just to fidget until they die."[7]

Seligman gets at a point that drives Joseph Campbell's Hero's Journey: we crave meaning. We will confront risk in order to find our purpose and to achieve victory. We would rather fight than fidget. When the motivation is right, as Sam's journey shows, we will face sacrifice, even death, in order to win, and fulfill a sense that life has meaning.

Without the adventure, we won't have meaning and won't have success. Samwell Tarly arrives at Castle Black a fidgeting mess, but this changes. Alliser Thorne pits the muscular Halder against Sam. The fat recruit is beaten to the ground. He wants to quit, but he doesn't. He builds an alliance with Jon.

Seligman points out that depressed people are "evenhanded in assessing success and failure."[8] This is an apt description of Sam when he arrives at Castle Black. He has no problem identifying himself as a *coward*. That honesty helps him with Jon, but honesty merged with deep pessimism won't secure the trust of colleagues. As Grenn points out after watching Sam take that first beating from Halder in the Castle Black yard, "'Nobody likes cravens,' he said uncomfortably. 'I wish we hadn't helped him. What if they think we're craven too?'"[9]

Jon makes an effort to connect with Sam in the dining hall, and asks him if he has seen the Wall. "'I'm fat, not blind,' Samwell Tarly said. 'Of course I saw it, it's seven hundred feet high.'"[10] Sam has the courage of self-assessment; he's honest, perceptive, has intellectual curiosity, and is fascinated by history. Since history is returning to Westeros in a big way with the reboot of the White Walkers, the loss of Sam would be the loss of a significant resource in confronting the threat.

There is a facial paralysis condition known as the Moebius syndrome. People with this affliction can't smile. Their faces are incapable of showing emotion. They are unable to reflect and react to positive emotion in a way that other people can recognize. It is very hard for them to have friendships. This is a tragic condition. As Seligman points out: "When the sequence of feeling a positive emotion, expressing it, eliciting a positive emotion in another, and then responding goes awry, the music that supports the dance of love and friendship is interrupted."[11] Despite his difficult experiences in Horn Hill and his first days at Castle Black, Samwell Tarly has the advantage of being able to smile. He finds his way forward in the dance of love and friendship. He builds a relationship with Jon and Maester Aemon. He finds a place for himself, despite constant challenges, such as when he returns with Gilly and Little Sam, only to be harassed. When two brothers of the Night's Watch attempt to assault Gilly in the Castle Black kitchen, Sam steps in to defend her. One of his "brothers" viciously beats him, but Sam perseveres.

OPTIMISM AND HAPPINESS

Seligman was asked to assist the United States Military Academy in helping new recruits at West Point persevere in the harsh, violent, demanding reality of training to be Army leaders. The key differentiator in why plebes chose to persevere through the brutal training of Beast Barracks, according to Seligman's research, was optimism. If they viewed everything that was negative as permanent, they quit. As with Sam at Castle Black and the plebes at West Point, optimism is the difference between the decision to fidget or fight. The good news is that "basic pessimism is not fixed and unchangeable. You can learn a set of skills that free you from the tyranny of pessimism and allow you to use optimism when you choose."[12] It takes conscious effort to build our optimism, but it can be done.

In *Learned Optimism: How to Change Your Mind and Your Life*, Seligman writes: "Optimism has an important place in some, though not all, realms of your life. It is not a panacea. But it can protect you against depression; it can raise your level of achievement; it can enhance your physical well-being; it is a far more pleasant mental state to be in."[13] He points out that pessimism also has a role. When the stakes are high, pessimism offers a cautioning element that can keep us from making poor decisions.

In *A Dance with Dragons*, the Dornishman Quentyn Martell travels to Meereen to persuade Daenerys to be his bride. Daenerys has just chosen to wed the crafty Hizdahr zo Loraq for political alliance. But even if Dany were still single, Quentyn, also known as *Frog*, would not have succeeded in his marriage quest. His link to Dorne has limited political appeal and he's not handsome. Quentyn also has an overabundance of optimism and it does not serve him well. He attempts to steal Daenerys's dragons. When confronting risky endeavors, optimism should be balanced with pessimism. Quentyn's journey ends with a dragon erasing him with fire breath.

In terms of optimism and pessimism in risky situations, Samwell Tarly finds that balance.

One of the challenges of operating with too much pessimism is that "depressed people often take much more responsibility for bad events than is warranted."[14] It is important to not see your situation as permanent. Sam sees his situation as permanent when he arrives at Castle Black, but once he crosses the Wall on the Great Ranging North, his excitement lifts him from obsessing about the permanence of his flaws. He develops what Seligman calls a *temporary style for bad events*.

It could be that when Sam swears himself to the Old Gods, he takes a step in ownership of his future that blurs the wounding insults of his father Lord Tarly. It could be that lifting the Night's Watch cloak from the dirt on the Fist of the First Men helps Sam out of the narrowness of what he has experienced up to that point of his life, connecting him with the history that fascinates him. He discovers dragonglass. It could be the action of knifing the White Walker; it could be his attraction for Gilly and willingness to put himself in harm's way to protect her and her infant. Sam changes. He chooses to believe that bad events can be averted; a negative future can be transformed. Sam is changed by this choice and starts to do better.

Sam has low self-esteem and critiques his ability to fight and do manual labor, but he develops a more important ability. He finds *temporary* and *specific*—to use Seligman's terms—ways to explain the negative. This is necessary to live with hope. He believes he can protect Gilly and Little Sam, and puts himself in harm's way to get them to the other side of the Wall. In Castle Black he continues to find ways to protect them in an environment that could turn violent at any moment. The negative isn't permanent. He believes he *will do better* and protect mother and child.

Optimism recognizes negative things as temporary and specific, not pervasive and permanent. This is not where Sam begins when Halder hammers him with a wood sword and his mouth fills with blood, but this is where Sam ends when he returns to Castle Black with Gilly and Little Sam. As Seligman puts it, "The pessimist seems to be at the mercy of reality, whereas the optimist has a massive defense against reality that maintains good cheer in the face of a relentlessly indifferent universe."[15] A shot of pessimism would have helped Quentyn Martell in Meereen, but the overwhelming waves of pessimism that kept Sam cowering in the dirt, unwilling to stand and fight, wouldn't have helped him face the White Walker. Optimism is the reason Sam wins Gilly and protects her and Little Sam.

A pessimistic explanatory style is the foundation of depressed thinking. "Depressed people cannot decide among alternatives."[16] Sam changed from a young man who saw no future for himself, who lived with the reality that his father hated him and would be pleased to kill him, to the Sam who decided between alternatives. He would help Gilly and Little Sam escape. He would keep them in Moletown. He would take them with him to stay with his parents in Horn Hill. He would change his mind and take them to the Citadel. He would choose to return with them to Winterfell. Each choice provided risks and rewards. Sam was optimistic and made decisions. He wasn't foolishly optimistic like Quentyn Martell. He balanced a realistic understanding of the perils with an ability to make important decisions. Sam focused on improving the future for himself, his friends, his lover, and her infant son.

THE GREAT RANGING NORTH AND OPTIMISM

Bivouacked at the Fist of the First Men, the isolated ruins of an ancient fort, a raised segment of terrain favored by Rangers when traveling in the badlands Beyond the Wall, Sam uncovers a cache of dragonglass—what the maesters call obsidian—stashed with a horn. The curious trove of black stone, carved into arrowheads and blades has been buried in a Night's Watch cloak. The cloak hasn't long been in the dirt. The material isn't rotted. Why did a Ranger bury this unusual stash? As Sam holds the dragonglass, a distant Night's Watch horn signals a dire warning that hasn't happened in over a thousand years: *White Walkers*.

After the bloodbath at Craster's Keep, Craster's daughter-wives warn Sam that he better escape with Gilly and the infant. Craster's blue-eyed sons will arrive, searching for the human child. "If you don't take him, *they* will."[17]

"Looking out for number one is more characteristic of sadness than of well-being."[18] Sam doesn't allow sadness to stop him. He chooses to help Gilly and Little Sam. But he is terrified on the attempt to escape the wights and White Walkers. He falls on his knees and prays to the Old Gods he chose over the Seven. "Whether Jon's gods had heard him or not he could not say."[19] Gods give strength. Sam knew the Seven had done nothing for him. The Old Gods might help.

Sam defends Gilly and Little Sam, knifing the White Walker under the tree where the ravens squawked in alarm. Samwell is far beyond worrying about his weaknesses. He is far more worried he will fail the woman he loves. In *Authentic Happiness*, Martin Seligman explains: "When we are happy, we are less self-focused."[20]

Positive emotions help people endure pain better and take more precautions to live a healthy life. Positive emotions can reverse negative emotions. Seligman makes two important points that relate to Samwell Tarly:

1) happy people handle bad things better, and

2) secure attachment connects us with people and makes us less self-focused.

But this doesn't mean positive emotions protect us from pain, suffering, and loss.

As Seligman writes, "Life inflicts the same setbacks and tragedies on the optimist as on the pessimist, but the optimist weathers them better."[21] This doesn't mean the optimist will avoid the fate that waits for each of us. "The good news is that pessimists can learn the skills of optimism and permanently improve the quality of their lives. Even optimists can benefit from learning how to change. Almost all optimists have periods of at least mild pessimism, and the techniques that benefit pessimists can be used by optimists when they are down."[22]

People struggling with challenges such as depression want the depression to lessen, but they often care about the fulfillment of meaning, of purpose. As Seligman puts it, "Experiences that induce positive emotion cause negative emotion to dissipate rapidly."[23] The fulfillment of meaning, the achievement of virtues and strengths that seemed out of reach, can be a barrier against psychological disorders. The positive emotion Samwell feels when Gilly trusts him and treats him with respect can provide a buffer against the residue of depression from his father's enthuiasm to murder him. Gilly's connection with him is an attachment that builds his resilience to lift the obsidian dagger against the White Walker.

Sam with Gilly and her baby is not looking out for number one. Negative emotions keep reminding us that we are engaged in a win-lose battle. Beyond the Wall—in an extreme win-lose environment—Sam is focused on helping people he wants to help.

Sir Richard Branson, entrepreneur, investor, philanthropist, and founder of Virgin Group, is quoted as saying, "My attitude has always been, if you fall flat on your face, at least you're moving forward. All you have to do is get back up and try again."[24] The cowardly disinherited former lordling that wouldn't defend himself on his first day at Castle Black can't persuade the conclave of archmaesters at the Citadel to realize the threat to humanity, yet he has come a long way from cowering in the dirt. The Sam that said "I never do better" has a new expectation of himself. He does better. He expects to keep doing better. His friends and his lover also expect him to do better.

Being a fat lordling dressed in Horn Hill finery didn't mean Sam couldn't or wouldn't fight. Sam was overwhelmed by pessimism. North of the Wall, Sam fights for his life and then fights for Gilly and Little Sam. Seligman suggests doing an exercise called "Your ABC Record." The goal is to recognize that there is a connection between adversity, one's beliefs about that adversity, and one's insights about the consequences.

EXERCISE #1: YOUR ABC RECORD

"Pessimists can in fact learn to be optimists . . . by learning a new set of cognitive skills."[25] The ABC Record (Adversity—Belief—Consequences) exercise is from Seligman's *Learned Optimism: How to Change Your Mind and Your Life*.[26] This is an exercise aimed to help us engage with adversity and practice not letting our thoughts instantly form beliefs that are counterproductive. This instant forming of thoughts into beliefs will often happen below the surface of our awareness. The problem is that these beliefs have consequences. "The beliefs are the direct causes of what we feel and what we do next."[27] What we feel and do next can range from the Sam who gave up in the dirt, his mouth bloodied in the Castle Black sparring pit, to the proactive Sam who chose to raise the dragonglass blade and kill the Other. Seligman's exercise is aimed at teaching us how to break the cycle of giving up. First, we need to see the relationship between adversity, belief, and consequence. Second, we need to see how this ABC dynamic happens in our own life, and then dispute the limiting beliefs and identify the energizing options that are available to us. The ABC Record exercise is focused on gaining clarity about the adversity you face, the beliefs you are linking to that adversity, and the consequences of those beliefs. Is the chain of connections true or built on unnecessary assumptions?

> **Step One**: Write down a moment of adversity you have faced in your life. This doesn't have to be a big adversity but could be as simple as a moment something didn't go right or someone treated you unfairly or in a way you didn't appreciate.
>
> **Step Two**: Write down what you thought when that event occurred.
>
> **Step Three**: Write down insights from that belief.

For example:

> 1) Your boss walks past you in the hall and doesn't say hello.
>
> 2) You think, "My boss is not satisfied with my work."
>
> 3) You feel: depressed and worried about your job.

Or:

> 1) Your boss walks past you in the hall and doesn't say hello.
>
> 2) You think, "My boss is overworked. I wonder what I can do to help?"
>
> 3) You feel: energized and eager to offer support.

It is important to separate the thoughts from the feelings. Feelings will go under C for consequences. Your feelings aren't your beliefs.

They are the way you interpret your belief of the adversity moment. Seligman suggests that pessimistic beliefs—or explanations—will encourage passivity or a powerless victim attitude. This is the Samwell Tarly who said to Jon Snow on his first day at the Night's Watch: "I never do better."[28]

If we can keep our ABC Record and recognize that our pessimistic beliefs are subjective and not necessarily true, we can raise our chance that our responses to Adversity—the decisions we arrive at with our Beliefs and Consequences—are optimistic and will energize us. We can take ownership for our beliefs and not have them just wash over us and overwhelm us.

There are two ways for us to handle our pessimistic beliefs. We can ignore them, distract ourselves, and move forward. Or we can dispute them. Seligman writes that "disputed beliefs are less likely to recur when the same situation presents itself again."[29] We can try to turn away from the negative belief, but we are much better off if we directly confront the belief. If we dispute a negative belief, we can often change our pessimistic interpretation into a positive one.

DISPUTE, DON'T JUST BELIEVE

We need to recognize that our beliefs are only beliefs, not facts. This is difficult. Over twelve years ago, I was forced to stop running and play basketball due to pain in my knees, hips, and legs. I believed this was the long-term trauma caused by a knee surgery I had gone through in my twenties. I didn't realize that one of my hips was, in the words of the first doctor I saw, "like the hip of a ninety-year-old man." I was forty-five years old.

The doctor, who looked to be in his midthirties, told me to get a cane and give up exercising until I could have surgery. He said I would probably be authorized for a hip replacement when I was closer to my midfifties. Ten years walking with a cane didn't seem a viable option to me, but I was caught in the belief that this was the only option. I was overwhelmed with the pessimistic belief my only option was a cane, painkillers, and waiting to age.

My first son had just been born two months earlier. It was difficult to see myself leaning on a cane for the first ten years of his life. People have faced worse, certainly, but was this reality? The consequences of my belief were confusion and increasing lack of motivation, verging on feelings of depression. After a variety of visits for different opinions, I was evaluated by a chiropractor who also specialized in sports therapy. He helped me dispute my beliefs. He worked with me on a variety of exercises to manage my hips and knees. I began taking demanding martial arts classes in kung fu, boxing, and jujitsu. Rather than exercise less, as I had been cautioned by the first doctor, I exercised more. It helped. I would later find out that I had an arthritic condition and the exercise was beneficial. I was able to dispute the belief and change the consequences.

The adversity was that I faced real pain and physical limitation. The belief, based on the first diagnosis, was that nothing could help me until I had surgery in ten years. The consequences were an assumption that I wouldn't find relief from the pain. The martial arts helped. My new doctor recommended immediate hip surgery. Within six years, I had two hip replacements and one knee replacement. The arthritic condition required exercise and surgery; resting my body only aggravated the condition.

The first hip replacement was hard to face, but the result was immediately beneficial. I still remember how I clung to what optimism was available through the coaching of my surgeon and chiropractor/physical therapist. I will never forget the optimism and happiness that washed over me the morning after the surgery. My original negative beliefs were not facts. They needed to be disputed.

Seligman recommends doing the ABC Record and then bringing in D—Disputation—and E—Energization. He doesn't recommend that you hunt for adversity but rather notice it when it arrives. Dispute the negative beliefs. Attack them and record your answers to ABCDE. The goal is to add the disputation to the first three stages, pushing back at the beliefs.

My first son is now thirteen years old; my basketball game isn't impressive, but I can manage half-court games with him and my ten-year-old son. I can hike with my dog. Ducking my head and hiding from the physical ailments had worked, until it didn't work. The adversity was real. The belief I had accepted from the first doctor's evaluation led to beliefs and consequences that triggered pessimism and a growing depression in me. I was like Sam in the dirt at Castle Black. My mouth was filled with blood and I didn't want to get up, but when I did, it was easier to fight. With the help of the right doctor, I could dispute the belief and find new consequences and new energy.

We don't have to be Samwell Tarly, slammed in the head through our helm, nose bleeding, fallen in the dirt, to be triggered by pessimism. Evolution has wound us up to be ready for threats. If we hadn't been good at avoiding threats, our DNA wouldn't be here, surviving in us. Habitual pessimistic thinking is the natural extension of a caution built deep inside of us to help us avoid being attacked by a predator. "Habitual pessimistic thoughts merely carry this useful process one detrimental step further. They not only grab our attention; they circle unceasingly through our minds."[30]

One of the ways to dispute this pessimistic noise is to fight past the tendency to believe the negative. The ABC Record exercise will help you respond to adversity with clarity and not spiral into negative consequences, based on beliefs that can be disputed. Energize yourself to take productive actions.

Dispute Optimism

There will be times in your work when it is helpful to dispute your optimism. As Seligman writes, "The genius of evolution lies in the dynamic tension between optimism and pessimism continually correcting each other."[31] As we move through the day, we balance venturing forward with optimism and retrenching with pessimism. This is a good thing. Seligman explains that pessimism offers a constructive element in our lives. Moments of pessimistic constraint can pull us back from the risk and help us think more carefully about our actions before jumping into a situation where we are not prepared.

It took close to four years of leading internal debate for Deloitte LLP's CEO, Barry Salzberg, to sell the U.S. firm of Deloitte on a transformational idea. It took time, but Salzberg succeeded. The idea was based on his decision to stop outsourcing all Deloitte's employee training. Salzberg believed the solution was to build and support a Deloitte training facility. "Believing that learning and development were critical parts of the people strategy refresh, Salzberg initiated a complete evaluation of Deloitte's learning and development agenda. At the annual partners, principals, and directors meeting in 2006, Salzberg held a session in which the attendees were asked to evaluate the fundamental question of whether a significant investment in learning and development should be in a physical university or a virtual one. They called it the bricks-versus-clicks debate."[32]

In 2009, the groundbreaking ceremony happened for Deloitte University, but when Salzberg discusses his leadership journey in the classroom, he explains why it almost didn't happen: he was too optimistic.

At a cocktail party the night before he was to make a presentation to the Board for approval of the project, he was approached by a colleague. She told him not to bring the project to the Board because it wouldn't pass. Barry was surprised. It seemed obvious that he was suggesting the right path forward for the firm. She said, "They haven't been on your journey."[33]

Salzberg worked all night with his team to adjust their presentation. He realized he wasn't going to reach his goal, and he needed to change his plan. Optimism almost killed the opportunity. He was thankful that an honest ally had cautioned him while there was still time. He needed to dispute his optimism. Once he did, and the presentation was adjusted, he asked the Board if they would join him on a journey of considering the choice of Deloitte University. The journey worked. Salzberg's willingness to dispute his optimism also allowed him the chance to use persuasion to confront his challenge.

Salzberg offers a related learning to apply to similar leadership challenges: "Never underestimate the importance of proper socialization of your stakeholders."[34]

EXERCISE #2: WHAT IS YOUR STORY?

Jim Loehr, founder of the Human Performance Institute, writes about our capacity to reshape the stories we use to understand our life. He offers two definitions for optimism. One, from psychologists Michael Scheier and Charles Carver, is *dispositional optimism*—which is the idea that we have enough resources in our world for everyone to benefit. This interpretation of optimism may be motivational in most twenty-first century economies but won't help much in Westeros or Essos, where almost every character struggles with the realities of a zero-sum game.

Loehr refers to a second option that fits into George R. R. Martin's fictional Known World yet it is also motivating for us in our world:

"The second definition, largely subjective, is that optimism represents a constructive way to partly neutralize bad events." Loehr argues for the latter definition because he suggests dangers can exist with too much optimism "once it strays far enough from reality." He argues we need to recognize consequences in order to guide ourselves to live our lives with clarity. "When there's too much negativity, the environment becomes toxic, granted, but when there's too much positive feedback, the environment departs from reality."[35] The challenge is to balance the optimistic with the pessimistic.

Seligman suggests that when you are in a situation focused on an achievement or improving the way you feel, including improving your health, use optimism. If you are stepping into a leadership situation that requires inspiring people, use optimism.

On the other hand, if your aim is to plan to confront risk or uncertainty, or if you are offering guidance to people facing a difficult future, and if you want to build sympathy with people who are confronting trouble, don't start with optimism. You might use it later, once empathy and confidence have been established. You should evaluate the cost of failure in a given situation. If the cost is high, optimism is the wrong strategy.[36]

In Sam's case, the pessimistic reality of death and betrayal is never far away. Sam balances optimism and pessimism. The optimism is necessary to encourage action. He also needs that optimism to be able to move forward and see past the pessimistic, low self-esteem his father's abusive parenting imposed on him, not to mention the reality of the White Walkers. Loehr asks the reader to apply honesty to appraising one's life, one's beliefs, and behaviors. Sam is honest.

Optimism doesn't forgive our bad habits, but it can help us respond to life-threatening challenges. Optimism can help us stand up, blood in our mouth, and keep fighting. This is what Loehr refers to when he talks about *taking control of your story*. We have the ability to redefine our story by asking ourselves what we believe and seeing if those beliefs stand up to the test of reality. We can train ourselves to push forward.

This requires bringing honesty to understand the old story that has been driving you, and recognizing your capacity to change it, rewriting yourself into a new story. Loehr's model for moving from the old story to the new story involves **Purpose—Truth—Action**. "With those three principles in your pocket, you can summon your deepest intelligence and wisdom to protect yourself from all forms of sinister indoctrination and faulty storytelling, bad influences from without and within; armed with those three principles, you are virtually guaranteed to keep your story vital, moving, productive, fulfilling."[37] I have used this structure in my work with graduate business students:

> **Purpose:** What is my ultimate purpose? What am I living for? Why do I do what I do?

> For Samwell Tarly, the answer has to do with his love for and protection of Gilly and her baby, plus his commitment to help Jon Snow protect humanity from the Night King.

> **Truth:** Is the story I'm telling true? Does it conform to known facts?

> Sam Tarly knows the threat of the White Walkers and the wights is true.

> **Action:** In the words of Jim Loehr: "With my purpose firmly in mind, along with a confidence about what is really true, what actions will I now take to make things better, so that my ultimate purpose and my day-to-day life are better aligned?"[38]

> For Samwell Tarly, this is exemplified by his choice to leave the Citadel, the center of higher learning, and return to work with his colleague Jon Snow to try to fulfill his purpose, under a recognition of the truth: the threat of the White Walkers.

ALIGNING YOUR STORY WITH YOUR ACTIONS

Fill out the following questions with the aim of getting perspective on how to align your purpose with the truth in order to guide yourself to the most effective choice of actions.

> **Purpose:** What is my ultimate purpose? What am I living for? What principle, what goal, what end?

Truth: Is the story I'm telling myself true? Does it conform to known facts? Grounded in objective reality?

Action: With my purpose firmly in mind, along with a confidence about what is really true, what actions will I now take to make things better, so that my ultimate purpose and my day-to-day life are aligned?

Loehr's **Purpose—Truth—Action** model reminds us to decide which of our habits contribute to our successful capacity to align our efforts with the results that matter to us. The point "is that one must hold one's story up as if against a three-part checklist: Your story must have purpose (can you name it?), your story must be true (is it?), you story must lead to hope-filled action (does it? what is it?). If you can't answer those three questions affirmatively, clearly, certainly, then your story will fail."[39]

There are always factors that are under our control. Are we spending our time with optimistic people or pessimistic people? Are we managing our emotions by building skills, exercising, being respectful about our health? Are we expanding our social network when opportunities arise; and, conversely, are we making sure we have time to recharge and be reflective when that is what we need to do for ourselves?

Our happiness can be impacted in different ways by the people in our personal and professional lives. We have to take responsibility to not fall into being a victim (or a version of what Littlefinger called "a piece") with regards to our happiness. If we can't help ourselves get up off the ground, our face bloodied, and step out to the heart tree and pray, we can't help those that look to us for support in our personal and professional lives.

We can't quit without paying a great price. If we lie down in the snow surrounded by wights north of the Wall, we will die. Gilly and her baby will also die. Jorah Mormont will die of greyscale. Many more will die. We can't abandon our happiness or we will abandon those who need us, those we will help. Understanding our *purpose* and the *truth* will give us clarity on the best course to take in terms of our *action*.

H = S + C + V

When Sam reaches the Citadel in *A Feast for Crows*, he is taken to meet Archmaester Marwyn, known as the Mage. Sam is shown an obsidian candle that burns with extreme colors. He is told that the flame is fed by the same magic of all Valyrian sorcery. "The sorcerers of the Freehold could see across mountains, seas, and deserts with one of these glass candles. They could enter a man's dreams and give him visions, and speak to one another half a world apart, seated before their candles."[40] The Mage tells Sam there is a conspiracy at the Citadel, a judgment against Targaryens that contributed to Aemon living out his life at Castle Black instead of serving as an archmaester in the capital of knowledge. The Mage and his assistant, Alleras, listen as Sam tells them Maester Aemon believed Daenerys was the prophesized leader who would save them all. The Mage doesn't buy it, repeating what he was once told by Gorghan of Old Ghis, "Prophecy will bite your prick off every time."[41] Then the Mage thinks again and decides on a course of action unclear to Sam. He tells Sam to go to the Citadel, to work and learn. He advises Sam to compliment the archmaesters but not to talk about dragons. In both the novels and the show, Sam has to find his way forward without much in the way of coaching or clear direction. He has his balance of optimism and pessimism, the equivalent of an internal obsidian candle. This helps guide him through risk and toward success.

We have a similar responsibility in terms of our happiness. We can't expect our happiness to be a gift from Horn Hill, Castle Black, or the Citadel. We can look for guidance to build our happiness threshold, but we should expect to be our own coach first. We need to find it ourselves. Our momentary happiness can be the gift to ourselves of our favorite food, or entertainment, or an item we purchase. This is not part of our *enduring happiness*. If tested on our happiness, about half of our score would be similar to the score of our biological parents. As Seligman puts it, "This may mean that we inherit a 'steersman' who urges us toward a specific level of happiness or sadness."[42] Seligman supports the idea that we need to appreciate what is good.

"Insufficient appreciation and savoring of the good events" is what leads us away from "serenity, contentment and satisfaction."[43] There is an equation for happiness. *Happiness* equals your biologically *set range* for happiness, plus your *circumstances*, plus what is under your *voluntary control*. $H = S + C + V$.

We can't change our biologically set range, but we can apply the two exercises in this chapter to work with the circumstances that we face and positively impact what is in our voluntary control.

We have a responsibility to lead the part of us that is Samwell Tarly. Pessimism has its place, but we will require optimism if we want to do better. When we demand and nurture optimism in ourselves and our colleagues, action follows. When Sam attacked the White Walker that slew Small Paul in *A Storm of Swords*, the voice in his head told him it was time to act. Was he a coward or was he brave? It didn't matter. What mattered is that he told himself to stop crying: it was time to fight. Sam knifes the White Walker. Sam opens his eyes as "the Other shrank and puddled, dissolving away. In twenty heartbeats its flesh was gone, swirling away in a fine white mist."[44]

Sam realizes the answer to the White Walker is obsidian—dragonglass. He falls in the snow and vomits. Grenn tells Sam they must find Lord Commander Mormont. Sam decides he will try. He won't die Beyond the Wall. He killed a White Walker. He will be mocked at Castle Black. Alliser Thorne will tauntingly call him *Slayer*. But he won't die in the snow.

It is almost dawn. "Sam kicked his left foot against a tree, to knock off all the snow. Then the right. 'I'll try.' Grimacing, he took a step. 'I'll try hard.' And then another."[45] Sam doesn't collapse into the waves of snow. Sam takes the frozen, exhausted steps that will lead him to what he hungers to find—a greater purpose that he can align with his truth and action. He also finds a romantic partner and a child who both need his protection, as humanity will also need his help against the danger that heads south in the long, cold night.

THE LEADER'S JOURNEY: RESCUE FROM WITHOUT AND CROSSING THE RETURN THRESHOLD

Jeor Mormont, the Old Bear, said: "On the Wall, we are all one house."[46] This house was the best place for Samwell Tarly to arrive. He didn't know it, but often we don't understand when we are involved in a shift that can either destroy us or direct us where we need to go to succeed. It is important to be aware and to be able to learn. Despite his initial pessimism, Sam is an exemplar in his capacity to decide, and despite his protestations of being cowardly, to act with courage. One lesson we can take from Sam is his ability to do much with less, in particular when it comes to moving past the disabling noise of our human attachment to fear and thoughts that derail us from our Hero's Journey.

When Sam arrives at the Citadel in *A Feast for Crows,* he tells himself he should have run off to the Citadel and serve as a novice. His father wouldn't have chased him down. *"I doubt he would even have troubled to search for me, unless I took a mule to ride. Then he would have hunted me down, but only for the mule."*[47] This is Sam listening to the discursive voices, the noise he must learn to dispute—the consequences of beliefs his father hammered into his young mind. Sam teaches himself a new story. At the Citadel, Sam sees acolytes waiting to pelt an older acolyte with rotting vegetables. The older novice is locked in stocks as punishment. "They all gave Sam curious looks as he strode past, his black cloak billowing behind him like a sail."[48] That moment of description tells us everything about the young man who turned to Jon Snow and said, "I never do better." Samwell *is* doing better.

In Campbell's *Rescue from Without,* leaders sometimes need to be called back into the action. This is because both success and failure can lead to isolation, confusion, and doubt. Sam goes to the Citadel and cures Jorah Mormont of the incurable greyscale. He attempts to persuade the archmaesters to confront the threat of the White Walkers. He fails, but he returns with books and the knowledge that Jon Snow has a true claim on the Iron Throne. The powerful, human guide that brings Sam back from the Citadel is not Archmaester Marwyn, Archmaester Ebrose, or any of the Conclave. The powerful guide that has offered Sam strength through his entire journey, from the moment he stepped into Craster's Keep, is the wildling Gilly. We may also decide that Sam's promise to the weirwood and the Old Gods has served him well in Westeros and in the territory Beyond the Wall. We know his ability to leverage optimism has helped him. We may decide that his *rescue from without* has been supported by both the woman and the Old Gods. The Seven gave Samwell Tarly very little, but the Old Gods with their bleeding red eyes in the weirwood groves appear to be watching and protecting Sam. Did they send the ravens that awoke him and Gilly as the White Walker approached when they were sleeping? Yes, they did.

The struggle against the Night King might serve all of us in the twenty-first century well as a reminder that we can pray to different gods and still be aligned together in our effort not to fall into the long winter where mothers smother their babies rather than listen to them weep and die from hunger or dead things in the snow. We can be different and still fight together.

We are all facing the hard reality of Campbell's Rescue from Without. We would like to huddle in our zones of comfort, maybe even fidget until we die, but this is not what the work of George R. R. Martin and Joseph Campbell recommends for us. In the words of Campbell: "Life will call. Society is jealous of those who remain away from it, and will come knocking at the door."[49]

Sam gains wisdom on each step of his Hero's Journey. He Crosses the Return Threshold and makes his way back to Winterfell with Gilly and Little Sam. He has found a way to continue to develop. He is driven by the desire to share his wisdom with the friend and leader who first inspired his commitment to a brotherhood: Aegon Targaryen.

Going Forward

Sam Tarly arrives at his new organization on the border of Westeros as a pessimistic, depressed loner, unwilling to defend himself. He fidgets. He doesn't choose to fight. He can't be depended upon in a crisis. He is a professed coward. He is a recruit in an organization that prioritizes the skill of fighting and the value of courage. He is in an organization where colleagues must depend on one another for support in dangerous situations. Sam is thumped on the helm with a stout wood sword; his mouth fills with blood; he makes no effort to defend himself and insists he will never improve. But he does improve.

Sam faces mockery when his reputation isn't aligned with the opinions of some of his colleagues and bosses. Alliser Thorne calls him Ser Piggy before the Great Ranging North. After Sam returns and word spreads that he killed a White Walker, Thorne calls him Slayer. Sam is beyond worrying about Thorne. He has returned with a woman and her child. He has also returned from his journey in the land of the Old Gods, and he doesn't see his flaws as permanent or pervasive. Confronted with an enemy far more powerful than the wildlings, Sam would be expected to retreat toward the desert sands of Dorne, with or without Gilly and Little Sam. Instead, he finds a way to operate with a reasonable level of happiness and a motivating belief in the possibility of an optimistic solution to the onslaught of the newly active, thousand-year-old enemy from north of the Wall. Sam lets go of negative beliefs and the consequences that will hold him back. He chooses optimism, balances it with a measure of pessimism, and searches for a solution. He understands his purpose. He decides on actions that could offer salvation to the threatened country of the people he loves and serves to protect.

RIDE DRAGONS!

HOW TO ACHIEVE PURPOSE

In *Leading from Purpose*, Nick Craig at the Harvard Business School writes, "No one can take your purpose away from you; it is your real identity. Purpose has deep resilience and staying power in a way that nothing else can or will."[1] Craig goes on to make the point that *purpose* is different from *objectives*. Daenerys wants to take the Iron Throne and control Westeros. That is her objective but not her purpose. Daenerys tells Tyrion, "Lannister, Targaryen, Baratheon, Stark, Tyrell. They're all just spokes on a wheel. This one's on top, then that one's on top and on and on it spins, crushing those on the ground."

BREAK THE WHEEL

Tyrion says it's a beautiful dream to stop the wheel, a dream others have dreamt before but couldn't make real. Dany says: "I'm not going to stop the wheel. I'm going to break the wheel."[2] This is her purpose: to break the cycle that continues to oppress the downtrodden, disenfranchised, and vulnerable.

Daenerys wants to put a system in place that treats all people fairly instead of marginalizing, enslaving, and taking advantage of them. Yet, she makes a leadership choice on the battlefield that calls this into question. She executes two prisoners who stand up to her authority. She could be seen to betray her leadership purpose, or she could be seen to make a difficult choice where the ends justify the means, and she proves her commitment to her purpose.

Queen Cersei's objective, on the other hand, is to defeat all of her enemies. Her purpose, which is also one of her top values, is *power*. Success for Cersei means retaining power and gaining more power. Cersei and Daenerys are competitors whose purposes are at odds. They must confront each other.

In the real world, we could also face competitors who oppose our objectives and our purpose. It is important to remember to use our values to drive our authenticity as leaders. This will help our colleagues choose to follow us into battle. Our authenticity will help us motivate our followers.

THE QUEEN WE CHOSE

In an organization that operates with traditional boundaries, "it is assumed that the leaders have the know-how to create a competitive corporation."[3] This is how Robert Baratheon, Eddard Stark, and Tywin Lannister would have led. This is how Cersei Lannister leads. Daenerys's leadership instincts are different. She is flexible about hierarchy. She wants a level of democratic agreement from her direct reports, even if she understands the final decision rests on her shoulders. In order to get people moving together in a demanding environment, Dany would agree there is risk in listening to your people's guidance, but there is risk in all decision making. If you have selected good advisors, listening to them is worth it because your team will be aligned; however, listening doesn't mean abdicating responsibility. *The Boundaryless Organization: Breaking the Chains of Organizational Structure* points out: "Understanding the *why*, they are more likely to accept the *what*."[4]

As a result she accepts Tyrion's plan for winning control of Westeros, despite his recent track record, which has involved tactical assumptions that didn't work out: 1) the slave masters in Meereen burned Daenerys's ships; and 2) the Iron Fleet was destroyed with her allies killed or captured.

The why of Tyrion's plan is something of an analytical chess move: outmaneuver the Lannisters and avoid the horror of annihilating the citizenry of Westeros with Daenerys's dragons. Tyrion believes the loss of life contradicts Daenerys's purpose. The what is to take Casterly Rock. The problem is, they don't test their assumptions as a group. Tyrion suggests a plan and heads nod in agreement. No feedback, no critical analysis, no suggestion of unconsidered options, no evaluation of the validity of Tyrion's assumptions—and Daenerys agrees. The plan sounds smart in the Chamber of the Painted Table, but it doesn't work on the battlefield.

As former undisputed world heavyweight champion Mike Tyson famously said, "Everyone has a plan till they get punched in the mouth." Asked by journalist Mike Berardino about the quote, Tyson explained, "If you're good and your plan is working, somewhere during the duration of that, the outcome of that event you're involved in, you're going to get the wrath, the bad end of the stick. Let's see how you deal with it. Normally people don't deal with it that well."[5] Daenerys Targaryen gets punched in the mouth.

Does she deal with it well?

As *Glamour* magazine wrote after the episode, "Dany has a new strategy, and it's called scorched earth."[6] Miyamoto puts it this way in *The Book of Five Rings*: "He who is shut inside is a pheasant. He who enters to arrest is a hawk."[7] Dany attempts the cautious civility suggested by Tyrion, but then she decides to be a hawk.

It would have been understandable if Daenerys had first erred due to overconfidence in her own power. Her first instinct was to attack King's Landing with her army and her dragons. That is the leadership decision that Yara Greyjoy wanted Daenerys to choose. As Galinsky and Schweitzer write, "Often, the powerful only see the rewards in their behavior and not the risks or even mortal consequences."[8] But Dany is careful with her power. She understands that power can intoxicate leaders. Dany surrounds herself with truth-tellers. She evaluates their guidance and attempts to make her best decision.

After Daenerys agrees with Tyrion's plan and her team leaves the Chamber of the Painted Table, Lady Olenna tells Daenerys, "Peace never lasts, my dear." The Queen of Thorns proceeds to offer Dany advice: "He's a clever man, your Hand. I've known a great many clever men. I've outlived them all. You know why? I ignored them. The lords of Westeros are sheep. Are you a sheep? No. You're a dragon. Be a dragon."[9] Daenerys takes in the message but sticks to Tyrion's plan.

After the plan fails and she's been punched in the mouth, Dany takes her dragon ride across the water to Westeros and boils Cersei's troops in their red cloaks and armor.

The Mother of Dragons stands on a bluff above the captured Lord Randyll Tarly and his son Dickon, Samwell Tarly's father and younger brother. Daenerys demands that both men pledge their fealty; Tyrion wants to prevent Daenerys from the public execution of a father and son. He whispers, "Your grace . . ." and tries to cool her resolve to take action. Daenerys is the strong leader with a vision of change that rallies people to support her because she presents herself as fighting for more than her self-interest. She is fearless, strong, and fair. Tyrion believes his boss is walking close to a moral misstep.

Lord Randyll is not an Unsullied ex-slave from Astapor, nor is he one of the King's Landing Smallfolk from Flea Bottom. He is the Lord of Horn Hill and a military man with a powerful reputation for competence in battle. He would be a great asset for Daenerys, but he won't kneel. He would also be an asset at the Night's Watch, but he points out to Daenerys that she has no right to make him take the black. Dany is faced with a choice. Should she execute the father and son that stand together and defy her? She issues the command for dragonfire to Drogon in High Valyrian: "Dracarys!" Dany follows through on the guidance from the Queen of Thorns. She decides to *be a dragon*.

Do the ends justify the means, or is she betraying her values and her purpose of defending the vulnerable?

Father and son are immolated. The rest of the soldiers kneel as quickly as it is possible to kneel. She has acted to gain a military advantage in her effort to reclaim the throne that was stolen in Robert's Rebellion from her father, King Aerys II. She rides her dragon into battle. The field is won. Jaime tells the defiant Queen Cersei about the impact of dragonfire in combat.

This result presents a leadership challenge: if Dany's objective is to take the Iron Throne, she can ride one dragon over the capital and do what her father had intended to do during the War of the Usurper: immolate the city. But this would be a violation of her purpose. This would not gain her the willing followership of King's Landing or Westeros. This would instead gain her a large population of people attempting to kneel as fast as possible. This is not the purpose she has been pursuing. She would not have broken the wheel; she would have become the wheel. Her followers in Essos chose to follow her because she stood for helping them. Dany needs to guide her team toward her purpose. If she chooses to burn city populations, she has become a version of her father—or worse than even Queen Cersei. To become more than a dragon wrangler who murders her way to power, she must be a leader that gains and sustains followership.

The majority of her followers—from the former slaves of Essos to leaders who sat on the Small Council and held positions of authority in Westeros, to the King in the North—trust her because they believe she stands for a vision that represents more than the application of her own power.

As Missandei explained, Daenerys is the queen they chose.

When Daenerys dreamed she was her brother, all those years before with the maegi in the black tent of witchcraft, she dreamed she would fulfill Rhaegar's leadership potential. Her challenge is to continue to be an authentic leader, rallying her followers to confront risk. She must drive change and align the skills, commitment, and innovation of her team in order to find solutions to the threats she faces. Daenerys Stormborn is the leader of an army and a political movement. It is good to have dragons, but she will also need authenticity and a method to drive change.

AUTHENTICITY

Professors Paul Ingram and Sheena S. Iyengar at Columbia Business School and Columbia Business School Ph.D. Yoonjin Choi, now an Assistant Professor at London Business School, researched the relationship between a leader's core values and their ability to project and operate with *authenticity*. The research provides empirical evidence that "individuals feel authentic engaging in an action that is motivated by their core values. Leaders who are 'true to their core values' are authentic because their actions are motivated by their core values and therefore, are self-determined."[10]

Being able to operate as an authentic leader is believed, both by researchers and senior managers, to be a necessary skill that can be the difference between success and failure. "For instance, one recent cross-national study of senior managers revealed that 83% saw authentic leadership as improving the performance of teams they lead, and 77% thought it improved their own performance."[11]

Choi, Ingram, and Iyengar point out that it isn't easy to define what being authentic means; and it's also not a given that feeling you are an authentic leader translates to your followers believing you are an authentic leader.

Bill George, in *True North*, as discussed in chapter 5 with regards to President Kennedy, suggests that authentic leaders have five qualities: 1) they pursue purpose with passion; 2) they practice solid values; 3) they lead with the heart; 4) they establish connected relationships; and 5) they demonstrate self-discipline.

George's definition is inspiring: "As they develop as authentic leaders, they are more concerned about serving others than they are about their own success or recognition. And they are constantly looking for ways to grow personally. Authentic leaders develop genuine connections with others and engender trust. Because people trust them, they are able to motivate people to high levels of performance by empowering them to lead."[12]

Choi, Ingram, and Iyengar point out that the idea of authenticity sounds clear but is tricky. "Being authentic sounds simple enough—be your true self. However, in reality, achieving felt authenticity or the sense of being one's true self is not easy, let alone conveying it to others."[13]

If we start with the idea that *authenticity* means being true to one's self, then Daenerys Targaryen is being true to herself when she defends the Lhazareen godswife who is being raped by the Dothraki after they destroyed her temple. Dany is also being authentic when she insists Mirri Maz Duur be allowed the opportunity to heal the wounded Khal Drogo. Dany makes a terrible mistake and she pays for it, but she is being true to herself.

The Dothraki think she is foolish to trust the Lhazareen godswife of the Great Shepherd, but Khal Drogo accepts Daenerys's decision to be treated by the sorceress. Authenticity is no guard against making mistakes.

Is Daenerys being authentic when she orders the execution of the captured Tarly soldiers? The surviving soldiers of Cersei's army instantly kneel, but has Daenerys won them to her side or just intimidated them into temporary followership? Has Daenerys betrayed her purpose, or is she pursuing her purpose with authenticity when she uses the power of her dragon to turn a captured army obedient?

Acting with authenticity in leadership allows our followers to understand why we are making decisions and have clarity on why they are choosing to follow us. The Mother of Dragons executes Randyll and Dickon Tarly. She recognizes she is in territory where her direct reports will question her choice. Still, she makes the choice. Was Tyrion right to caution the Mother of Dragons? Or was Daenerys right?

Daenerys has always understood the power of messaging authenticity. She walked into the Dothraki funeral pyre and emerged naked, unburnt, with her baby dragons. She tested herself in a public way that built her followership. This commitment by Dany and her survival gives her a confidence and causes her to continue to act with belief in her values as she makes her way to Qarth to Slaver's Bay to Dragonstone to Westeros.

Choi, Ingram, and Iyengar's research suggests "the perception of authenticity, at least in the realm of leadership, is affected by a leader's ability to manage and convey an image to others."[14] Communication in front of an audience is a powerful way to convince potential followers of one's authenticity. It is possible that Daenerys was derailed by the loss of Highgarden and the Ironborn ships to Euron, and this is why she executed the Tarlys. It is also possible she realized she needed to make this message to regain her followers' belief in her commitment and ability to achieve her objectives and fulfill her purpose.

When the leader's values are being affirmed, "values affirmation makes values-based motivation salient for leaders and therefore makes leaders more focused on their core values when communicating their decisions to followers as well as when they are implementing their decisions."[15] In other words, when Dany gets on her dragon and flies into combat in Westeros, she fulfills all of her values, from Equality through Responsibility, Courage, and Power to Freedom. This affirmation could put her into Galinsky and Schweitzer's cautionary space of over-believing in her own power, or it could make her values salient and drive her forward to confront her enemy. Daenerys understands her dragons are both her children and her weapon. They are a game changer. She holds back until she decides her authentic response is to put strategizing aside and fight. She made a choice on the battlefield, aware she leads an army in support of a transformational purpose: *to break the wheel*. If Lord Randyll Tarly wanted to survive, or if he only wanted his son Dickon to survive, he should have bent the knee. He should have taken the black. He had followed Jaime's promises and abandoned the Queen of Thorns and Highgarden for promises of increased wealth and status. Tyrion had a point, but Daenerys had to lead her army and a captured army. Lord Randyll Tarly and his son were killed by Lord Tarly's unwillingness to bend the knee. Daenerys

Stormborn, the Mother of Dragons, could have sent a message of forgiveness and attempted to leverage the Tarlys as a living resource. She chose to send the message to both her followers and her enemies that she was in the game to win.

It is possible that standing above the captured army and two rebellious prisoners that Daenerys reflected upon her values and made an authentic decision. It is also possible that she was derailed by power and acting as the daughter of the Mad King. Time will tell.

Queen Cersei and the Mother of Dragons are both courageous, successful leaders who operate with different levels of authenticity. Both act true to their beliefs; the difference is that Queen Cersei's decisions are devoid of interest in aligning her followers with her strategy and plans. Cersei would not fulfill Bill George's five categories of being an authentic leader. When she agrees to partner with Daenerys, Jon Snow, and the rest, she lies. Cersei's leadership is not driven by any purpose to help the people she leads. She doesn't care about anyone else. Daenerys does care. Dany attempts to fulfill all five of Bill George's categories.

In *Why Should Anyone Be Led by YOU? What It Takes to Be an Authentic Leader*, authors Rob Goffee and Gareth Jones emphasize the importance of understanding our life experience. Authentic leaders are willing to identify and leverage their differences and push themselves beyond their comfort zones. We see that in Westeros and Essos with both Cersei and Daenerys. They are fighting for the top leadership role in an environment where ambition can get one killed.

Leadership was not handed to either of these women. They had to fight for it. Cersei acquires her freedom and regains her leadership role by igniting the Great Sept of Baelor in wildfire. Daenerys rides her dragon into battle. Both women understand how their past experiences have provided challenges and resources. Cersei learned from her influential, powerful, and successful father. Daenerys didn't have the opportunity to learn from her brother Rhaegar or from her father, King Aerys II. Dany has chosen to try and learn about both men, including their strengths and weaknesses. Ser Barristan Selmy, who served her father as Lord Commander of the Kingsguard, was a resource until the Sons of the Harpy murdered him. Jorah Mormont has also helped her learn from her history.

Both women have a trait Goffee and Jones say is fundamental to authentic leadership: "They are comfortable with their origins."[16] This comfort doesn't mean they relish what they experienced, but they attempt to respond to it. Cersei is more reactive in this front. She visited the maegi, Maggy the Frog, and was told that all three of her children would die early. This haunted her and has proven true. Cersei was able to accept her relationship with Jaime and come to terms with her unpleasant marriage, although this involved instigating the death of her husband.

Cersei approaches any confrontation by attacking. She learned this from Tywin. The Lannisters always pay their debts. This applies to owing money, and it applies to lashing out at any challenge to their authority or legacy.

Daenerys can attack, but she also listens and learns. When Lord Varys tells Dany the people of Westeros await her heroic return, she remembers Illyrio Mopatis in Pentos promising Viserys that the Westerosi women sewed dragon banners and the men raised secret toasts in his honor. "They are your people, and they love you well."[17] Magister Illyrio had said, persuading the vain Viserys—but not his observant sister.

Daenerys is effective at the skill of being self-aware and being able to disclose to trusted advisors what concerns her. She is aware that she wants to take Daario on the journey to Westeros, but she understands she will need to be free of obligations to a romantic partner. She doesn't want to leave Daario. She turns to Tyrion for guidance.

It is hard to see Cersei leaving anything she wants, until the exact moment she doesn't want it anymore. Cersei only sacrifices when her actions have forced a sacrifice upon her, such as the deaths of her children.

Both women understand that authenticity in leadership requires performance. They confront the challenges of these moments in both their choice of clothing and their willingness to send the appropriate message, both verbally and through action. One can argue that Daenerys makes a leadership error when she immolates the Tarlys, but she is taking the moment seriously in terms of how her performance will be interpreted by her followers. Goffee and Jones refer to this ability as being able to *know yourself* and *show yourself*, but just enough.

Both women learned another quality Goffee and Jones identify as critical to authentic leadership: the importance of taking risks. Cersei lives this out. She has to live this out. Her partnerships, as she learned from Tywin, are all realpolitik. When she works with the Freys or the Iron Bank or Euron Greyjoy, the partnerships are transactional. She will take risks, but they are for her own interest and don't prioritize any cause beyond her self-aggrandizement. This is where Cersei diverges from the Goffee and Jones model.

Goffee and Jones argue that authenticity requires that the leader *care*. "Real leaders genuinely care about their cause."[18] They make the persuasive point that the verb *care* in English can be seen as describing a softly emotional tendency or action, but when leadership is involved, it's difficult to care about your people. "When we show what we care about, we become vulnerable. It is this vulnerability that entails personal risk. The capacity to do this means leaders are prepared to use their passions to stretch the performance of others and to challenge established organizational dogma."[19] Goffee and Jones use the term *tough empathy*, which means helping your team stay focused on the goal. It means being clear on the task, the people, and the overall purpose.

Cersei's purpose appears to be to gain power—to gain revenge on her enemies and continue to stand at the top of the org-chart with a glass of red wine. Daenerys's purpose, which is clear to all of her chosen followers, is to break the cycle that continues to oppress the vulnerable and downtrodden. Risk is necessary to achieve her purpose. "There is some superordinate desired end state, which energizes the leader who in turn gives energy to followers. Effective leaders really *care* about this goal. They care enough to reveal their authentic selves."[20] Dany cares. She is energized to break the wheel.

Bill George writes in *True North* about how motivation to become a leader often develops from confronting risk. Both Cersei and Daenerys accepted the risk in front of them before they pursued the role of queen regnant. Cersei had crossed a moral line by drugging King Robert's wine, but when the Hand of the King tells her she should take her children and run, she decides to stay and fight. She develops confidence she can handle the job when she is Queen Regent for King Joffrey. We may not agree with her leadership decisions, but after her imprisonment by the High Sparrow, we can agree that Cersei didn't lose confidence in her abilities to navigate the risk, and achieve her freedom, and lead from the Iron Throne.

On the Dothraki Sea, Daenerys leans into her role as khaleesi, embracing the Dothraki culture. She tries to convince Khal Drogo to sail across the poison water and take the Iron Throne. After she realizes what she has lost to the maegi, Dany decides to ramp up the risk she will face and fight for what she believes in, even if it means delaying her objective to win the Iron Throne.

Bill George quotes the late John Gardner, a former US Marine in World War II, who went on to become the president of the Carnegie Corporation and secretary of Health, Education and Welfare in the Johnson administration. Among other accomplishments, Gardner continued to encourage leaders to move into public service. "There were some qualities that life was waiting to pull out of me."[21] As George explains, "When leaders step out of their comfort zones to take on new challenges, they often discover capabilities they did not know they had." It is important to take risks because "you may be surprised to find leadership abilities you did not know you had."[22] Your leadership effectiveness depends on operating with high motivation and utilizing your full set of skills. You need to discover them and that often happens during challenges. This is true of both Daenerys and Cersei.

Our core values represent what we think is most important. Daenerys believes strongly in the right for all people to live in freedom and not be victimized by slavery. Freedom is one other core value. We are faced with situations that might—or might not—reflect a clean alignment with our values and the actions we decide are correct. When Grey Worm and Daario capture a Son of the Harpy, Daenerys pushes back against the request from a freed Meereenese slave that the Son of the Harpy be executed for murdering the Unsullied warrior, White Rat. Daenerys insists on a fair trial instead of a lynching. She is encouraged by Ser Barristan Selmy, who is known throughout the Seven Kingdoms as Barristan the Bold, to be a leader that controls the instinct to exercise power.

Barristan the Bold was friends with her brother Rhaegar and reported to her father, the Mad King. He tells Dany that her father always delivered the justice he thought people deserved. He had the power to commit these judgments, and he did horrible acts, often to innocent civilians.

Daenerys has been forced to confront situations that do not align with her values. As with any leader, she is motivated and convincing to her followers when she acts with self-determined reasons that are driven by fulfilling her core values. As with her decision to execute the Tarlys, this isn't always easy. It also isn't always clear if a leader's decisions are aligned with their values. She may have made a mistake to ignore Tyrion's plea to offer money. She chose to secure the commitment of her captured soldiers. She was in combat. She wanted to win for her followers.

When leaders create clarity that show their actions and values are aligned, it is noticeable to followers that the leader's choices aren't the result of some external pressure (rewards, punishment, social pressure, or a sense of obligation). The leader finds enjoyment or inherent satisfaction, and it is noticeable to followers.[23]

The Mother of Dragons sends a clear signal of alignment when she descends from the sky on her dragon.

Daenerys understands communicating in nonverbal ways; this includes her commitment to dress as a Dothraki when she is the khaleesi, to dressing in the required tokar in Meereen, to making a strong choice in clothing as a show of strength on Dragonstone. She also challenges her followers to express their opinions. She may not take their advice, but she requests that opinions be voiced. As a woman who grew up with no belongings or family beyond her older brother, Viserys, and her claim as the daughter of King Aerys II, she presents herself as a symbol of Targaryen legacy, beauty, strength, and power. She understands that in the Known World leadership is a responsibility, and success in leadership must be earned, and the message she sends matters.

Daenerys has fought for a leadership role that many people have attempted to deny her. Daenerys was bartered by Illyrio Mopatis and her brother as a bride to Khal Drogo for the promise of an army. Her brother, the Beggar King, told Daenerys: "I'd let his whole *khalasar* fuck you if need be, sweet sister."[24] Viserys is not the last man who attempts to marginalize Daenerys through insults and betrayal. In Qarth, Xaro Xhoan Daxos from the Summer Isles attempts to charm her, promising her ships and marriage, only to steal her dragons. Dany locks him up to die in his vault.

In Astapor, she is insulted by the Good Master Kraznys mo Nakloz, who fails to imagine she might understand Valyrian. Dany turns his Unsullied against him. She immolates the Khals who attempt to imprison her with the *dosh khaleen* in the Dothraki capital of Vaes Dothrak. Dany continues to pursue what she believes is her right: leadership. She believes it is her duty to lead from the Iron Throne, taking back what was stolen from her family; yet, she wants to lead without making the mistakes of the previous leaders in her family. She believes in the value of freedom for all. She continues to liberate and sees that as her purpose: to break the wheel that subjugates the vulnerable.

The key finding in the Choi, Ingram, and Iyengar paper is that "leaders can feel authentic and be perceived as authentic by followers by activating personal values that are central to their self-concept using a values-affirmation exercise where they remind themselves of their core values for a few minutes."[25] Dany will need to remind herself of her core values as her challenges escalate in Westeros. As the daughter of King Aerys II, Daenerys has a justified claim to become the Protector of the Seven Kingdoms. Her authentic leadership might be part of the answer to the problem that heads south. She needs to not get derailed by Queen Cersei or other distractions, but stay on her purpose to guide herself and her followers. "Leaders' behaviors often stem from multiple motivations because they manage multiple constituents."[26] Dany has different constituents and needs to work to keep them all focused on the main threat. "Leaders may intend to be authentic, act accordingly and feel authentic in the process but be viewed as inauthentic by followers who misread leaders' intentions."[27] Dany has the skill to align her powers of communication with her values and bring out full commitment from a diverse group of followers, but she can't take their followership for granted.

Dany will need all of the authenticity she can leverage to sustain her working relationships, her team's commitment, and possibly build any available new partnerships in Westeros or Essos. The Mother of Dragons has Dothraki bloodriders, her Unsullied army, access to the King in the North's sworn banners, and wildlings. She has two dragons left. The Night King has a dragon and he can ride it. It is possible he also has precognition and can predict how to maximize his success in future combat situations. This is one argument for his convenient access to ice-javelins and huge chains when it was time to capture Viserion.[28] Daenerys and her team face a serious challenge.

Bill George writes: "Brilliance comes only from exploiting your strengths."[29] He explains: "When you find a role that meshes your motivations with your capabilities, you will discover the sweet spot that maximizes your effectiveness as a leader."[30]

Daenerys Targaryen has been driven by her purpose to *break the wheel*. Her leadership strength of authenticity has been significant to her success. Her followers chose her. She has been able to lead herself and she has built followership. She should remember to step away from the fray, when possible, even for a few minutes, and reflect on her values. This self-management could contribute to leveraging her authenticity during the stressful times that will confront her and her team.

She should remember, with regards to her values, the advice of the Queen of Thorns: *Be a dragon!* She must balance this power with her humanistic goals.

Choi, Ingram, and Iyengar wrote: "By thinking about core values for a few minutes, leaders can effectively activate their values and make values-based motivation salient and experience authenticity as a result."[31]

Remember to reflect on values to get clear on the right decisions to drive motivation; rally the team by communicating and acting in a way that shows your team that your decisions are "emanating from the leader's core self."[32] When it is time for you to lead, bring your team with you and challenge your Night King!

EXERCISE #1: VALUES REFLECTION TO INDUCE AUTHENTICITY

In order to leverage the recommendation to reflect on your core values, particularly during key moments in your leadership journey, reflect on the values exercise that you completed in chapter 1.

- Remind yourself how you selected those values.

- Why do you find those values fulfilling?

- What has it felt like in the past when you have achieved your top value in pursuit of a goal?

- What difficulties have you faced in authentically living your values?

- What did it feel like when you ultimately achieved your goal?

When we look at the proposed core values for Daenerys Targaryen, we see *Freedom* at the top, with *Equality* at the bottom of her hierarchy, as follows.

DAENERYS

Freedom

Power

Courage

Responsibility

Equality

Daenerys believes all people deserve an equal chance. She takes the *Responsibility* on her shoulders to work to deliver the value of *Equality*. The final value that encompasses her values structure is *Freedom*. This value captures the core value that satisfies her in the most fundamental way. She has delivered on *Freedom* when she liberates the slaves in Meereen, which has required for her a commitment to the belief in *Equality*, as well as the *Courage* to face the challenge. She also recognizes that *Power* is achieved when she fulfills her commitment to *Equality*, *Responsibility*, and *Courage*. Daenerys riding her dragon in the sky is a manifestation of her fulfillment of her values.

When the Mother of Dragons finds herself facing the Night King and his new weapon, a blue-eyed Viserion, it will be important for her to remember why she has fought this long and hard to attempt to regain Targaryen control of the Iron Throne. She wants to break the wheel. Her ultimate value of *Freedom* will be fulfilled if she can deliver *Equality* to the people who have been crushed under the wheel. That wheel has taken on an icier, uglier reality. Daenerys can revisit her values to find the strength and focus to be her authentic self against great danger. When she rides her dragons, and reflects on why she must break the wheel, she will activate her values and experience authenticity.

EXERCISE #2: COMFORT WITH ORIGINS AND EASE WITH MOBILITY

In *Why Should Anyone Be Led by YOU?*, the authors recommend steps you can take to build comfort with your origins, including strengthening what Goffee and Jones call "an ease with mobility." The goal of the former is to be able to be natural, understand what shaped you and what you stand for, recognizing that you are the sum of your experiences. The goal of ease with mobility means to move through different social, geographical, organizational environments, and stay grounded. It isn't effective for a leader if they are derailed as they move into environments where they are unfamiliar. In Westeros, it is probably not surprising that, with the exception of being jailed and forced on her Walk of Atonement past the mocking, insulting citizenry, Cersei doesn't leave the confines of her safe zone: the Red Keep and the connected buildings. Cersei doesn't show ease with mobility. Daenerys, from her immediate commitment to embrace her role as khaleesi through her time on Slaver's Bay in Essos, to her black, caped arrival on Dragonstone, and confidence to travel Beyond the Wall to protect Jon Snow and his men, exemplifies ease with mobility.

The authors recommend the following five steps to build comfort with origins and ease with mobility:[33]

1) **Seek out new experiences and new contexts:** "This can involve changes as small as seeking to lead outside your function or as large as seeking to lead in an entirely different context." An important example in *Game of Thrones* is when Tyrion decides to visit the Wall at Castle Black. He is driven by curiosity. This effort, which could have been seen as a waste of time, prepared Tyrion years later to advise Daenerys about his positive memory of Jon Snow.

   To develop self-knowledge, it helps to avoid comfort zones and related routines that don't intrigue our curiosity.

2) **Get honest feedback:** "Effective leaders seek out sources of straight feedback." In Columbia Business School's Executive Education programs, participants ask their colleagues at work—boss, peers, and direct-reports—to fill out surveys and provide feedback on their leadership. These *360 reports* are part of a feedback process used in many organizations. They are a useful mechanism for executives to gain insight into areas where they have shown strength in leadership, and areas where they can focus their effort and develop. The Advanced Management Program has also used coaches to maximize the benefit of this process. Goffee and Jones also recommend the benefit of gaining feedback from trusted colleagues, family, and friends.

   Jon Snow doesn't want to listen to the advice he first gets at Castle Black from Donal Noye. "The armorer leaned close. 'You're no lordling. Remember that. You're a Snow, not a Stark. You're a bastard and a bully.'"[34] Jon is shocked, argues back at the accusation, but he later chooses to defend Samwell Tarly and his Brothers of the Night's Watch with more EQ. Jon Snow's ability to accept and learn from critical feedback has great impact on the fate of the Seven Kingdoms.

3) **Explore biography:** "Self-knowledge grows from coming to terms with the events that make us what we are." Reflect on

the experiences that have shaped you. There are different exercises to explore your past history. A simple approach is to write a line on a piece of paper and write the date of your birth at the bottom of the line to create a *Lifeline*. Then move up the line and mark different events you remember from your life. I was taught this exercise close to twenty years ago and have used it in classrooms with senior executives and graduate business students for many years. If you have done a version of this exercise, do it again. You can repeat the exercise and elicit new, useful insights as you remember events that influenced you.

This Lifeline exercise will open your eyes to the unique experiences that have shaped your development; as well as provide you with experiences you can use in conveying your leadership ideas to a range of colleagues, including situations where you are leading "up" to a boss, "across" to a peer, or "down" to a direct report. These stories will also help you communicate to customers. Think of the message you want to convey to your customer and the value represented, and then look on your Lifeline for a story from your past that supports the intended message.

When Daenerys questions Lord Varys at Dragonstone about his role in sending an assassin to kill her, she uses a story from her past, about the vanity of her brother, to convey to Varys that she won't be conned through lies and false compliments. She also demands of Varys that he promise to treat her with complete honesty and confront her if she makes poor leadership decisions. She uses a moment from her Lifeline to convey a message about a value that matters to her in a leadership context: honesty.

4) **Return to roots:** "Spend time with people who know you without the trappings of organizational power." Being in my late fifties, I realize that time with friends from past periods of my life helps me with both *comfort of origin* and *ease with mobility*. It can be rewarding to revisit past adventures and challenges, recognizing how you helped each other out, stood by each other, experienced life together, and are able to revisit the experiences years later and share what you each learned.

Given the weight of leadership responsibility on the surviving children of Winterfell, one can't say they have escaped what Goffee and Jones call "the trappings of organizational power." To the contrary, they have fought against impossible odds to achieve organizational power against the betrayal of Theon and the murderous behavior of the Freys, the Lannisters, and the Boltons. Yet, there is a return to roots that happens when the Stark children, now grown, can reconnect with a home they all believed was gone forever. They are able to let their guard down (a little) and support one another (a lot) in Winterfell.

5) **Find a third place:** This idea, espoused by the American sociologist and writer Ray Oldenburg, suggests that we can benefit from places—not social media—to connect with people and develop outside of the obligations of family and work. As Director of Columbia's senior leadership program, I call each executive in the months that precede the launch of the program. One of the questions I ask is about what interests them outside of work and family. What kinds of hobbies or activities engage them? As one would imagine, with a global cohort of executives, there are traditional sports, such as golf and football communities, as well as more solo interests, such as reading and cooking, but there is almost always something—a group, place, or activity—that serves as their version of Oldenburg's *third place*.

The third place for Samwell Tarly involves books. For Arya there are the early, contemplative moments where we watch her train with her sword, Needle; for Tyrion, books, and also his social interactions, which one might tend to judge but which still fall into the third-place concept. For Daenerys, her third place is being with her dragons, helping her dragons, riding her dragons.

The above five steps will help one prepare to be comfortable with origins, as well as be at ease with mobility. These are steps to help you know yourself and leverage the ability to show yourself in support of your authenticity. This will support the leadership requirement to take risks, which will contribute to success at being authentic and driving change to achieve purpose.

DVP > C

Columbia Business School professor Joel Brockner suggests a process to lead successful change initiatives. The structure for the process is DVP > C. In *The Process Matters*, Brockner writes: "Although trying to bring about change is not for the faint of heart, I do not mean to suggest that any one person has to be great at all of the things that go into a well-managed change process. I am simply saying that all aspects of the DVP > C framework need to be present."[35]

Professor Paul Ingram writes: "Organizational change is one of the hardest things for leaders to achieve, whether it involves a group, a division, or an entire company. Companies are made up of individuals, and everyone knows from personal experience just how hard it is to change."[36] If we want to drive change in order to achieve our purpose, we can support our authenticity by remembering an equation to achieve organizational change: **DVP > C**.

D is for Dissatisfaction with how things are, **V** is for a Vision of the future, and **P** is for Process to reach that vision. If one of these categories hasn't been effectively communicated by the leader, the followers won't be able to push past their resistance to **C,** the Cost of Change. Ingram explains: "If the product of the first three factors is greater than the cost (both economic and psychological) of change, then change becomes possible. Yet if any one of those three factors is absent, the product will be too low to overcome the resistance."[37]

Many years ago, a young McKinsey & Company consultant Wolfgang Bernhard, just two years out of Columbia Business School, confronted this problem when he saw an opportunity to lead a process improvement initiative at the Stuttgart transmission plant of Mercedes, but he faced resistance. "'It was difficult,' said Bernhard, 'because the people thought everything was great.'" Paul Ingram writes how the Mercedes employees didn't see the reason to confront the challenge on improving their processes. "They hadn't been given a compelling argument for change or a vision for the future."[38] A leader won't succeed in driving change if their followers don't recognize dissatisfaction at the current situation. Bernhard needed to create a compelling argument for change.

Ingram points out two effective ways to create dissatisfaction:

1) **Give employees information about how bad things currently are and contrast those facts with desired results**. This is what Jon

Snow, Daenerys, and the team attempt to achieve when they bring the wight back to King's Landing.

2) **Change managers can emphasize the positive results to be gained**. This may require the leader to show followers the gap between a satisfactory present and an aspirational future. When Missandei tells Davos and Tyrion on Dragonstone that Dany's followers have chosen her, she underscores how Daenerys has succeeded on this part of driving dissatisfaction. After the successful liberation of Meereen, Dany's followers get in ships and cross the Narrow Sea to engage in another war. They do this because they believe the success in Meereen is a step toward a greater achievement in Westeros. They believe in her mission.

Wolfgang Bernhard created dissatisfaction by using both of these strategies. He understood, despite advice from a McKinsey partner to pressure the resisters, that applying pressure wouldn't build commitment. He showed his colleagues that the situation was worse than they imagined, and he gave them an example of how much better their processes could be. He told them "if they didn't increase their productivity, their transmissions would not be competitive and they would fall drastically behind the competition."

"'For that reason,' said Bernhard, 'I took the team to Japan and looked at the Japanese process. After that trip, it was completely clear to them that if they don't get their productivity up, they have no chance.'"[39] Bernhard had gained buy-in on the D for dissatisfaction.

Bernhard was able to help his team understand a way to identify the future state. This is the V for vision. The case references change guru John Kotter's premise that "behavior change happens mostly by speaking to people's feelings."[40] Gaining commitment to achieve an identifiable future state requires a balance of aspiration and specificity. "We set ourselves a target of increasing productivity by 25%. Everyone said, 'It's impossible.' There was a culture of quibbling over 2.5 or 2.6% changes. Motivation was there after the Japan trip. Within a year we hit our 25%!"[41] In order to create a commitment that is greater than people's resistance to change, leaders need to support that dissatisfaction and vision with a process.

After Bernhard's trip to Japan with his team, he gained their commitment to reach for the 25 percent target. Success would involve the buy-in of roughly three thousand employees. How did he get the P for process to reach down through all the layers in the organization? "'In Mercedes,' said Bernhard, 'we selected people . . . from among the blue collar workers. We also had town hall meetings to present our overarching reasons to everyone, but [we used this] small involved group to create an active change process.'"[42] The ideal in a participatory change movement is to listen to everyone affected and use their feedback; this includes making sure to engage the most resistant people in the organization.

John Kotter notes that when change must happen quickly, this may justify more centralized decision making. Leaders face the challenge to gain full buy-in, with the choice of using feedback to succeed at gaining commitment. They also need to recognize when the situation requires centralized decision making and speed.[43] Additional process encouragements include: 1) think of mechanisms—such as "report cards"—that can help support the process; 2) remove barriers to change (culture, resources, etc.); and 3) be patient.

In the world of fire and ice, this $DVP > C$ equation has dictated Daenerys's whole life. She has led her way through the various cities, villages, deserts, and veldts of Essos to Dragonstone in an attempt to change not just the organizational leadership of Westeros but also to take on the organizational threat of the White Walkers.

From the moment Dany stepped into Khal Drogo's funeral pyre, she has committed to finding a leadership solution to D for herself and her followers. Since the incompetency of her brother Viserys became clear on the Dothraki Sea, her V has been to retake the Iron Throne, either at the side of a romantic partner or as the leader of the invasion. When she lands in Dragonstone, V is still about bringing a new kind of equitable leadership to Westeros. This V will be magnified in importance with her recognition of the Night King and his army.

Achieving P has required the Mother of Dragons to adapt to various constraints, pressures, and opportunities, but she has benefitted from her willingness to drive a *participatory change effort*. At some point in the future, P will have to address the kind of political structure she believes can "break the wheel." In Meereen, she attempted to be a benevolent queen regnant. It is possible she will stick with that model, although it's also possible, given her openness to listening to advisors, that she will select a new form of government. But this focus on **P** is down the road. First Dany must focus on a **P** that can combine with **D** and **V** and rally all available resources to confront the terror of the White Walkers. It is time to win and not die.

We see the equation in action when Daenerys's team delivers a wight to Cersei in the remains of Maegor's Dragonpit on Rhaenys's Hill in King's Landing. Team Targaryen traveled Beyond the Wall to bring back proof to Cersei that the challenge presented by the competition can't be ignored. Jon tells Cersei, referring to the reanimated corpse shuddering and screeching in the dirt, "If we don't win this fight, then that is the fate of every person in the world."[44] These two conflicting political organizations, one under the Dragon banner, the other under the Lion banner, appear to partner in a joint venture to stop the Night King. Cersei betrays their verbal contract. The future could be barren, icy cold, and dark. As the King Beyond the Wall, Mance Rayder said regarding the Night King's advantage with his wight technology: "We're all the same to them. Meat for their army."[45]

Dany must remember that she holds the power of centralized decision making, but her team's opportunity for success may arrive, as Wolfgang Bernhard recommends, by cutting across silos and creating interdisciplinary teams to facilitate change. The answer to the challenge doesn't have to be discovered by Dany. It could come from any of her expanded team of allies, either individually or working together.

EXERCISE #3: DVP > C

Consider a leadership challenge you face with your team or organization—or a personal challenge you want to confront—and fill out the four categories. This can be answered as if you are communicating to colleagues or advising yourself.

D (Dissatisfaction)	*V (Vision)	*P (Process)	>C (Cost of Change)

Example: Theon uses DVP > C to convince the Ironborn to help him rescue Yara from their uncle, Euron Greyjoy:

D (Dissatisfaction)	*V (Vision)	*P (Process)	>C (Cost of Change)
We don't have a leader we respect. Euron will just use us to promote his own interests. We trusted Yara and would have died for her. Who can we follow?	Yara is the leader we trust and respect. She is the one who can bring the Iron Islands the reputation and resources we deserve. She is the leader who will help us live with honor.	Theon will lead them forward to rescue Yara from Euron. He stood up as a true Ironborn and defeated Harrag, who is a strong warrior.	The cost of change is possible death. If we do this wrong, Euron will kill us. But we are willing to risk our lives to preserve the legacy of the Ironborn.

REAL WORLD: SELLING SODA IN IRAQ

I taught a session last year in an executive education program at Columbia Business School. One of the participants, Reda, a Moroccan national, had taken a leadership role with an organization in Iraq, a country dealing with a variety of postwar issues. The company's products include popular beverages, snacks, and food. I wrote Reda and asked for his thoughts on the value of the DVP >C model.

D—Dissatisfaction—Reda said when his team took over the company, the mission was, in his words, "totally lost." The organization was unfocused and the engagement and effort with the customers was flawed. The work environment was based on fear and punishment. People acknowledged it was an uncomfortable place to work. The recruitment process was random and not merit-based. Reda and the senior-executive team led a deep dive to rediscover the mission. The exercises involved sharing what was important to them about the organization, their professional work, and their aspirations for the organization. People gained clarity on what they were dissatisfied with in the organization and this motivated them to work on the vision and process.

V—Vision—To rally around a vision, the team used their core values as leadership drivers. They identified the core values, placing them in a hierarchy and supported them with leadership behaviors. An example of this is how they identified the importance to the team of the value of "respect." A way to support the value of respect is to also operate with the values of being "resilient" and "doing your best." They made these sets of related values actionable by the leadership behavior of compensating people fairly.

Reda explained, "I have inherited from my family that under-paying or not rewarding sufficiently is a form of lack of respect—literally, 'stealing sweat.'"

They worked through the values to understand the vision, and this provided them with leadership behaviors, such as fair compensation, that helped them with the P—Process.

P—Process—As Reda wrote: "All important decisions are benchmarked against our values." They decided to embrace conflict and make it part of the process. Healthy debate is a part of their process. The daily mind-set is focused on acknowledging the importance of healthy conflict. Related to this, Reda said that the process is focused on coaching.

The process also involved specific actions: 1) eliminating underperforming units; 2) reducing complexity and eliminating excess cost; 3) eliminating bureaucracy; and 4) focusing on the "front line," the part of the company that actually touches the customer.

They were able to create an environment where continuous learning with healthy conflict and coaching, complemented with human warmth, allowed them to deliver quality to their customers. Values are supported by leadership behaviors. They were able to remove the fear from both employees and customers that the organization would act unfairly. Reda feels they have been successful at implementing transparency and authentic leadership through the company.

The DVP>C model shows how Reda's organization could confront the need to change and achieve the motivation, clarity, and actions to win.

PURPOSE AND AUTHENTICITY: GET IN THE ARENA

Daenerys has the Targaryen dragon magic. She has an immunity to fire. Dragons trust her. She is also a woman with a vision. She is committed to deliver leadership that will benefit all. Lady Olenna's advice to *be a dragon* will help at key moments, but it won't bring the complete achievement of purpose that has driven Daenerys since her vision in the maegi's tent the night her son, Rhaego, was stillborn with dragon wings. Daenerys also needs to lead her dragon insincts.

Nick Craig writes: "*Purpose* is a sharp sword. Once you know what your purpose is, you also know immediately when you are leading from it and when you are not. The moment you find your purpose is a moment of waking up; once awake, you see."[46] He compares this waking up to standing in the arena that Teddy Roosevelt referred to in his famous lines about stepping into the battle to achieve, recognizing that errors will be part of your fight. Roosevelt's message still reminds us to fight and not criticize. If failure happens, at least fail *while daring greatly*. Credit belongs to the leaders and followers who recognize the necessity of the challenge and enter into the arena.

There will be dust and sweat and blood on your face, but the credit goes not to a critic analyzing from a safe spot; the credit, as Roosevelt emphasized, goes to the warrior who *strives valiantly*. Dany's purpose won't be easy, but she is a leader who is not afraid to step into the arena. She will fight as a dragon. She will also lead.

Our purpose matters to us, and has the potential to matter to our colleagues, community, and the world. "Purpose doesn't wait or care about the plan, it whispers in our ear and says . . . *follow me*. Leading isn't about going where everyone else is going, it's about creating something that didn't previously exist."[47] Purpose calls us into action.

Will we choose the purpose that Cersei chooses when she lies about her commitment to stop the White Walkers? Will we focus our effort on the consolidation of our power?

Or will we make the choice Daenerys makes and commit to break the wheel and also stop the White Walkers? Will we choose power or community?

Daenerys captures the complete definition from Bill George for an authentic leader: "As they develop as authentic leaders, they are more concerned about serving others than they are about their own success or recognition. And they are constantly looking for ways to grow personally. Authentic leaders develop genuine connections with others and engender trust. Because people trust them, they are able to motivate people to high levels of performance by empowering them to lead."[48]

We will see if Queen Daenerys Stormborn of the House Targaryen, the First of her Name, Queen of the Andals, the Rhoynar and the First Men, Lady of the Seven Kingdoms and Protector of the Realm, Lady of Dragonstone, Queen of Meereen, Khaleesi of the Great Grass Sea, the Unburnt, Breaker of Chains and Mother of Dragons[49] brings victory to herself and her followers. Will she win or die?

THE LEADER'S JOURNEY: MASTER OF
TWO WORLDS AND THE FREEDOM TO LIVE

In *The Art of What Works,* Professor William Duggan cites Joseph Campbell's *Creative Mythology*. Campbell refers to Leonardo da Vinci offering a line of wisdom that applies both to Duggan's concept of strategic intuition and to Campbell's seventeen-stage Hero's Journey: "As you cannot do what you want, want what you can do."[50] Find out what you can do and then set about getting it done.

Even Napoleon also understood a leader must find a way to merge the journey with the possible.

Both Daenerys Targaryen and Cersei Lannister are leaders at the point where it should become clear to each of them that they have a chance to save humanity. This is a larger goal than Daenerys's focus on helping the downtrodden. This is a larger goal than Cersei's pursuit of personal power and family legacy. Both women began their journeys years earlier in an attempt to save themselves from an unforgiving world. Now they face a situation that is captured perfectly by Ser Davos Seaworth, the Onion Knight.

"If we don't put aside our enmities and band together, we will die. And then it doesn't matter whose skeleton sits on the Iron Throne."[51]

Many of us won't face stakes so high. We will start our Leader's Journey, pursuing our purpose without being sure where the journey will take us. Nick Craig quotes a moment of dialogue from the 1988 interview of Joseph Campbell by television journalist Bill Moyers.

Bill Moyers: "Unlike the classical heroes, we're not going on our journey to save the world, but to save ourselves."

Joseph Campbell: "And in doing that, you save the world."[52]

Campbell believes that the movement through the Hero's Journey is a process we should all accept in order to bring *boons* back to our community and to fulfill our capacity as leaders. The Hero's Journey is the Leader's Journey. The Master of Two Worlds and the Freedom to Live are the final stages. In these final stages, we have reached a capacity to get past what we want and we have accepted what we have learned by pursuing what we can do. We are at a stage in our journey that Leonardo da Vinci would understand.

Campbell called the sixteenth stage of the journey Master of Two Worlds. This can be represented by a transcendental religious figure. These figures might have once lived as people, but for us, they are symbols of our own journey. We only know God in a certain way: "Symbols are only the vehicles of communication; they must not be mistaken for the final term, the tenor, of their references. No matter how attractive or impressive they may seem, they remain but convenient means, accommodated to the understanding."[53] Campbell argues that our symbols of spiritual ideals need to be "translucent, as that it may not block out the very light it is supposed to convey."[54] The light is what is important, not the symbol. Campbell wants us to remember that the symbol is a symbol. The figures we look at for help in understanding religion are signs for a journey we can't fully understand, at least, not right now. We must go on the journey first; understanding may follow in a brief epiphany or for eternity.

Campbell suggests there is a possibility of living with a peacefulness that comes from letting go of desires, fears, and attachments; accepting a quality inside ourselves that is anonymous. Campbell writes that the meaning of all religious practices is to reach this state. "His personal ambitions being totally dissolved, he no longer tries to live but willingly relaxes to whatever may come to pass in him; he becomes, that is to say, an anonymity. The Law lives in him with his unreserved consent."[55]

Daenerys becomes Campbell's signal for her followers. She doesn't represent one of the gods of the Known World, but a better future. She is a real woman, and she is a story that people can imbue with their values, aspirations, and commitment.

Leadership isn't about constant followers having constant access, and it's not about a constant fulfilling of one's wants and desires. Leadership is about service. It is what Campbell writes about in the opening of Master of Two Worlds. It requires "freedom to pass back and forth across the world division;"[56] it is an ability to dance in different roles, delivering what is needed. It is also the ability to become a story that others tell in order to deliver the important message and fulfill a transformation in people's lives. This idea would please Daenerys and her colleagues who have fought against the uglier manifestations of power.

For those who survive the Night King's invasion, they will live out their days in the Known World, and they will live in the histories of Westeros and Essos. They will also live in us as we pursue our struggles and reach for the way to exist with, and not be consumed by, our hopes and fears.

They are fiction and they are symbols of our own authenticity. If we reflect on their stories, we can tune up our own values and improve our own leadership. This is important for us, our colleagues, our communities, and for the world. As Goffee and Jones put it, "As traditional hierarchies disintegrate, only leadership can fill the void. Without a clearly articulated purpose, meaning is elusive. Leadership provides that articulation."[57]

Freedom to Live, the last stage of the journey, builds on that positive spiritual anonymity of the stage known as Master of Two Worlds. When it's time for Freedom to Live, the goal is to dispel the need to believe that each of us is somehow, in Campbell's words, "an exceptional phenomenon in the world, not guilty as others are, but justified in one's inevitable sinning because one represents the good."[58] We're not. Every creature in life has a connection with the death of other creatures and we may refuse to accept this reality of our engagement with the transitory world, yet we are a part of it. We live off creatures and people. We can learn to do this in a sustainable, humane way, but that depends on acknowledging the truth of death and life, and finding our way without needing to believe we are the special answer. We are part of it all.

Time passes and imperishable life lives on through us, and dies in us, and lives on past us. At this seventeenth stage, we have gone on a great adventure, sacrificed, confronted danger, learned, and returned with good things for our community . . . and we may have another journey and another journey, but at some point we will face mortality. We aren't an "exceptional phenomenon."

It is possible, as is written in the *Bhagavad Gita* (2:22–24) that: "Even as a person casts off worn-out clothes and puts on others that are new, so the embodied Self casts off worn-out bodies and enters into others that are new. Weapons cut It not; fire burns It not; water wets It not; the wind does not wither It. This Self cannot be cut nor burnt nor wetted nor withered. Eternal, all-pervading, unchanging, immovable, the Self is the same for ever."[59] This may be true. I have no idea, but Freedom to Live encourages us to embrace this possibility and let go of our fear of death, embrace our anonymity, be in this life with dreams but not enslaved by desires; don't anticipate the future or regret the past. This is our time to have the freedom to live. Religious paths can guide us. Their truths are available now and may be proven when we die. We may find heaven. We may find incarnation. I may find myself in the roots of a Coachella Valley creosote. This moment we breathe is our freedom. This is our freedom to live.

If we must face the Night King, the White Walkers, the wights, and the blue-eyed dragon, then face them and fight. The result of our miraculous passage on our Leader's Journey is that we have reached this moment and we understand we are here. There is no time that is better or more pure. We are free. We have made mistakes and bad decisions. We have felt regret and remorse, but we should remember the guidance from Lord Varys to Tyrion in Pentos: "I never said you were perfect."[60]

GOING FORWARD

Comfort with origins and ease with mobility are two important qualities of the authentic leader. These capabilities can be developed. Queen Cersei struggles with her ease with mobility. This has caused her to stay blind to the true threat. She doesn't want to recognize the danger of the Night King and hides from reality.

Daenerys Stormborn could have made different choices. She could have hidden from her legacy as the, apparently, last living heir to the Targaryen claim on the Iron Throne. She could have interpreted the loss of her *sun and stars*, Khal Drogo, and their unborn *Stallion Who Mounts the World*, Rhaego, as a reason to become uneasy with mobility. Instead, Dany committed to learning from her origins and continuing her journey across Essos and back to Westeros. Dany embraces origins and commits herself to mobility. She enters new cultures and transforms them with her leadership.

Taking personal risks is critical for an authentic leader. "Real leaders genuinely care about their cause."[61] This might sound mundane, yet Daenerys's followers understand what she cares about achieving. She will die if that's what it takes to break the wheel. The former slaves of Essos believe her and will die for her, too. Missandei, from Naath, repeats the qualities that motivate Daenerys and motivate her followers.

In the contemporary business world, a short leadership message that conveys the objectives, and values of a leader is known as an "elevator speech." Missandei shares her elevator speech about Daenerys with the Onion Knight, Ser Davos Seaworth, and with Jon Snow on the external walkway on Dragonstone. It is a simple message and Missandei conveys it with enthusiasm and conviction. She is persuasive and Ser Davos jokes that he wished he, too, was following Daenerys.

Now that her three children are dead, what cause does Queen Cersei genuinely care about achieving? She claims to be pregnant. Her followers are all weaponized direct reports or people she has a transactional relationship with to win at a zero-sum game. Cersei cares that in the game of thrones, you win or you die. She doesn't want to die. She is genuine and consistent in her commitment to power, but her type of leadership attracts followers signed on for a paycheck, not followers willing to sacrifice themselves to break the wheel and defend humanity from the true threat. Will Cersei face the true threat? Will Dany and Jon win? Winter is coming.

Leadership is for a purpose and that purpose requires risk. Bring what Goffee and Jones call *tough empathy* to your leadership. Be yourself, be authentic, and be focused on your objectives and purpose.

Remember to use DVP to overcome resistance to change. Remember to tune up your authenticity by taking time to activate your values. This will put you in the best place to convey your leadership messages. Encourage your followers to understand what you stand for as a leader. Help them choose your purpose, so they can commit to your objectives . . . and fight with you for freedom and equality. Purpose leads you where you want to go. As Nick Craig says, "*Purpose* is a sharp sword."[62]

Carry your sharp sword into battle and ride dragons.

ACKNOWLEDGMENTS

A few years back, I received an email from an editor, Stephen S. Power. He suggested I take the methodology of my Columbia Business School MBA elective—Leadership Through Fiction—and write a leadership book examining leadership decisions by the characters in *Game of Thrones*. This suggestion appealed to me for two reasons. First, writing this book would be its own game of thrones. I would either win or die. It sounded like an exciting and daunting challenge. Second, I now had a way to convince my wife, Sherelle, to watch the HBO series *Game of Thrones*.

We started watching the show. Sherelle was initially skeptical of the epic fantasy . . . and then she was hooked. We read George R. R. Martin's books. We rewatched the show. We reread the books. *Win or Die* is very much a coproduction supported by Stephen's vision, his enthusiasm, and his editing, and by Sherelle's encouragement, partnership, and attention to detail. I owe my thanks to both of them for their effort. Also, I want to offer my gratitude to Janine Barlow and everyone at US Macmillan, St. Martin's Press, and Thomas Dunne Books for their gracious and calm support through the process of creating and completing this project.

I also want to thank friends who offered encouragement, humor, advice, and support along the way, including Dan Halpern, the mentor, poet, and editor who ran the Columbia School of the Arts MFA writing program when I attended in 1985–1987, and takes time to meet me near the Brooklyn Bridge to talk about writing and life. Three writers from that MFA program—Campbell McGrath, Betsy Lerner, and Dean Smith—have kept my courage from failing at certain low points during the writing of this book. They offered me their confidence and pushed me forward. In my writing efforts, Campbell has always been a vocal supporter, as have actor and writer Max Martini and stuntman, actor, and military advisor Freddie Joe Farnsworth. Another writer, my friend since the eighth grade, Pete Magill, promised me on numerous occasions that I would complete the book and feel good about the effort. He offered tips, encouragement, and humor. I've been blessed with the continuous support of great friends from my hometown of La Cañada Flintridge, as well as from my undergraduate days at the University of California at Santa Cruz.

Friends made more recently have also offered support, including Todd Zarfos, vice president of Boeing Commercial Airplanes. Todd participated in my classes and offered guidance on both my teaching and chapters in this book. Dr. Andrew Kassinove offered detailed notes and encouragement over lunches in Palm Springs. Juergen Weigand also offered notes over dinners in Harlem. I was also encouraged at the crossroads of my leader's journey by publishing industry C-suite executive and literary editor David Shelley. The photographer Mark Shaw has been a constant source of encouragement to me on both fiction and nonfiction projects. He lugged his equipment up from Brooklyn to the Essex Hotel in Manhattan to devote an afternoon shooting portrait shots of me for this book.

I want to thank all of the MBA and EMBA students that brought their intellectual curiosity to Leadership Through Fiction. In particular, three students—Xiohan Huang, Erinmichelle Perri, and Chelsey McGinnis—completed independent study projects on *Game of Thrones*. Their enthusiasm for the intersection between leadership and *Game of Thrones* was one more motivation to stay committed on bringing this book to completion. I have had exceptional students who have served as teaching assistants for the course and offered their coaching support to my teaching efforts. Two of my business education colleagues with backgrounds in teaching and performing arts, Bob Kulhan (writing and improvisation), and Jeff Golde (theater) also helped me stay on my path.

During my thirty years of varied employment with Columbia Business School, I have had many mentors, friends, and allies. I won't present a list of names, but want to thank my first boss in the field of executive education: Mary Anne Devanna. She passed away many years ago and still inspires me. She set the bar high in leadership. She instilled in me a strong pride in the business school effort to educate leaders. I think she would be proud of those who have followed in her role at CBSEE. It is a demanding job, often subject to criticism, but it is an important role that impacts leaders across all continents. In my early days I was also supported by faculty in various roles who saw potential in me, including, just to name a few: John Whitney, Grant

Ackerman, Joel Brockner, Ralph Biggadike, Don Hambrick, Michael Fenlon, Bill Klepper, Rachel Ciporen, and longtime friend and mentor David Lewin. Kent Linder first encouraged me in the nineties to consider connecting my interests in story-writing with executive education; a few years later, he helped me develop my first class session. Ten years ago, Hitendra Wadhwa invited me to work with him teaching two three-day workshops in Mumbai. His leadership development interests influenced my personal growth and current teaching focus. I was supported by educators, including John Kerrick, Whit Mitchell, Manny Elkind, Matthias Ehrhardt, and many more names. More recently, I have benefitted from the intellectual support of a number of current professors at Columbia Business School, many of them generous enough to offer feedback on this book, as well as allow me to reference their content.

It was very motivating when Dean Glenn Hubbard and Janet Horan created an official position for me at the school that didn't previously exist. Thanks in part to that job, for over a decade, I have been in a leadership role on a demanding, rewarding team, serving as program director of the Advanced Management Program. In delivering these four-week senior executive programs, I have been fortunate to follow the world-class leadership of Professor Paul Ingram, and work with two exceptional colleagues: Alberta Barron and Howie Berg. I offer a humble thank-you to the vice dean of executive education, Dil Sidhu, for his support, and a thank-you to my colleagues at CBSEE for their support and friendship; they have offered support of my teaching and this book. I also want to honor the memory of Professor Casey Ichniowski. As chair of the Management Division, Casey provided the chance for me to introduce a leadership elective based on fiction. He took a gamble on a relative unknown. The class has been running for more than seven years and catalyzed this book.

I was fortunate to grow up in a home filled with books and a respect for reading. My parents, Robert and Elizabeth Craven, and my sisters, Janet Bernstein and Caroline Craven, have always expressed pride at my adventures in writing. My brother-in-law, Jeff Bernstein, has been a rock of support, humor, and a coadventurer in listening to live music. My in-laws, the Messer family in Canada, have been enthusiastic supporters from the true north. My two sons, Gram, age thirteen, and Walker, age ten, were concerned that I wouldn't complete this book in the assigned time. They were always understanding when

I said work had to take priority over basketball games in our driveway. Their pride at this accomplishment has made the whole effort worth it.

It is 100 percent guaranteed that I will keep thinking of people that should be acknowledged for contributing to this book. If you read this far and are not on this list, you should be.

My final thanks go to George R. R. Martin, Bantam Books, and all that supported the writing and publishing of his amazing epic fantasy series: A Song of Ice and Fire . . . and to the showrunners, David Benioff and D. B. Weiss and everyone involved with the brilliant HBO show *Game of Thrones*. The Known World of Westeros and Essos is a compelling, daunting, and energizing landscape that mirrors challenges we all face. The creativity of the novels and show are a true gift. Immersing in that world has been intoxicating, addictive, and fulfilling.

I hope this book offers you the courage and wisdom to pursue your ambitions, both for your own accomplishment and so you can offer support to those who depend on your leadership. As Arya Stark reminds us: "A bruise is a lesson . . . and each lesson makes us better." We won't achieve unless we step forward on our journey. I have had my share of bruises and want to thank everyone who has helped me respond to this Call to Adventure.

—Bruce H. Craven
Desert Hot Springs, California
November 15, 2018

Notes

Preface and Chapter 1. Don't Be Ned Stark!

1 George R. R. Martin, *A Storm of Swords* (New York: Bantam Books, 2000), p. 725.

2 Ibid.

3 Joseph Campbell, *The Hero with a Thousand Faces* (Princeton: Bollingen Series, 1949), p. vii.

4 George R. R. Martin, *A Game of Thrones* (New York: Bantam Books, 1996), p. 408.

5 Ibid., p. 38.

6 Ibid., p. 162.

7 Ibid., p. 295.

8 Ibid., p. 259.

9 Ibid., p. 271.

10 Paul Ingram, "Value Cards and Knowing Yourself," in *Research for Action* ebook, (*IEDP Developing Leaders*, Columbia Business School), p. 9. https://go-execed.gsb.columbia.edu/columbia-ResearchforAction-eBook.

11 William D. Guth and Renato Tagiuri, "Personal Values and Corporate Strategy," *Harvard Business Review*, (September 1965).

12 Ibid.

13 Ingram, "Value Cards and Knowing Yourself," p. 5.

14 Ibid., p. 6.

15 Shalom H. Schwartz, "An Overview of the Schwartz Theory of Basic Values," *Online Readings in Psychology and Culture*, 2 (1) (2012): https://doi.org/10.9707/2307-0919.1116, p. 3.

16 Ibid., p. 4.

17 Ibid.

18 Ibid.

19 Ralph H. Kilmann, "Toward a Unique/Useful Concept of Values for Interpersonal Behavior: A Critical Review of the Literature on Value," (Graduate School of Business, University of Pittsburgh, *Psychological Reports*, 1981), p. 942.

20 Ibid., p. 941.

21 Martin, *A Game of Thrones*, p. 14.

22 Schwartz, "An Overview of the Schwartz Theory of Basic Values," p. 4.

23 Martin, *A Game of Thrones*, p. 53.

24 Ibid., p. 407.

25 Ibid.

26 Ibid., p. 408.

27 Campbell, *The Hero with a Thousand Faces*, p. 58.

28 Ibid., p.51.

29 Ibid., pp. 59–60.

30 Martin, *A Game of Thrones*, p. 53.

31 Ibid.

Chapter 2. See True!

1 Martin, *A Game of Thrones*, p. 300.

2 Ibid., p. 403.

3 Ibid., p. 217.

4 Ibid., p. 28.

5 Ibid., p. 195.

6 Ibid.

7 Ibid., p. 418.

8 Ibid., p. 635.

9 Ibid., p. 629.

10 Ibid., p. 669.

11 Ibid., p. 672.

12 Ibid., p. 673.

13 Ibid., p. 674.

14 Ibid.

15 Bill George with Peter Sims, *True North: Discover Your Authentic Leadership* (San Francisco: Jossey-Bass, 2007), pp. 124–25.

16 Warren Bennis, *On Becoming a Leader* (New York: Basic Books, 2003), p. 135.

17 Diane Coutu and Carol Kauffman, "What Can Coaches Do for You?," *Harvard Business Review* (January 2009), p. 4.

18 Michael W. Morris, "The Craft of Coaching," Columbia CaseWorks, Columbia University, 2009. (www8.gsb.columbia.edu/caseworks), case number 090418, p. 1.

19 Coutu and Kauffman, "What Can Coaches Do for You?," p. 3.

20 Morris, "The Craft of Coaching," p. 1.

21 Bruce Craven, Class Journals, 2018.

22 Morris, "The Craft of Coaching," p. 2

23 Matthias Ehrhardt, "Stories Are Bridges from One Mind to Another," Columbia Coaching Conference 2016, pp. 2–6.

24 Morris, "The Craft of Coaching," p. 7.

25 Ibid., p. 6.

26 Martin, *A Game of Thrones*, p. 446.

27 Ibid., p. 447.

28 Angela Duckworth, *Grit: The Power of Passion and Perseverance* (Toronto: HarperCollins, 2016), p. 54.

29 Martin, *A Game of Thrones*, p. 284.

30 Musashi Miyamoto, *The Book of Five Rings* (Books Pub, 2018), Apple Books, chapter 1, "The Ground Book."

31 Ibid., chapter 2, "The Water Book."

32 Martin, *A Game of Thrones*, p. 444.

33 Ibid., p. 288.

34 Jay M. Jackman and Myra H. Strober, "Fear of Feedback," *Harvard Business Review* (April 2003), p. 3.

35 Ibid.

36 Miyamoto, *The Book of Five Rings*, chapter 2, "The Water Book."

37 "No One," *Game of Thrones*, Season 6, Episode 8, HBO, 2016.

38 Joseph Campbell, *Pathways to Bliss: Mythology and Personal Transformation* (Novato: New World Library, 2004), p. 108.

39 Ibid.

40 Nick Craig, *Leading from Purpose: Clarity and the Confidence to Act When It Matters Most* (New York: Hachette Books, 2018), pp. 30–31.

41 Campbell, *The Hero with a Thousand Faces*, p. 71.

42 Ibid., p. 72.

43 Ibid., p. 69.

44 Ibid., p. 71.

45 Ibid., p. 82.

46 Ibid.

47 Yamamoto Tsunetomo, *The Hagakure: A Code to the Way of the Samurai*, trans. by Takao Mukoh (Tokyo: The Hokuseido Press, 1980), p. 71.

48 Ibid., p. 81.

49 George R. R. Martin, Originally published in *The Faces of Fantasy: Photographs by Patti Peret* by Patti Peret (1996), www.georgerrmartin.com/about -george/on-writing-essays/on-fantasy-by-george-r-r-martin/.

Chapter 3. Be a Player, Not a Piece!

1 Martin, *A Game of Thrones*, p. 58.

2 Ibid., p. 399.

3 Ibid., p. 394.

4 Angela Lee Duckworth, "Grit: The Power of Passion and Perseverance," TED Talks Education, https://www.ted.com/talks/angela_lee_duckworth_grit_the _power_of_passion_and_perseverance.

5 Ibid.

6 Josh Waitzkin, *The Art of Learning: An Inner Journey to Optimal Performance* (New York: Free Press, 2007), p. 112.

7 Ibid., p. 113.

8 Ibid., p. 33.

9 Emilia Lahti, "What is Sisu?," https://www.emilialahti.com/what-is-sisu.

10 Marta Velázquez, "Sisu: Beyond Perseverance," *Positive Psychology News*, December 15, 2014, https://positivepsychologynews.com/news/marta -velazquez/2014121530618.

11 Emilia Lahti, "Sisu - transforming barriers into frontiers," TEDx Turku, https://www.youtube.com/watch?v=UTlizGyf5kU.

12 Wikipedia: Sisu.

13 "NORTHERN THEATRE: Sisu," *Time*, January 8, 1940, content.time.com /time/magazine/article/0,9171,763161,00.html.

14 Lahti, "Sisu - transforming barriers into frontiers."

15 Rick Hanson, *Resilient: How to Grow an Unshakable Core of Calm, Strength, and Happiness* (New York: Harmony Books, 2018), p. 2.

16 Viktor E. Frankl, *Man's Search for Meaning* (Boston: Beacon Press, 2006), p. 5.

17 Duckworth, *Grit: The Power of Passion and Perseverance*, p. 54.

18 Frederick Douglass, *Narrative of the Life of Frederick Douglass, An American Slave* (New York: Barnes & Noble Classics, 2003, orig. pub. 1845), p. 68.

19 Ibid., p. 69.

20 Ibid.

21 Ibid., p. 89.

22 Ibid., p. 92.

23 AMP Follow-up Coaching Conversation with David Russell, October 10, 2017.

24 Ibid.

25 Jim Loehr, *The Power of Story: Rewrite Your Destiny in Business and in Life* (New York: Free Press, 2007), p. 204

26 Ibid., p. 133.

27 Ibid., p. 144.

28 Duckworth, *Grit: The Power of Passion and Perseverance*, p. 53.

29 His Holiness the Dalai Lama, translated and edited by Jeffrey Hopkins, *How to Expand Love: Widening the Circle of Loving Relationships* (New York: Atria Books, 2005), p. 99.

30 Ibid., p. 109.

31 Martin, *A Storm of Swords*, p. 692.

32 Campbell, *The Hero with a Thousand Faces*, p. 90.

33 George R. R. Martin, *A Feast for Crows* (New York: Bantam Books, 2005), p. 472.

34 "The Dragon and the Wolf," *Game of Thrones*, Season 7, Episode 7, HBO, 2017.

35 Ibid.

36 *Joseph Campbell and the Power of Myth with Bill Moyers*, Apostrophe S Productions, Inc & Public Affairs Television, Inc, 1988.

37 Campbell, *Pathways to Bliss*, p. xxiii.

38 Ibid., p. xxi.

39 Ibid., p. xxiv.

40 *Joseph Campbell and the Power of Myth with Bill Moyers*.

41 Ibid.

42 "The Dragon and the Wolf," *Game of Thrones*.

Chapter 4. Be More Than a Sword-Hand!

1 George R. R. Martin, *A Clash of Kings* (New York: Bantam Books, 1999), p. 599.

2 Ibid., p. 601.

3 Seneca, *Letters from a Stoic* (Enhanced Media, 2015), Apple Books, "Letter XLVIII—On Quibbling as Unworthy of the Philosopher."

4 Martin, *A Storm of Swords*, p. 344.

5 Ibid.

6 Ibid., p. 421.

7 Daniel Goleman in "What Makes a Leader?," HBR's *10 Must Reads: On Emotional Intelligence*, 2015 (originally 1996), p. 1.

8 Daniel Goleman, Richard Boyatzis, and Annie McKee in "Primal Leadership: The Hidden Driver of Great Performance," HBR's *10 Must Reads: On Emotional Intelligence*, 2015 (originally 2001), p. 24.

9 Travis Bradberry and Jean Greaves, *Emotional Intelligence 2.0* (San Diego: TalentSmart, 2009), p. 32.

10 Ibid., p. 24.

11 Daniel Goleman, *Working with Emotional Intelligence* (New York: Bantam Books, 1998), p. 22.

12 Ibid., p. 317.

13 Bradberry and Greaves, *Emotional Intelligence 2.0*, p. 21.

14 Goleman, "What Makes a Leader?," p. 21.

15 Bradberry and Greaves, *Emotional Intelligence 2.0*, p. 19.

16 Ibid., p. 20.

17 Martin, *A Clash of Kings*, p. 440.

18 Martin, *A Game of Thrones*, p. 561.

19 Seneca, *Letters from a Stoic*, "Letter III—On True and False Friendship."

20 Martin, *A Game of Thrones*, p. 672.

21 George R. R. Martin, *A Dance with Dragons* (New York: Bantam Books, 2011), p. 304.

22 Martin, *A Game of Thrones*, p. 451.

23 Ibid., p. 44.

24 "Dark Wings, Dark Words," *Game of Thrones*, Season 3, Episode 2, HBO, 2013.

25 Ko Kuwabara, "Building Success Habits: Networking and the Science of Self-Change," 2017, Columbia CaseWorks of Columbia University (www8.gsb.columbia.edu/caseworks), case number 130402, p. 1.

26 Martin, *A Game of Thrones*, p. 47.

27 Ibid., p. 206.

28 Martin, *A Clash of Kings*, p. 635.

29 Tarun Khanna, "Contextual Intelligence," *Harvard Business Review* (September 2014), p. 11.

30 Warren Bennis and Joan Goldsmith, *Learning to Lead: A Workbook on Becoming a Leader* (New York: Basic Books, 2010), p. 50.

31 Ibid.

32 Ibid.

33 Khanna, "Contextual Intelligence," p. 4.

34 Ibid.

35 Bennis and Goldsmith, *Learning to Lead*, p. 56.

36 Ibid.

37 Campbell, *The Hero with a Thousand Faces*, p. 97.

38 Ibid., p. 105.

39 Ibid.

40 Ibid., p. 108.

41 Ibid.

42 Ibid., p. 101.

43 Ibid., p. 109.

44 George R. R. Martin, Elio M. García, Jr., and Linda Antonsson, *The World of Ice & Fire: The Untold History of Westeros and the Game of Throne* (New York: Bantam Books, 2014), p. 31.

45 Campbell, *The Hero with a Thousand Faces*, p. 118.

46 Ibid., p. 111.

47 Ibid., p. 115.

48 Ibid., p. 114.

49 Ibid., p. 120.

50 Ibid., p. 121.

51 Ibid.

52 Ibid.

Chapter 5. Ride to Meereen!

1 George, *True North: Discover Your Authentic Leadership*, p. 106.

2 Ibid., p. 109.

3 Ibid., p. 106.

4 Martin, *A Clash of Kings*, p. 634.

5 "Valar Dohaeris," *Game of Thrones*, Season 3, Episode 1, HBO, 2013.

6 Martin, *A Game of Thrones*, p. 103.

7 George, *True North: Discover Your Authentic Leadership*, p. 148.

8 Ibid., p. xxxii.

9 Simon Sinek, *Start with Why: How Great Leaders Inspire Everyone to Take Action* (New York: Portfolio/Penguin, 2009), p. 69.

10 Daniel Ames, Malia Mason, and Dana Carney, "A Primer on Personal Development," 2008, Columbia CaseWorks of Columbia University (www8 .gsb.columbia.edu/caseworks), case number 080403, p. 3.

11 "Fire and Blood," *Game of Thrones*, Season 1, Episode 10, HBO, 2011.

12 Ames, Mason, and Carney, "A Primer on Personal Development," p. 6.

13 Ibid.

14 Ibid., p. 9.

15 Ibid., p. 8.

16 Ibid., p. 9.

17 Ibid.

18 Ibid., p. 10.

19 Ibid.

20 Ibid., p. 1.

21 "The Wars to Come," *Game of Thrones*, Season 5, Episode 1, HBO, 2015.

22 Ames, Mason, and Carney, "A Primer on Personal Development," p. 2.

23 Ibid.

24 Graham Allison and Philip Zelikow, *Essence of Decision: Explaining the Cuban Missile Crisis* (Addison-Wesley Educational Publishers, 1999), p. 81.

25 Ibid., p. 107.

26 Sheldon M. Stern, *The Week the World Stood Still: Inside the Secret Cuban Missile Crisis* (University Press Audiobooks, 2012), Presented by Audible .com.

27 Allison and Zelikow, *Essence of Decision*, p. 97.

28 Ibid., p. 100.

29 Ibid., p. 104.

30 Arthur M. Schlesinger Jr., in Foreword, Robert F. Kennedy, *Thirteen Days: A Memoir of the Cuban Missile Crisis* (New York: W. W. Norton, 1999), p. 12.

31 Ibid.

32 Sheldon M. Stern, *The Cuban Missile Crisis in American Memory: Myth Versus Reality* (Stanford: Stanford University Press, 2012), p. 45.

33 Ibid., p. 100.

34 Morten T. Hansen, "How John F. Kennedy Changed Decision Making for Us All," *Harvard Business Review*, November 22, 2013.

35 Ibid., p. 3.

36 Ernest R. May and Philip D. Zelikow, *The Kennedy Tapes: Inside the White House during the Cuban Missile Crisis* (New York: W. W. Norton, 2002), p. 145.

37 Ibid., p. 146.

38 Judd Apatow, *Sick in the Head: Conversations About Life and Comedy* (New York: Random House, 2015), p. 415.

39 Ibid.

40 Martin, *A Game of Thrones*, p. 269.

41 Adam Galinsky and Maurice Schweitzer, *Friend & Foe: When to Cooperate, When to Compete, and How to Succeed at Both* (New York: Crown Business, Penguin Random House, 2015), p. 139.

42 Ibid., p. 142.

43 Ibid., p. 145.

44 Ibid.

45 Ibid., p. 156.

46 Ibid.

47 "Hardhome," *Game of Thrones*, Season 5, Episode 8, HBO, 2015.

48 Galinsky and Schweitzer, *Friend & Foe*, p. 158.

49 Ibid.

50 Adam Galinsky, "How to Speak Up for Yourself," TED, December 16, 2016, https://www.youtube.com/watch?v=MEDgtjpycYg.

51 "Hardhome," *Game of Thrones*.

52 "The Winds of Winter," *Games of Thrones*, Season 6, Episode 10, HBO, 2016.

53 Campbell, *The Hero with a Thousand Faces*, p. 145.

54 Ibid., pp. 130–31.

55 Ibid., p. 131.

56 Ibid.

57 Ibid., p. 132.

58 Ibid., p. 147.

59 Ibid., p. 160.

60 Ibid., p. 162.

61 Ibid., p. 165.

Chapter 6. Don't Walk, Fly!

1 Martin, *A Game of Thrones*, p. 6.

2 Ibid.

3 Ibid., p. 7.

4 Richard J. Davidson, "Training Your Brain to be Flexible" in Daniel Goleman et al., Building Blocks of Emotional Intelligence Books; *Adaptability: A Primer* (More Than Sound, LLC, 2017), ebook.

5 George Kohlrieser, "A Mindset of Adaptability" in *Adaptability: A Primer*.

6 "The Climb," *Game of Thrones*, Season 3, Episode 6, HBO, 2013.

7 Richard Boyatzis, "Developing Adaptability" in *Adaptability: A Primer*.

8 Martin, *A Storm of Swords*, p.100.

9 Ibid., p. 107.

10 Ibid., p. 108.

11 Daniel Goleman, "Adaptability: An Introduction" in *Adaptability: A Primer*.

12 Ibid.

13 Ibid.

14 MacNN Staff, "RIM Thought iPhone Was Impossible in 2007," *MacNN*, December 22, 2010, http://www.macnn.com/articles/10/12/27/rim.thought .apple.was.lying.on.iphone.in.2007/.

15 Bruce Craven, Class Journals, 2018.

16 Rita Gunther McGrath, *The End of Competitive Advantage: How to Keep Your Strategy Moving as Fast as Your Business* (Boston: Harvard Business Review Press, 2013), p. 56.

17 Adam Lashinsky, "'Old Codger' Adobe Pulls Off Rare Tech Transformation," *Fortune*, June 15, 2018, fortune.com/2018/06/15/old-codger-adobe-pulls-off -rare-tech-transformation/.

18 Kara Sprague, "Reborn in the Cloud," *Digital McKinsey*, McKinsey & Company, July 2015, https://www.mckinsey.com/business-functions/digital -mckinsey/our-insights/reborn-in-the-cloud.

19 Ibid.

20 Ibid.

21 Andrew S. Grove, *Only the Paranoid Survive: How to Exploit the Crisis Points that Challenge Every Company* (New York: A Currency Book, Doubleday, 1996), p. 110.

22 Áine Cain, "Jeff Bezos's Productivity Tip? The '2 Pizza Rule,'" *Business Insider, Inc.*, June 7, 2017, https://www.inc.com/business-insider/jeff-bezos -productivity-tip-two-pizza-rule-html.

23 Ibid.

24 Ibid.

25 "Dark Wings, Dark Words," *Game of Thrones.*

26 Mark Randall, "How We Funded 1,000 Experiments" video, https://kickbox .adobe.com/what-is-kickbox.

27 "Home," *Game of Thrones*, Season 6, Episode 2, HBO, 2016.

28 Ashley Morton, "Isaac Hempstead Wright on the 'Fine Balance' of Playing Bran," *HBO-Making Game of Thrones* blog, August 9, 2017, http://www .makinggameofthrones.com/production-diary/isaac-hempstead-wright-on -the-fine-balance-of-playing-bran.

29 "Books: Uppie's Goddess," *Time*, November 18, 1957, http://content.time .com/time/magazine/article/0,9171,868072,00.html.

30 Upton Sinclair, *I, Candidate for Governor: And How I Got Licked* (Berkeley: University of California Press, 1994, originally published 1934), p. 109.

31 Bruce Craven, Class Journals, 2018.

32 Rita Gunther McGrath, "Vacation Edition: Snow Melts from the Edges," *RGM Newsletter* (August 2018), https://mailchi.mp/ritamcgrath/vacation -edition-snow-melts-from-the-edges.

33 Amanda Lotz, "The Unique Strategy Netflix Deployed to Reach 90 Million Worldwide Subscribers," *The Conversation*, April 4, 2017, theconversation .com/the-unique-strategy-netflix-deployed-to-reach-90-million-worldwide -subscribers-74885.

34 Ibid.

35 Joanna Robinson, "*Game of Thrones* Show-Runners Get Extremely Candid About Their Original 'Piece of Sh—t' Pilot," *Vanity Fair*, February 3, 2016, https://www.vanityfair.com/hollywood/2016/02/game-of-thrones-original -pilot-bad.

36 Ibid.

37 Ibid.

38 Richard Boyatzis in "Developing Adaptability" in *Adaptability: A Primer.*

39 Paul Gilbert and Choden, *Mindful Compassion: How the Science of Compassion Can Help You Understand Your Emotions, Live in the Present, and Connect Deeply with Others* in "The Four Noble Truths and Modern Psychology," Apple Books (Oakland, CA: New Harbinger Publications, 2014).

40 Rick Hanson, *Just One Thing: Developing a Buddha Brain One Simple Practice at a Time* in "Be Grateful," Apple Books (Oakland, CA: New Harbinger Publications, 2011).

41 Ibid.

42 Sprague, "Reborn in the Cloud."

43 Ibid.

44 Martin, *A Dance with Dragons*, p. 380.

45 Campbell, *The Hero with a Thousand Faces*, p. 160

46 Ibid.

47 Ibid., 161.

48 "The Lion and the Rose," *Game of Thrones*, Season 4, Episode 2, HBO, 2014.

49 Campbell, *The Hero with a Thousand Faces*, p. 167.

50 Ibid., p. 173.

51 Ibid., p. 182.

52 "The Door," *Game of Thrones*, Season 6, Episode 5, HBO, 2016.

53 Ibid.

54 Campbell, *The Hero with a Thousand Faces*, p. 188.

55 Ibid., pp. 189–90.

56 Daniel Goleman, "Conclusion" in *Adaptability: A Primer*.

57 Sprague, "Reborn in the Cloud."

Chapter 7. Don't Get Assassinated!

1   Ryan W. Quinn and Robert E. Quinn, *Lift: The Fundamental State of Leadership* (Oakland: Berrett-Koehler Publishers, Inc., 2015), p. 8.

2   Ibid., pp. 8–9.

3   Martin, *A Dance with Dragons*, p. 175.

4   Martin et al., *The World of Ice & Fire*, p. 222.

5   Martin, *A Dance with Dragons*, p. 453.

6   Ibid., p. 715.

7   Ibid.

8   William Duggan, *Napoleon's Glance: The Secret of Stragegy* (New York: Thunder's Mouth Press, Nation Books, 2002), p. 3.

9   Michael E. Porter, "What Is Strategy?" in HBR*'s 10 Must Reads On Strategy* (Boston: Harvard Business Review Press, 2011), p. 8.

10 Willie Pietersen, *Strategic Learning: How to Be Smarter Than Your Competition and Turn Key Insights into Competitive Advantage* (Hoboken: John Wiley & Sons, 2010), p. 6.

11 Martin et al., *The World of Ice & Fire*, p. 146.

12 Pietersen, *Strategic Learning*, p. 7.

13 Ibid., p. 12.

14 Ibid., p. 7.

15 Ibid.

16 Ibid., p. 8.

17 Bruce Craven, Class Journals, 2018.

18 Pieterson, *Strategic Learning*, p. 13.

19 Bruce Craven, Class Journals, 2018.

20 Pieterson, *Strategic Learning*, p. 24.

21 Ibid., pp. 26–27.

22 Lauri Harrison, "Zappos Creates Value that Truly Develops Customer Loyalty," *Marketing Trend Watcher*, May 26, 2012, marketingtrendwatcher .blogspot/2012/05/for-past-3-semesters-ive-been-fortunate.html.

23 Ibid.

24 Pietersen, *Strategic Learning*, p. 24.

25 Ibid., p. 106.

26 Martin, *A Dance with Dragons*, p. 714.

27 Harry Kraemer, "How Ford CEO Alan Mulally Turned a Broken Company into the Industry's Comeback Kid," *Quartz*, June 18, 2015, https://qz.com /431078/how-ford-ceo-alan-mulally-turned-a-broken-company-into-the -industrys-comeback-kid/.

28 "The Way Forward; Ford & Alan Mulally," *Mainland Ford* blog, December 15, 2015, https: //www.mainlandford.com/blog/the-way-forward/.

29 Marli Guzzetta, "The 4 Keys to One of the Biggest Turnarounds in Business History," *Inc. 5000, Inc. Magazine* (October 12, 2017), https://www.inc.com /marli-guzzetta/how-alan-mulally-turned-ford-around-inc5000.html.

30 Ibid.

31 Ibid.

32 Martin, *A Dance with Dragons*, p. 781.

33 Ibid., p. 782.

34 Ibid.

35 Ibid., p. 913

36 Ibid.

37 Campbell, *The Hero with a Thousand Faces*, p. 193.

38 Ibid.

39 "Oathbreaker," *Game of Thrones*, Season 6, Episode 3, HBO, 2016.

40 Ibid.

41 Bruce Craven, Class Journals, 2018.

42 George, *True North*, p. 46.

43 Bennis, *On Becoming a Leader*, p. xx.

44 Ibid., p. xxi.

45 Joanna Robinson, "*Game of Thrones*: Jon Snow's Alive But Not Necessarily Well," *Vanity Fair*, May 1, 2016, https://www.vanityfair.com/hollywood/2016 /05/game-of-thrones-jon-snow-alive-melisandre-resurrected-ghost-warg.

46 Martin, *A Game of Thrones*, p. 79.

47 Martin, *A Dance with Dragons*, p. 374.

48 Martin, *A Game of Thrones*, p. 81.

49 "Eastwatch," *Game of Thrones*, Season 6, Episode 3, HBO, 2016.

50 "Oathbreaker," *Game of Thrones*.

51 Martin, *A Dance with Dragons*, p. 268.

52 Ibid.

53 Ibid., p. 710.

54 Ibid., p. 715.

Chapter 8. Find Dragonglass!

1 Martin, *A Game of Thrones*, p. 221.

2 Ibid., p. 105.

3 Duggan, *Napoleon's Glance*, p. 17.

4 William Duggan, *Strategic Intuition: The Creative Spark in Human Achievement* (New York: Columbia University Press, 2007), p. 60.

5 William Duggan, *The Art of What Works: How Success Really Happens* (New York: McGraw-Hill, 2003), p. ix.

6 William Duggan, *The Seventh Sense: How Flashes of Insight Change Your Life* (New York: Columbia University Press, 2015), p. 72.

7 Ibid., p. 79.

8 Martin, *A Game of Thrones*, p. 434.

9 Duggan, *Strategic Intuition*, p. 9.

10 Ibid., p. 19.

11 Ibid., p. 58.

12 Adrian Gilbert, "Siege of Toulon," *Encyclopaedia Britannica*, https://www
    .britannica.com/event/Siege-of-Toulon.

13 Duggan, *Strategic Intuition*, p. 58.

14 Ibid., p. 59.

15 Duggan, *Napoleon's Glance*, p. 19.

16 Duggan, *Strategic Intuition*, p. 75.

17 J. Christopher Herold, ed., *Mind of Napoleon: A Selection of His Written and
    Spoken Words* (New York: Columbia University Press, 1955), pp. 43, 240.

18 Brian Jay Jones, *George Lucas: A Life* (New York: Little, Brown and Com-
    pany, 2016) Apple Books, chap. 6, "Bleeding on the Page: 1973–1976."

19 Ibid.

20 Ibid.

21 Ibid.

22 Ibid.

23 Ibid., chap. 7, "'I Have a Bad Feeling About This': 1976–1977."

24 Ibid.

25 John Baxter, *George Lucas: A Biography* (London: HarperCollins, 2012),
    Apple Books, chap. 15, "Saving *Star Wars*."

26 Jones, *George Lucas: A Life*, chap. 6.

27 Baxter, *George Lucas: A Biography*, chap. 15.

28 Jones, *George Lucas, A Life*, chap. 6.

29 Ibid.

30 Walter Isaacson, *Steve Jobs* (New York: Simon & Schuster, 2011), p. 94.

31 Ibid., p. 97.

32 Ibid., p. 100.

33 Ibid.

34 Duggan, *Napoleon's Glance*, p. 272.

35 Isaacson, *Steve Jobs*, p. 101.

36 Ibid., p. 113.

37 Duggan, *Strategic Intuition*, p. 101.

38 Gary Wolf, "Steve Jobs: The Next Insanely Great Thing," *Wired*, February 1,
    1996, https://www.wired.com/1996/02/jobs-2/.

39 Isaacson, *Steve Jobs*, p. 96.

40 Ibid., p. 118.

41 Ibid., p. 100.

42 Jones, *George Lucas: A Life*, chap. 7.

43 Duggan, *Strategic Intuition*, p. 75.

44 Martin, *A Dance with Dragons*, p. 589.

45 Ibid., p. 588.

46 Ibid., p. 770.

47 Martin, *A Storm of Swords*, p. 529.

48 Campbell, *The Hero with a Thousand Faces*, p. 207.

Chapter 9. Kill the White Walker!

1   Martin E. P. Seligman, *Authentic Happiness: Using the New Positive Psychology to Realize Your Potential for Lasting Fulfillment* (New York: Free Press, 2002), p. 35.

2   Ibid.

3   Ibid., p. 38.

4   Martin E. P. Seligman, *Learned Optimism: How to Change Your Mind and Your Life* (New York: Vintage Books, 2006), p. 107.

5   Seligman, *Authentic Happiness*, p. 37.

6   Ibid., p. ix.

7   Ibid.

8   Ibid., p. 38.

9   Martin, *A Game of Thrones*, p. 221.

10   Ibid., p. 223.

11   Seligman, *Authentic Happiness*, p. 42.

12   Seligman, *Learned Optimism*, p. 16.

13   Ibid.

14   Ibid., p. 52.

15   Ibid., p. 111.

16   Ibid., p. 58.

17   Martin, *A Storm of Swords*, p. 380.

18   Seligman, *Authentic Happiness*, p. 43.

19   Martin, *A Storm of Swords*, p. 529.

20   Seligman, *Authentic Happiness*, p. 43.

21   Seligman, *Learned Optimism*, p. 207.

22   Ibid.

23   Seligman, *Authentic Happiness*, p. xii.

24   Brainy Quote, https://www.brainyquote.com/quotes/richard_branson_770402.

25   Seligman, *Learned Optimism*, p. 5.

26   Ibid., pp. 210–17.

27   Ibid., p. 211.

28   Martin, *A Game of Thrones*, p. 221.

29   Seligman, *Learned Optimism*, p. 217.

30   Ibid.

31   Ibid., p. 114.

32   Boris Groysberg, Maureen Gibbons, and Joshua Bronstein, "Building a Developmental Culture: The Birth of Deloitte University," Harvard Business School, Case 411-059, October 2010. (Revised May 8, 2017.), p. 5.

33   Bruce Craven, Class Journals, 2016.

34   Ibid.

35   Loehr, *The Power of Story*, pp. 83–84.

36   Seligman, *Learned Optimism*, pp. 208–09.

37   Loehr, *The Power of Story*, p. 138.

38 Ibid., p. 139.

39 Ibid., pp. 139–40.

40 Martin, *A Feast for Crows*, p. 682.

41 Ibid., p. 683.

42 Seligman, *Authentic Happiness*, p. 47.

43 Ibid., p. 70.

44 Martin, *A Storm of Swords*, p. 208.

45 Ibid.

46 Martin, *A Game of Thrones*, p. 431.

47 Martin, *A Feast for Crows*, p. 677.

48 Ibid.

49 Campbell, *The Hero with a Thousand Faces*, p. 207.

Chapter 10. Ride Dragons!

1 Craig, *Leading from Purpose*, p. 5.

2 "Hardhome," *Game of Thrones*.

3 Ron Ashkenas, Dave Ulrich, Todd Jick, and Steve Kerr, *The Boundaryless Organization: Breaking the Chains of Organizational Structure* (San Francisco: Jossey-Bass, 2002), p. 46.

4 Ibid.

5 Mike Berardino, "Mike Tyson Explains One of His Most Famous Quotes," *Sun Sentinel*, November 9, 2012, http://articles.sun-sentinel.com/2012-11-09 /sports/sfl-mike-tyson-explains-one-of-his-most-famous-quotes-20121109_1 _mike-tyson-undisputed-truth-famous-quotes.

6 Elyse Roth, "'Game of Thrones' Season 7 Episode 4 Recap: Daenerys Finally Rode a Dragon into Battle," *Glamour*, August 6, 2017, https://www .glamour.com/story/game-of-thrones-season-7-episode-4-recap-dragon -battle.

7 Miyamoto, *The Book of Five Rings*, chap. 3, "The Fire Book."

8 Galinsky and Schweitzer, *Friend & Foe*, p. 50.

9 "Stormborn" *Game of Thrones*, Season 7, Episode 2, HBO, 2017.

10 Yoonjin Choi, Sheena S. Iyengar, and Paul Ingram, "The Authenticity Challenge: How a Value Affirmation Exercise Can Engender Authentic Leadership," Working Paper, Columbia Business School, pp. 10–11.

11 Ibid., p. 2.

12 George, *True North*, pp. 205–06.

13 Choi, Iyengar, and Ingram, "The Authenticity Challenge," p. 2.

14 Ibid., p. 36.

15 Ibid., p. 15.

16 Rob Goffee and Gareth Jones, *Why Should Anyone Be Led by YOU?: What It Takes to Be an Authentic Leader* (Boston: Harvard Business School Press, 2006), p. 52.

17 Martin, *A Game of Thrones*, p. 28.

18 Goffee and Jones, *Why Should Anyone Be Led by YOU?*, p. 61.

19 Ibid., p. 63.

20 Ibid.

21 George, *True North*, p. 115.

22 Ibid., pp. 114–15.

23 Choi, Iyengar, and Ingram, "The Authenticity Challenge," p. 10.

24 Martin, *A Game of Thrones*, p. 31.

25 Choi, Iyengar, and Ingram, "The Authenticity Challenge," p. 35.

26 Ibid., p. 1.

27 Ibid., p. 6.

28 Stephan Roget, "This Fan Theory About the Night King and His New Dragon Is Blowing Up on Reddit," *Total Nerd*, from Ranker, 2018. https://www.ranker.com/list/the-night-king-dragon-fan-theory/stephanroget.

29 George, *True North*, p. 113.

30 Ibid., p. 115.

31 Choi, Iyengar, and Ingram, "The Authenticity Challenge," p. 13.

32 Ibid., pp. 15–16.

33 Goffee and Jones, *Why Should Anyone Be Led by YOU?*, pp. 56–57.

34 Martin, *A Game of Thrones*, p. 153

35 Joel Brockner, *The Process Matters: Engaging and Equipping People for Success* (Princeton: Princeton University Press, 2016), Yuzu ebook, chap. 3, "Making Change Happen: It's All (or at Least Largely) in the Process."

36 Paul Ingram, "Organizational Change: The DVP > C Formula," Columbia CaseWorks of Columbia University, 2013; www8.gsb.columbia.edu/caseworks, case number 080412, p. 2.

37 Ibid., p. 2.

38 Ibid., p. 1.

39 Ibid., p. 4.

40 Ibid., p. 5.

41 Ibid.

42 Ibid.

43 Ibid.

44 "The Dragon and the Wolf," *Game of Thrones*.

45 "Walk of Punishment," *Game of Thrones*, Season 3, Episode 3, HBO, 2013.

46 Craig, *Leading with Purpose*, p. 248.

47 Ibid., p. 6–7

48 George, *True North*, p. 206.

49 Zoltán Szászi, comment on "What is the full title of Daenerys Targaryen?," *Quora*, August 9, 2018, https://www.quora.com/What-is-the-full-title-of-Daenerys-Targaryen.

50 Duggan, *The Art of What Works*, p. ix.

51 "The Queen's Justice," *Game of Thrones*, Season 7, Episode 3, HBO, 2017.

52 Craig, *Leading with Purpose*, p. 210.

53 Campbell, *The Hero with a Thousand Faces*, p. 236.

54 Ibid.

55 Ibid., p. 237.

56 Ibid., p. 229.

57 Goffee and Jones, *Why Should Anyone Be Led by YOU?*, p. 7.

58 Campbell, *The Hero with a Thousand Faces*, p. 238.

59 Ibid.

60 "The Wars to Come," *Game of Thrones*, Season 5, Episode 1, HBO, 2015.

61 Goffee and Jones, *Why Should Anyone Be Led by YOU?*, p. 61.

62 Craig, *Leading with Purpose*, p. 248.

INDEX